a sense of
urgency

JOHN
KOTTER

a sense of
urgency

HARVARD BUSINESS PRESS
BOSTON, MASSACHUSETTS

No part of this publication may be reproduced, stored in or introduced into a retrieval system, or transmitted, in any form, or by any
means (electronic, mechanical, photocopying, recording, or otherwise), without the prior permission of the publisher. Requests for permission should be directed to permissions@hbsp.harvard.edu, or
mailed to Permissions, Harvard Business School Publishing, 60 Harvard Way, Boston, Massachusetts 02163.

ISBN-13 (U.S. edition): 978-1-4221-7971-0
ISBN-13 (India edition): 978-1-4221-5230-0

Library of Congress Cataloging-in-Publication Data
Kotter, John P., 1947–
  A sense of urgency / John Kotter.
    p. cm.
  U.S. edition ISBN-13: 978-1-4221-7971-0
  1. Organizational change. I. Title.
  HD58.8.K673 2008
  658.4'06—dc22
                                        2008011152

The paper used in this publication meets the requirements of the
American National Standard for Permanence of Paper for Publications and Documents in Libraries and Archives Z39.48-1992.

contents

contents

preface

This is a book about a seemingly narrow issue—creating a high enough sense of urgency among a large enough group of people—but an issue I have come to believe is of overriding importance in a fast-moving, turbulent era. When the urgency challenge is not handled well, even very capable people and resource-rich organizations can suffer greatly. When the challenge is handled well, even those who face formidable obstacles can produce results we all want for our careers, employers, and nations.

My path to these conclusions began eleven years ago with the publication of *Leading Change*. That book was based on the analysis of about one hundred efforts in organizations to produce large-scale change: implementing new growth strategies, putting in new IT systems, reorganizing to reduce expenses. Incredibly, we found that in over 70 percent of the situations where substantial changes were clearly needed, either they were not fully launched, or the change efforts failed, or changes were achieved but over budget, late, and with great frustration. We also found that in about 10 percent of the cases, people achieved more than would have been thought possible. Surprisingly, at least to us, in those 10 a similar formula was used in virtually all instances, a formula I described as eight steps, the first of which was creating a sufficiently high sense of urgency.

Six years ago, Dan Cohen and I published a follow-up study in a book called *The Heart of Change.* Here we conducted hundreds of interviews to document small but important stories within each phase of large change efforts. We found the same appalling 70 percent figure, the same inspiring 10 percent, plus a powerful role that emotions played in the most successful cases. Two years ago, Holger Rathgeber and I published this material as a fable—*Our Iceberg Is Melting*—that made complex ideas about change more accessible and highlighted the emotional lessons of *Heart of Change* with a story about emperor penguins, using color illustrations, and with colorful characters.

While writing the fable, it first occurred to me how often I was being asked, "What is the single biggest error people make when they try to change?" After reflection, I decided the answer was that they did not create a high enough sense of urgency among enough people to set the stage for making a challenging leap into some new direction.

Both to test this observation and to probe deeper into the issues, I began to systematically ask managers a new set of questions: How high is the sense of urgency among relevant people around you? How do you know this assessment is accurate? If it is too low, why? If it is too low, what exactly are you doing to change this fact? What specific actions are you taking? How successful or unsuccessful are your actions? If you are unsuccessful, what seem to be the consequences to your organization (and to your own career!)? If you are succeeding, what exactly are you doing? From these discussions emerged a number of interesting conclusions.

First, I became more than ever convinced that it all starts with urgency. At the very beginning of any effort to make changes of any magnitude, if a sense of urgency is not high enough and complacency is not low enough, everything else becomes so much more difficult. The difficulties add up to produce failure, pain, disappointment, and that distressing 70 percent figure.

Second, complacency is much more common than we might think and very often invisible to the people involved. Success easily produces complacency. It does not even have to be recent success. An organization's many years of prosperity could have ended a decade ago, and yet the complacency created by that prosperity can live on, often because the people involved don't see it. A smart, sophisticated manager can be oblivious to the fact that two levels below him in the hierarchy is an organization so complacent that his dreams of the future will never be realized. That same manager can sometimes be just as oblivious to the fact that he too is being dangerously complacent.

Third, the opposite of urgency is not only complacency. It's also a false or misguided sense of urgency that is as prevalent today as complacency itself and even more insidious. With a false sense of urgency, an organization does have a great deal of energized action, but it's driven by anxiety, anger, and frustration, and not a focused determination to win, and win as soon as is reasonably possible. With false urgency, the action has a frantic feeling: running from meeting to meeting, producing volumes of paper, moving rapidly in circles, all with a dysfunctional orientation that often prevents people from exploiting key opportunities and addressing gnawing problems.

Fourth, mistaking what you might call false urgency from real urgency is a huge problem today. People constantly see the frenzied action, assume that it represents true urgency, and then move ahead, only to encounter problems and failures not unlike what would happen if they were surrounded by complacency. Task forces underperform. Enterprises underperform. People are hurt, sometimes badly.

Fifth, it most certainly is possible to recognize false urgency and complacency and transform each into a true sense of urgency. There is a strategy. There are practical tactics. The bulk of this book describes these methods.

Sixth, urgency is becoming increasingly important because change is shifting from episodic to continuous. With episodic change, there is one big issue, such as making and integrating the largest acquisition in a firm's history. With continuous change, some combination of acquisitions, new strategies, big IT projects, reorganizations, and the like comes at you in an almost ceaseless flow. With episodic change, the challenge of creating a sufficient sense of urgency comes in occasional spurts. With continuous change, creating and sustaining a sufficient sense of urgency are always a necessity. These two different kinds of change will continue to challenge us, but in a world where the rate of change appears to be going up and up, we are experiencing a more global shift from episodic to continuous, with huge implications for the issue of urgency and performance. *Put simply, a strong sense of urgency is moving from an essential element in big change programs to an essential asset in general.*

I have talked about urgency before as a part of the eight steps of successful change. So what is new here? Readers of my past books on leadership and change should think of this book as digging much deeper than I have before into a topic that I now see as much more important than before. Here I offer a broader and deeper view of urgency, including a clear distinction between constructive true urgency and destructive false urgency; an expanded set of tactics for creating true urgency; and numerous examples gathered in just the past few years of complacency problems and solutions.

The many stories in this book are about failures and successes. At least one is about a sixty-two-year-old CEO, another about a twenty-seven-year-old recent university graduate. The failures are cautionary. Many of the successes, I think, are inspiring. Probably three-quarters of these stories are based on U.S. organizations, but I have little doubt that the basic points apply across cultures.

So many people contribute to a book such as this that any attempt at listing names seems to me totally inadequate. So I will not try. I just offer heartfelt thanks to them all.

—John Kotter
Cambridge, Massachusetts

it all starts with a sense of urgency

We are much too complacent.

And we don't even know it.

yes, urgency is relevant, but . . .

"A sense of urgency is important, of course," he tells me. "Complacency is a disaster these days. But complacency is a relatively minor issue for us. Better execution of our innovation initiative is our challenge."

He's a smart man, and his competitors do not understand the opportunities nearly as well as he does. Nor are they inclined to take new actions when profits are good, as he is doing. But there is no question that his firm is not executing his very clever initiative well. Why? Look around him and you find employees who think they innovate just fine. They don't tell the boss that, but that's what they honestly believe. You find people who think "the innovation thing" is the latest flavor-of-the-month, which will come and go. So, quite rationally, they see no point in wasting time on it. You find people making lists, writing papers on innovation, to-ing and fro-ing, but it's all driven by anxiety and is largely focused on making sure a new initiative does not hurt them. You find angry people who feel the innovation program is being crammed down their throats. They act, all right, and with energy, but to covertly undermine the initiative. Our man doesn't see any of this clearly, not least because others around him don't either. Under these circumstances, execution is, and will certainly remain, a great problem.

"Urgency is not the issue," she tells me. "People know we are in trouble and need to change. The economic evidence in our sector of health care is everywhere. We have a burning platform. Our old complacency is, for all practical purposes, entirely gone. Communicating the new strategy is now the big challenge."

From where she sits, her views seem valid, and most are. The good news: she has a growth strategy that could make her enterprise highly successful. The bad news: the complacency, which she thinks is gone, is alive and very well. Why? Lazy or less-than-competent employees? There are some people who will not win any talent contests, but that's not her problem.

Two levels below this manager, employees are living in a different world. Some of them are never exposed to the flames coming from investment analysts or the blistering comments coming from customers. They don't live on a burning platform but instead in a building that seems to require no renovation, at least on their floor. The few people who do have smoke pouring into their offices are furious that somebody has started a fire. But instead of demonstrating a real sense of urgency to solve the problem, starting *today*, they complain. "Yeah," the angry accountant tells me, "we need major changes in marketing. You wouldn't believe what those people do!"

"I think we could do with a little less urgency," he says, almost defiantly. "We're running so fast and long that we are completely stressed out. We can't take this much longer."

Go check, and you find people are running and they are stressed out. But this man, and almost everyone else around him, is mistaking the enormous amount of activity as a sign of a real sense of urgency. It's not. It's just frenetic activity, with people trying to cope with fifteen issues, few of which are central to his organization's success. All this action is exhausting employees and actually killing true and positive urgency. Who can feel absolutely determined to deal *now* with the central issues facing an organization after racing into nine meetings on nine different topics in the space of one day?

"Within a month, we are going to have to lay off two or three thousand people," he tells me. "What's really terrible," he adds with great frustration, "is that if we had acted a year ago, we probably wouldn't be in this mess." Why did they not act a year ago? I ask. He's a man of action, not reflection, so he struggles with the question. Finally: "With 20/20 hindsight," he tells me, "I would say complacency. And some arrogance." And why was the firm complacent and arrogant? "Too much success in the past," he says. "I would bet that's it."

It's a good bet.

complacency and false urgency

We have a serious problem. It could grow more serious in the future if we don't act now. What many people often see as the solution is not the solution. It can actually make matters worse. There is a real solution. You can find it in use today. It can produce the achievements we all want for organizations, nations, and ourselves.

The problem is complacency. We have all seen it. Yet we underestimate its power and its prevalence. Highly destructive complacency is, in fact, all around us, including in places where people would deny it, deny it, and deny it still more.

With complacency, no matter what people say, if you look at what they do it is clear that they are mostly content with the status quo. They pay insufficient attention to wonderful new opportunities and frightening new hazards. They continue with what has been the norm in the past, whether it's short hours or long, suits or jeans, a focus on products or systems or not much of anything. As an outsider, you may correctly see that internal complacency is dangerous, that past successes have created sluggishness or arrogance, but complacent insiders—even very smart people—just don't have that perspective. They may admit there are difficult challenges, but the challenges are over there in that other person's department. They think they know what to do and they do it. In a world that moves slowly and in which you have a strong position, this attitude certainly is a problem, but no more so than a dozen other problems. In a fast-moving and changing world, a sleepy or steadfast contentment with the status quo can create disaster—literally, disaster.

Far too often, managers think they have found the solution to this problem when they see lots of energetic *activity*: where people sometimes run from meeting to meeting, preparing endless PowerPoint presentations; where people have agendas containing a long list of activities; where people seem willing to abandon the status quo; where people seem to have a great sense of urgency. But more often than not, this flurry of behavior is not driven by any underlying determination to move and win, *now*. It's driven by pressures that create anxiety and anger. The resulting frantic activity is more distracting than useful. This is a false sense of urgency that may be even *more* destructive than complacency because it drains needed energy in activity and not productivity.

Since people mistake the running-around for a real sense of urgency, they sometimes actually try to create it. The frustrated boss screams "execute." His employees scramble: sprinting, meeting, task-forcing, e-mailing— all of which create a howling wind of activity. But that's all it is, a howling wind or, worse yet, a tornado that destroys much and builds nothing.

The real solution to the complacency problem is a *true* sense of urgency. This set of thoughts, feelings, and actions is never associated with an endless list of exhausting activities. It has nothing to do with anxious running from meeting to meeting. It's not supported by an adrenalin rush that cannot be sustained over time. True urgency focuses on critical issues, not agendas overstuffed with the important and the trivial. True urgency is driven by a deep determination to win, not anxiety about losing. With an attitude of true urgency, you try to accomplish something important each day, never leaving yourself with a heart-attack-producing task of running one thousand miles in the last week of the race.

In a turbulent era, when new competitors or political problems might emerge at any time, when technology is changing everything, both the business-as-usual behavior associated with complacency and the running-in-circles behavior associated with a false sense of urgency are increasingly dangerous. They are not only torpedoes that will eventually sink ships, they are often stealth torpedoes, and that makes them doubly dangerous.

In bold contrast, a true sense of urgency is becoming immeasurably important. The results of my recent research on this point are exceptionally clear. Real urgency is an essential asset that must be created, and re-created, and it can be. I'll show you how.

a true sense of urgency

The dictionary tells us that urgency means "of pressing importance." When people have a true sense of urgency, they think that action on critical issues is needed *now*, not eventually, not when it fits easily into a schedule. *Now* means making real progress every single day. *Critically important* means challenges that are central to success or survival, winning or losing. A sense of urgency is not an attitude that I must have the project team meeting today, but that the meeting must accomplish something *important* today.

Urgent behavior is not driven by a belief that all is well or that everything is a mess but, instead, that the world contains great opportunities and great hazards. Even more so, urgent action is not created by feelings of contentment, anxiety, frustration, or anger, but by a gut-level determination to *move, and win, now*. These feelings quite naturally lead to behavior in which people are alert and proactive, in which they constantly scan the environment around them, both inside and outside their organizations, looking for information relevant to success and survival. With complacency or false urgency, people look inward, not out, and they miss what is essential for prosperity.

With a real sense of urgency, when people see an opportunity or a problem of significance to their organization, and others don't, they quite naturally search for effective ways to get the information to the right individual—and not when they meet him or her next month. With a true sense of urgency, people want to come to work each day ready to cooperate energetically and responsively with intelligent initiatives from others. And they do. People want to find ways to launch smart initiatives. And they do. They don't move at thirty-five miles per hour when sixty-five is needed to win.

A real sense of urgency is a highly positive and highly focused force. Because it naturally directs you to be truly alert to what's really happening, it rarely leads to a race to deal with the trivial, to pursue pet projects of minor significance to the larger organization, or to tackle important issues in uninformed, potentially dangerous ways.

It is often believed that people cannot maintain a high sense of urgency over a prolonged period of time, without burnout. Yet with all the alertness, initiative, and speed, true urgency doesn't produce dangerous levels of stress, at least partially because it motivates people to relentlessly look for ways to rid themselves of chores that add little value to their organizations but clog their calendars and slow down needed action. People who are determined to move and win, now, simply do not waste time or add stress by engaging in irrelevant or business-as-usual activities.

True urgency is not the product of historical successes or current failures but the result of people, up and down the hierarchy, who provide the leadership needed to create and re-create this increasingly important asset. These sorts of people use a strategy that aims at the heart as well as the mind. They use four identifiable sets of tactics. As you will see shortly, we know what these people do, and what many others could do.

A real sense of urgency is rare, much rarer than most people seem to think. Yet it is invaluable in a world that will not stand still. Complacency is pervasive, in part because it simply is not seen, even by many smart, experienced, and sophisticated people. A false sense of urgency is pervasive and insidious because people mistake activity for productivity.

complacency, false urgency, and true urgency

	Complacency	A False Sense of Urgency	A True Sense of Urgency
	More pervasive than people recognize, insidious, and *often invisible to insiders*	Also pervasive, insidious, and *often seen, incorrectly, as a true sense of urgency*	Rare and *immeasurably important in a rapidly changing world*
Roots	Successes: real, or perceived wins, usually over a period of time	Failures: recent problems with short-term results or long-standing, incremental decline	Leadership: people not only at the top but up and down the hierarchy who create true urgency and re-create it when needed
People Think	"I know what to do, and I do it."	"What a mess this is."	"Great opportunities and hazards are everywhere."
People Feel	Content with the status quo (and sometimes anxious of the unknown)	Very anxious, angry, and frustrated	A powerful desire to move, and win, *now*

	Complacency	A False Sense of Urgency	A True Sense of Urgency
Behavior	Unchanging activity: action which ignores an organization's new opportunities or hazards, focuses inward, does whatever has been the norm in the past (many meetings or no meetings, 9 to 5 or 8 to 6).	Frenetic activity: meeting-meeting, writing-writing, going-going, projects-projects, with task force after task force and PowerPoint to the extreme—all of which exhausts and greatly stresses people.	Urgent activity: action which is alert, fast moving, focused externally on the important issues, relentless, and continuously purging irrelevant activities to provide time for the important and to prevent burnout.

the consequences of little true urgency in an era of change

We live in an age when change is accelerating. This observation, hardly new news, cannot be overemphasized. The argument that change is always with us, or that change is cyclical, misses the point entirely. Both may be true over a millennium. But for now, and for the next five or ten years, the rate of change will continue to go up and up, with huge consequences for nearly everyone.

New technologies alone can affect all organizations, even firms in older and mature industries. Globalization can open markets that, to be exploited, demand new offices, factories, employees, and more. International political turbulence can upset the most carefully crafted plans. A merger can produce a gigantic competitor overnight. Countless statistics demonstrate these trends. Two of my favorites: patents filed in the United States have gone from 132,000 in 1986 to 211,000 in 1996 and on to 452,000 in 2006, showing both huge increases and an accelerating rate of growth. Total merger and acquisition activity in the United States has gone from $173 billion in 1986 to $469 billion in 1996 to $1,484 billion in 2006, again huge jumps and an increasing rate of increase.

External change must be seen to be acted upon. With an insufficient sense of urgency, people don't tend to look hard enough or can't seem to find the time to look hard enough. Or they look and do not believe their eyes, or do not wish to believe their eyes. Even if seen correctly, and in time, external change demands internal change. More processes need to be made more efficient. New work methods and products must be created. Organizations need to be reorganized to focus more on customers or growth. With complacency or false urgency, none of these changes happens fast enough, smart enough, or efficiently enough. From years of study, I estimate that today more than 70 percent of needed change either fails to be launched, even though some people clearly see the need, fails to be completed, even though some people exhaust themselves trying, or finishes over budget, late, and with initial aspirations unmet. A 70 percent failure rate is an *enormous* drag on a company, a government, an economy, or a society. Investors are obviously hurt, but the pain goes in all directions: to employees, customers, our families.

We know it does not have to be this way. I have documented many cases where people have handled the challenges of a changing world remarkably well. In virtually all these cases, people use a basic formula, a pattern with eight steps that I have described at length in three of my books: *Leading Change*, *The Heart of Change*, and *Our Iceberg Is Melting*. Used correctly, this method can produce inspiring results. The first step in that formula involves creating and sustaining a sense of urgency that is as high as possible, among as many people as possible.

Most organizations handle step 1 poorly. Many fail elsewhere too. Smart people put the wrong group in charge of a new initiative. They don't get the change vision entirely right. They greatly undercommunicate to people who need to buy in. They don't eliminate enough obstacles for those people trying to execute a change. They don't achieve enough short-term wins to give them credibility and momentum. They let up before the job is done. They don't make the right moves to make a change stick. But the very best available evidence, everything I have seen in my work over the years, suggests that *the number-one problem they have is all about creating a sense of urgency— and that's the first step in a series of actions needed to succeed in a changing world.*

it all starts with urgency

1. **A sense of urgency:** Winners *first* make sure that a sufficient number of people feel a true sense of urgency to look for an organization's critical opportunities and hazards *now*.

2. **The guiding team:** With a strong sense of urgency, people quickly identify critical issues and form teams that are strong enough, and that feel enough commitment, to guide an ambitious change initiative, even though the team members may already be overworked or overcommitted.

3. **Visions and strategies:** Strong and highly committed teams orchestrate the effort to find smart visions and strategies for dealing with a key issue—even when the best strategies are elusive.

4. **Communication:** High-urgency teams inherently feel a need to relentlessly communicate the visions and strategies to relevant people to obtain buy in and generate still more urgency in their organizations.

5. **Empowerment:** Those with a true sense of urgency empower others who are committed to making any vision a reality by removing obstacles in their paths—even if it's very difficult to remove those obstacles.

6. **Short-term wins:** High-urgency teams guide em-powered people to achieve visible, unambiguous short-term wins that silence critics and disarm cynics.

7. **Never letting up:** After initial successes, groups with a true sense of urgency refuse to let their organizations slide back into a comfortable com-placency. They expand the effort, working on every phase of the challenge, and never let up until a vision is a reality.

8. **Making change stick:** High-urgency organizations feel compelled to find ways to make sure any change sticks by institutionalizing it into the structure, systems, and, most of all, culture.

a problem and its solution

A big reason that a true sense of urgency is rare is that it's not a natural state of affairs. It has to be created and re-created. In organizations that have survived for a signif-icant period of time, complacency is more likely the norm. Even in organizations that are clearly experienc-ing serious problems, devastating problems, business-as-usual can survive. Or it can be replaced by hundreds of anxiety-filled, unproductive activities that are mistaken for a real sense of urgency. And in organizations that handle episodic change well, with a big initiative every five years or so, you can still find a poor capacity to deal with continuous change because urgency tends to collapse after a few successes. This last point is exceptionally important because we are moving from episodic to continuous change. With this shift, urgency will move from being an important issue every few years to being a powerful asset *all the time*.

The urgency question is not limited to any particular class of organization or group. Insufficient urgency, with all of its consequences, can be found in winners and losers, businesses and governments. It can undermine a plant, an office, or a whole country. Conversely, in all of these situations, a high sense of urgency can help produce results, and a whole way of life, that we all desire.

For the past thirty-five years I have been studying what people actually do to help their organizations perform well, no matter how difficult the circumstances. My work has led me to this topic and to this book. In the pages that follow, you will find dozens of stories about urgency, complacency, and false urgency. I will describe a strategy and four sets of tactics I have seen people use to create a strong sense of urgency and an unexpectedly high level of performance—with benefits flowing to investors, employees, national economies, and their own careers. A few of these methods are relatively obvious. A few are totally counter-intuitive. Some seem to be virtually a secret.

The good news here—and there is good news—is that a changing world offers not only many hazards but wonderful opportunities. Such is the very nature of shifting contexts. To capitalize on the opportunities requires any number of skills and resources. But it all begins with a high enough sense of urgency among a large enough group of people. Get that right and you are off to a great start. Get that right and you can produce results that you very much want, and the world very much needs.

complacency and *false* urgency

The first step in creating a true sense of urgency is to deeply understand its opposites: complacency and false urgency.

be clear about what complacency is

The dictionary says *complacency* is "a feeling of contentment or self satisfaction, especially when coupled with an unawareness of danger or trouble." For our purposes here, two words in that definition are especially important. The first is *feeling*. Complacency is not only a thought. It's very much a feeling. It is usually less a matter of conscious, rational analysis than unconscious emotion. As you will see, this point is extremely important because people usually treat complacency as a state of mind that can be changed solely with "the cold, hard facts." The second key word is *self*. Complacency is a feeling that a person has about his or her own behavior, about what he or she needs to do or not do. This point is also extremely important, because it is possible to see problems and yet be astonishingly complacent because you do not feel that the problems require changes in your own actions.

Almost always, complacent individuals do not view themselves as complacent. They see themselves as behav-

complacency

The odds are overwhelming that there is some around you!

where does complacency come from?

Complacency is almost always the product of success or perceived success. Complacency can live on long after great success has disappeared. Perceptions do not have to be accurate.

how do the complacent think?

The complacent virtually never think they are complacent. "I'm doing what's right." "Sometimes it isn't easy, but I know what to do and I do it—or if I can't entirely do it, the problem is created over there (in that department, by my boss, by competitors that don't play fair, etc.)."

what do they feel?

At a very basic, gut level, the complacent are content with the status quo. Sometimes they cling to what exists because they are afraid, often *irrationally* afraid, of the personal consequences of change.

how do the complacent behave?

The best way to identify the complacent is by what they do instead of what they say (though words can be revealing).

The complacent do not alertly look for new opportunities or hazards facing their organizations. They pay much more attention to what is happening internally than externally. They tend to move at thirty miles an hour even when fifty is clearly needed to succeed. They rarely initiate or truly lead. Most of all, they do what has worked for them in the past.

who can be complacent?

The assembly line worker, you, me, our bosses, *anybody*!

ing quite rationally, given the circumstances. They can sometimes be aggravatingly creative in justifying their point of view. You offer "the facts" about a threat or opportunity. They come up with their own highly selective data and think to themselves that you worry too much. These people can sometimes be hard to spot because they look rational, thoughtful, and prudent. Worse yet, they can see themselves as rational, thoughtful, and prudent.

If you confront people with your observation that they are being complacent, almost without fail they will think you are wrong. Often, they will be offended (seriously offended) or wonder what your real agenda is. Even in cases where problems are very hard to deny, complacent people will often say, in essence, "Of course we have challenges and problems." Probe with questions, and you will learn that the complacent think that others, and not themselves, are failing to face the challenges and problems. If those others would change, all would be well.

Very, very smart people can be astonishingly complacent in the face of needed change. There are many reasons, and none more important than historical success. With sufficient success, the threats from outside are, or once were, conquered. With no need to focus outward, eyes shift inward to manage a larger and larger organization. Competitive instincts can also easily turn inward, creating bureaucratic politics. As a result, new problems or opportunities in the outside world are not seen clearly, if at all. Complacency grows, leading to even less interest in or focus on outside reality, leading to still more complacency.

be clear about what is a false sense of urgency

False urgency is a condition that is very different from complacency. While complacency embraces the status quo, false urgency can be filled with new activities. While complacency often has a sort of sleepy quality, false urgency is filled with energy. While complacency is built on a feeling that the status quo is basically fine, false urgency is built on a platform of anxiety and anger.

Anxiety and anger drive behavior that can be highly energetic—which is why people mistake false for true urgency. But the energy from anger and anxiety can easily create activity, not productivity, and sometimes very destructive activity.

With anger at the bosses, the union, or the marketing department, people spend their time racing around, often looking for and using the corporate equivalent of firearms. They create battles that get the company nowhere. They waste hours developing long PowerPoint presentations to shoot down good ideas from other units in the organization. They hold meeting after meeting strategizing

false urgency

The odds are reasonably high that there is some around you!

where does false urgency come from?

False urgency is almost always the product of failures or some form of intense pressure that is put on a group.

how do people think?

Those with a false sense of urgency do not think that all is well. They may think that the situation they are in is a mess. They may think their boss is applying ridiculous pressures on them.

what do they feel?

Those with a false sense of urgency tend to be very anxious, angry, frustrated, and tired.

how to fight the union, even if the latter prefers peace. They go through the motions, using passive aggression to stall projects (as in "Oh, was I supposed to have that done today?"). They create destructive conflict, such as pounding the table so that a sensible meeting is impossible. All this takes time and energy, but it is wasted energy—not in the service of mobilizing people to grab opportunities or duck hazards.

how do they behave?

Those with a false sense of urgency behave in ways that can *easily* be mistaken for people with a real sense of urgency because they are very active.

But with a false sense of urgency, the action is much more activity than productivity. It is frenetic. It is more mindless running to protect themselves or attack others than purposive focus on critical problems and opportunities. Run-run, meet-meet, talk-talk, defend-defend, and go home exhausted.

who can they be?

The assembly-line worker, you, me, our bosses, *anybody!*

One source of anger is failed attempts to change in the past. People become so frustrated by earlier efforts that they can actually become mad when you point to an important new issue. Another source is current difficulties, which people rarely tend to think are their fault.

The anxiety driving false complacency is very different from anger, yet the ultimate effects can be very similar. With anxiety, people eventually come to worry most about their jobs, their careers, and the future of their work groups. They become preoccupied searching for nearby personal dangers. They can spend hours seeking safe retreats. A worried mind, racing around looking for a safe retreat, will never act with a true sense of urgency.

Fear and anxiety have many sources, but, once again, just as with anger, earlier failed change efforts loom large. If people are hurt when they are asked to make sacrifices for the general good, and yet the sacrifices go on and life does not become better, they can become very anxious. Experience teaches them that the best way to react to new initiatives is to protect themselves, so they do anything the powerful ask, even if it is a total waste of time, or they just flee the building.

Just as with people who are complacent, those acting with a false sense of urgency often don't see it. The human capacity to hide feelings of fear and anger from others, and themselves, can be astonishing at times.

look for the red flags (they are always there)

Although feelings can be invisible, behavior is not. Know what to look for and you will always be able to see a lack of urgency. The red flags are always there.

An example: The company was a technology enterprise with products in the general arena called data warehousing. The firm had been very successful, but margins and market share were slipping. The enterprise had lost its industry leadership in technological breakthroughs, especially in the application of emerging nanotechnologies to its products.

red flag number 1: Instead of saying, "We have to deal with this as fast as possible both to stop the slide and to position ourselves for the future," and then behaving that way, the executive committee asked the chief strategy officer to talk to respected consulting companies and solicit proposals from them. Four months later, after receiving and evaluating those proposals, the committee selected a consultant to do an analysis of the business and to recommend changes. Nine months after that, the consultants produced a draft of a new strategy for the enterprise.

red flag number 2: After studying the consultant's report, the CEO, with help from his aides, created a task force of carefully chosen people to roll out the strategy and put the company back on firm footing. Out of the top ten people in the firm, two were on the task force. The CEO was not.

red flag number 3: The members of the task force had difficulty coordinating calendars to set up their first meeting. Four weeks after they were charged with their task, they met for the first time.

red flag number 4: At that first meeting, the discussion of how to implement the new strategy slid back and forth into a discussion of what exactly the strategy was and whether it was the right one. No one came out and said, "We are floundering and we don't have time to do so." No one said, "I'm not sure I understand the one-hundred-page document from the consultants, and you have to help me immediately or I am useless on this committee." Certainly no one said, "Why am I on this committee?" or "What kind of a power game is being played out here by the two contenders to succeed the CEO?" The four people who thought the firm had been clearly moving much too slowly, that hiring the consultants was not smart, and that putting only two executive committee members on the task force was a major mistake—these four individuals at times looked as if they wanted to throw chairs against the wall. But they did not, and the other eleven did not seem to share those feelings. Or they were not sure what to do. So they did nothing.

red flag number 5: No decision was made at the first task force meeting except that it must have another meeting. People were asked to pull out their appointment books. Not everyone had his or hers. After hemming, hawing, and negotiating, the members set a time in four weeks to meet again. Two people did not say so, but they knew they would have to miss the meeting because of prior commitments.

red flag number 6: Between the first and second meetings, very little happened except behind-the-scenes chatter about why those on the task force were selected and why the specific consulting firm was chosen. Among some people, conversations began about who was to blame for the firm's eroding position. No one acted on these conversations. They only complained.

red flag number 7: At the second meeting, a sub–task force was created for "communication of the new strategy." Discussing who should be on this committee took up most of the meeting. One person asked, with a look of pure exasperation, "But what exactly do we have to communicate?" The task force ran out of time before this issue received much attention.

red flag number 8: Six months after the second task force meeting, margins and market share continued to slip. Some improvement had been made in technological development, but not much, and certainly not as a result of any actions by the task force. A frustrated CEO began to meet with the task force head more regularly, sought advice from another consultant, and spent an increasing amount of time preparing to explain all this to his board of directors. When it became known that the CEO was not happy, sub-task forces were formed, projects were launched, more meetings were held, papers were written and distributed. The VP of sales presented to the executive committee a sixty-slide presentation crammed with data, the logical conclusion of which suggested the problems were all in product development. That set off a frenzy of activity in product development, virtually none of which was driven by a desire to better understand the customer issues, build better products, and win the competition in the industry.

The problems throughout this scenario relate to too much complacency, too much false urgency, too little true urgency. If the top team members had a greater sense of urgency at the start, they would have found a way to spend much more time focusing on critical strategic issues. They would have felt compelled to do so. They would never have delegated the challenge to a consultant and waited nine months for results. They would never have tossed the consultant's report to a task force of fifteen people, only two of whom came from the top management team.

If most of those on the task force had a strong sense of urgency, they would not have struggled to find times to meet. People would have canceled appointments to make way for what clearly seemed of greater priority. They would have felt compelled to do so even if it created conflict with those who wanted the task force members at those other meetings.

With sufficient urgency, at the very first session most task force members would have clearly and quickly turned the conversation into a candid assessment of the situation. The others would have felt compelled to listen and contribute. "We are in an unacceptable position. We have seen evidence for more than a year that we must change both the product development and selling processes. We cannot delay anymore. The health of the firm, jobs, and our own pride are all at stake. These changes affecting our marketplace are a challenge for all our competitors. If we can leap ahead faster than others, we can achieve a stronger position than in the past. But we have to start *now*."

If the urgency had been high enough, even before the very first session some of the task force members would have been talking about the makeup of their new group and would have tried to change it. They would have both seen the problem and tried to solve it—despite political, cultural, or bureaucratic barriers. That's what a sense of urgency does.

With a true sense of urgency, departments would not have invested time in shooting at each other. They would not have set up ten more sub-task forces with ambiguous charters, an additional burden of many dozens of

finding complacency and false urgency

— useful questions —

- Are critical issues delegated to consultants or task forces with little involvement of key people?

- Do people have trouble scheduling meetings on important initiatives ("Because, well, my agenda is so full")?

- Is candor lacking in confronting the bureaucracy and politics that are slowing down important initiatives?

- Do meetings on key issues end with no decisions about what must happen immediately (except the scheduling of another meeting)?

- Are discussions very inwardly focused and not about markets, emerging technology, competitors, and the like?

- Do people spend long hours developing Power-Point presentations on almost anything?

- Do people run from meeting to meeting, exhausting themselves and rarely if ever focusing on the most critical hazards or opportunities?

- Are highly selective facts used to shoot down data that suggests there is a big hazard or opportunity?

- Do people regularly blame others for any significant problems instead of taking responsibility and changing?

- Does passive aggression exist around big issues ("Oh, was that due today? I wasn't told")?

- Are failures in the past discussed not to learn but to stop or stall new initiatives?

- Do people say, "We must act now!" but then don't act?

- Do cynical jokes undermine important discussions?

- Are specific assignments around critical issues regularly not completed on time or with sufficient quality?

meetings, and hundreds of uncoordinated assignments. They would have felt driven to implement or improve the strategy recommended by the consultants, and as soon as possible. Since they still had their regular jobs to do— making and selling and keeping the books for the current products—they would have stopped low-value-added activities so that all the work could realistically be done without their burning out.

In this case the firm was hurt, careers were damaged, a number of customers could not achieve their plans without the products they had been promised, and stockholders lost, on average, about 35 percent of their investment. It was a lose-lose situation. In the short-term, the only winner was the firm's number-one competitor.

Over a longer period of time, this firm gained ground, propelled by a respected brand, economies of scale, and very good people. But the problems along the way were both terrible and unnecessary. For stockholders, employees, and locked-in customers, it should not have been that way. And it didn't have to be that way. The signs were clear. They could have been seen. Why weren't they? People underestimated the importance of real urgency, particularly as an essential requirement at the very beginning of their effort to solve serious problems. People didn't see the initial complacency. They didn't look very hard for it, either. In a few cases, managers saw the early red flags but did not know what to do, or thought they knew but took ineffective action. Some people thought the flurry of activity that eventually emerged was a sign that complacency was dying and urgency was growing—but it was not. All these mistakes are correctable deficiencies, the correction of which will only grow in importance in a faster-moving, more turbulent twenty-first-century world.

help others (including bosses) to see the problem

Not only are the deficiencies correctable, but the solution does not require a CEO with the talent of Winston Churchill.

Caroline Ortega works for a smaller version of the data warehousing company. She is twenty-seven years old. Her firm recently faced a change challenge equally as difficult as the one faced by the other larger firm. Caroline's company also made a very similar set of initial mistakes, first and foremost trying to charge forward with far too little urgency among management and staff. At Caroline's level in the company—this was her second job out of college—there was an odd mixture of frustration, arrogance, and a tendency to blame other departments or senior management for any perceived problems. Virtually no one seemed to know much about a "high level" task force except that it appeared to achieve very little.

Because Caroline did see red flags—many red flags—she decided to gather from friends what they knew about the executive committee. The consensus opinion was that the chief administrative officer (CAO) in charge of HR, legal, facilities, and so on was the most open minded, the least status conscious, the most approachable, and seemingly close to the CEO. Caroline asked for and, with little difficulty, was granted an appointment with the CAO. She requested thirty minutes. The actual meeting went on for an hour and a half.

Over the following three weeks, the CAO arranged a series of informal lunches with people at Caroline's level. He frequently visited other buildings in the large corporate headquarters campus. He talked extensively to four middle managers he had known since the firm's earliest days twenty-seven years ago. He asked for recent written reports associated with new product marketing activities, large-systems product development programs, and a quality improvement effort in the North American plants—all difficult reading because of the complexity of the technologies involved. He then canceled a trip to Europe and had a long dinner with the CEO.

Over the next month, an alarmed CEO rearranged his schedule to allow for a series of lunches, meetings, visits to other facilities, and an examination of certain reports that would never have reached his level in the firm. With increasing clarity about the scope of the complacency problem, he noticed for the first time how much the company's newspaper was filled with "happy talk" and devoid of serious information about customers, the industry, and the firm's challenges. With newfound determination, the CEO began taking action. He immediately restructured the high-level task force. He made major changes in the agenda for the upcoming yearly top management meeting. He shifted the tone of his comments in public. He looked for ways to expose other executive committee members to what he had seen and heard. Recognizing with clarity for the first time just how relentlessly one of the members of his executive team defended the status quo, disrupting tough conversations about the need for organizational changes and creating within his division an astonishingly low sense of urgency, the CEO handled the problem with uncharacteristic speed and decisiveness (the senior vice president took an early retirement).

It's a long story, as they all are. But the summary is this. Because of these and many more actions, coming first from the CEO and CAO and then from others, a sense of true urgency within the firm began to rise with surprising speed. Then, over the next two years, changes were made in how products were designed, manufactured, sold, and serviced (the latter being a much greater problem than the CEO had ever contemplated). As a result, margins improved significantly, technological leadership was regained, only one small layoff was required, and the stock did not crash as a few analysts had predicted.

Many people deserve credit for providing the needed initiative in this story, especially the CAO and the CEO.

But it was young Caroline's leadership that was arguably the single most important contribution, a fact that did not go unnoticed by the man who ran the firm.

The solution to the urgency problem often starts with one person. It could be a CEO. It could be a Caroline. Whichever the case, the person *does see* the complacency, *does see* the false urgency, and is willing to act. We need many more of these people.

increasing true
urgency

one strategy and four tactics

An increasingly popular management tool is the *business case.* Typically, in a business case, facts and figures, economic analysis, and qualitative logic are used to demonstrate that an issue is important and that a particular course of action should be taken. If not explicitly, at least implicitly, business cases try to reduce complacency by saying, "What we are doing is no longer what we will need in the future. If you look at the data, you'll find there is a much better way to operate. Here is the proof." Sometimes business cases try to redirect the dysfunctional activity associated with false urgency by saying, in effect, "Yes, we are in a mess. The way out is for us to focus our activities on doing such and such. Here is the analysis that logically supports that conclusion."

For our purposes, a careful examination of business cases is very useful because it tells us much about the best strategy for creating a heightened sense of urgency. This examination helps because, as a powerful urgency-raising tool, exceptionally well-researched business cases far too often fail miserably.

how and why a business case fails

The new head of information technology was smart, well educated at a prestigious eastern university, and deeply convinced that his firm's antiquated systems needed a major overhaul. Much better software was on the market to help sales management, plant management, financial reporting, and e-learning. Cheaper and faster servers were available. More effective firewalls were being sold. The IT problem inside the company was already serious, in his judgment, and would become intolerable within two to three years.

Fully recognizing that his firm's management would not see the hazards with the clarity that he did, would never support the huge allocation of scarce resources to solve the IT problem, and would be highly reluctant to suffer the headaches that came with all major computer system changeovers, he readily agreed when his CEO asked him to create the case for change and present it to the executive committee. Working with his direct reports and a well-known consulting firm, the man gathered a great deal of data and used it to demonstrate that the firm's current systems and hardware were fast becoming a serious problem. He also identified alternative courses of action, analyzed the costs and benefits of each, and developed an extremely well-thought-out proposal. A lengthy document was created to show the skeptical that expensive new systems were needed and to demonstrate to the anxious that the right systems were available and could be implemented with minimum disruptions.

The final report was nearly one hundred fifty pages long. In meticulous detail, the issues were defined. The firm's systems were compared to what was known of comparable systems in competing organizations and with best practices outside the industry. The market and economic consequences for the recommended changes were assessed and, whenever possible, quantified. The consequences of not changing, or of delaying, were also assessed, with an emphasis on economic estimates. A recommendation was made in some detail—equipment, vendors, cost. A return on investment estimate was presented and defended. A plan for implementation was outlined in moderate detail, with a timetable and an explanation for how disruptions could be minimized during changeover.

The executive committee discussed the case in a number of meetings over a three-month period. Many questions were asked, but the thorough case addressed most with no more than "If you'll turn to page 62, you will see that . . ." When a consensus appeared to emerge over a slightly modified version of the plan, the CEO gave his approval to proceed.

In a series of six speeches made by the IT head, the case was presented to groups of senior managers in the firm's six divisions. Each session included dozens of detailed PowerPoint slides and an opportunity for questions and answers. Although many concerns were raised, generally about disruptions during the changeover, most people appeared to agree, if only reluctantly, that the changes were necessary. When the CEO was convinced that enough people were on board, execution of the plan began.

A year later, when the huge project began to run into the kinds of problems that seem inevitable in IT system changeovers—problems that were for the most part anticipated in the original business case—criticisms grew and cooperation waned. Just as more assistance was needed to deal with growing problems, less was made available. As a result, the project began to miss more and more target dates and to run more and more over budget. Grumbling grew even louder. The frustrated head of IT pointed out, given any opportunity, that the logic in the original case was still valid. His support nevertheless continued to decline.

The project was eventually completed one year later than originally projected, at a 40 percent cost overrun, and with a functional capacity around 70 percent of what had been promised. The head of IT moved on to another company.

I have left out all detail here—industry, size of organization, number of organizational units spread out over what geography—because the same basic story can be found in nearly any industry, country, or level of government. And the basic lessons are the same everywhere.

The business case clearly played an important role in launching the IT effort. Almost no one knew enough about IT to see what was possible or to appreciate all of the dangers of continuing with the current systems. Even those managers who knew that their IT system was inadequate were not sure what to do. Because the demands for capital always exceeded what budgets could accommodate, any inclination to allocate huge sums for IT was very low. The thoughtful, thorough, and quantitative business case made sense to many of these people or, if not completely persuasive, at least assured them that someone had done the homework. Not all the junior IT staffers agreed on the technical aspects of the recommendation, but none could offer a more thoroughly researched alternative.

Likewise, among those managers who were terrified at the scope of the project and the possibilities for disruption, none had the expertise or time to offer a well-done counter case. Taken as a whole, the "buy in" seemed sufficient to move forward.

But the buy in was almost entirely *intellectual*. Yes, people thought, the figures do add up. Yes, the arguments sound logical. The return on investment analysis is probably as rigorous as can be done under these sorts of circumstances. There will be disruptions during implementation, but the plan has offered methods—hard to tell how sound—for dealing with the distractions. I'm not thrilled about the cost and potential problems, people often thought, but a solid case has been built that the alternative—doing little or nothing—is riskier. I suppose there is an economic or strategic opportunity to be had here. Okay. I guess.

The problem in stories like this is not that the case is weak, poorly thought out, or not supported with sufficient facts. The fundamental problem is that the case is *all head and no heart*.

aim for the heart

Underlying the urgent behavior that makes organizations succeed in a turbulent world is not only a set of thoughts. It's not only, "There is a great opportunity or hazard (in IT, for example) and therefore logically we must deal with it." Underlying a true sense of urgency is a set of *feelings*: a compulsive determination to *move, and win, now*. When it comes to affecting behavior—creating alert, fast-moving actions that are focused on an important issue, relentlessly launching needed initiatives or co-operating with the initiatives of others, pushing to achieve more ambitious goals despite the obstacles, trying to achieve progress each and every day, constantly purging low-value activities so that time is available to do all this—feelings are more influential than thoughts. This was the central conclusion I first fully understood as a result of the research reported in my book *The Heart of Change*. This is a perspective that is rarely acknowledged in the classroom or the boardroom.

For centuries we have had the expression in English, "Great leaders win over the hearts and minds of others." The expression is not, "Great leaders win over the minds of others." More interesting yet, the expression is not that great leaders win the minds and hearts of others. Heart comes first.

More than thoughts in the mind, it is feelings in the heart that create the unchanging behavior of complacency, the unproductive flurry of behavior that is a false urgency, or the powerfully useful actions of true urgency. This is not to say that thoughts are unimportant.

If I think I know what to do, and I am already doing it, those thoughts will support complacent, unchanging actions. If I think we are in a frightening mess, that idea can easily lead to an often-wasteful frenzy of activity. If I think that there are exciting opportunities and great hazards out there, that belief can produce more true urgency. But whether it's a contentment with the status quo, anger and anxiety, or a determination to move and win, *now*, those emotions influence action even more.

History is filled with examples that support this conclusion. Martin Luther King Jr. did not reduce anger among blacks and contentment or anxiety among whites by announcing on the Washington Mall, "I have a strategic plan." A mind-driven case for change could easily be made, and was made by many people at the time: treatment of blacks was inconsistent with some of the country's most long-cherished values, and inconsistencies have pernicious effects; wasting black talent undermined the country's interests; angry conflict among blacks and whites wasted resources and hurt people; un-Christian behavior toward blacks undermined Christianity itself and its foundation that served society. King's speech addressed all these points briefly, but mostly it pounded away at people's gut-level feelings with poetic rhetoric and passionate words about justice and morality. He hit hearts in a way that converted anger and anxiety into a commitment to move, do the right thing, and *now*. He hit hearts in a way that converted complacency into real urgency. Tens of millions of people not at the rally that day saw the speech on TV or heard it on the radio. Urgency went up, essential action followed, and legislation that would probably have failed the year before was passed into law.

Mindless emotion is not the point. Generally, the challenge is to fold a rational case directed toward the mind into an experience that is very much aimed at the heart. The winning strategy combines analytically sound, ambitious, but logical goals with methods that help people experience new, often very ambitious goals, as exciting, meaningful, and uplifting—creating a deeply felt determination to move, make it happen, and win, now.

Tactics that aim at the heart, and successfully increase urgency, all seem to have five key characteristics.

First, they are thoughtfully created human experiences. Documents, abstract ideas, or data sets may play a role and usually do, but how effectively is determined by many choices that shape what people experience. How should a report called a business case be written? Short, long, with illustrations, with exhibits, or with any color graphics? How should it be delivered—in paper form, as a speech, in a small group meeting with much Q&A? To whom should it be given—top management, everyone? At what time should it be delivered—7:00 a.m., 7:00 p.m.? By whom should it be presented—the CEO, the head of a task force? In what setting should it be delivered—the annual top management meeting, the weekly communication event in the company cafeteria? What nonverbal signals should be included—lots of smiles or frowns or passion? All these choices, and more, determine how, if at all, the heart is moved. A brilliant business case, packaged and delivered in the wrong way, can create indifference, suspicion, anger, or cynicism—none of which will produce a sense of urgency to make a group, enterprise, or nation prosper.

Second, effective experiences work appropriately on all our senses. People not only hear, but they see something in front of them or in their mind's eye that helps raise urgency. They are not only told; they are shown. They might even smell or feel something of relevance, as, for example, in a visit to a factory. These sorts of sensory experiences can be powerful. Taken as a whole, they can be compelling, surprising, or dramatic in ways that deeply influence our emotions, and not only the way we think.

Third, the experiences are not designed to create just any emotional reaction. They do not convert a contentment with the status quo into the anger and anxiety associated with false urgency. They do not convert fear back into complacency. They do make people feel that despite past failures, this time they can get it right. They do make people feel that despite creating a difficult situation, a crisis might be a blessing in disguise. They make change-weary, cynical people believe that this will not be a repeat of a painful or ridiculous past. Experiences succeed in these ways because information is sent by someone with confidence, credibility, passion, conviction, or a highly visible sense of urgency (I'll have much more to say about this later).

Fourth, the experiences are rarely, if ever, explained. They don't need to be. You don't find people saying, "Sarah, I am handing you this document as you walk out the door to the airport because I know that on the plane you are much more likely to read it in one sitting, which will make the new goals much more dramatic and emotionally appealing than reading the paper in twenty-minute segments over the course of a week." You probably wouldn't say, "David, we're going to stand next to workers on the factory floor, and not just look at the floor from the factory manager's office, because I need you to smell it down there, hear the grunts and groans, and, frankly, find yourself feeling very uncomfortable." The point is not to be covert or manipulative. It's to avoid trying to say explicitly what is difficult to say, is difficult for the other person to understand, and does not need to be said.

Fifth, the experiences almost inevitably lead us to raise our sights, to emotionally embrace goals beyond maintaining the status quo, beyond coping with a difficult situation, beyond incremental adjustments to what we now do. Ultimately, it is that gap between what exists and what you want—not only what you think is logical—and between the reality today and a deeply meaningful aspiration that generates the determination associated with a sense of urgency.

an example of the basic strategy

Here is one of my favorite examples of an effective heart-head, urgency-raising strategy.

At the annual top management meeting of a well-known company, two division managers were both on the agenda to make speeches. One was positioned in the afternoon of the first day, the other the morning of the second. The audience was made up of 150 of their peers, their subordinates, as well as their boss.

Manager number one walked to the podium with his notes. He asked for the lights to go down and he began his speech. A new, information-rich PowerPoint slide appeared every thirty to sixty seconds. Many slides were filled with numbers and charts. He looked at his notes about one-third of the time, the slides another third, and what he could see of the audience (the lights were down) the final third. Although he was no doubt a bit nervous because he rarely made important speeches in front of important audiences, he nevertheless was remarkably articulate. It helped that he clearly knew the material he was offering very well. It also helped that he could turn and look at a slide if he began to forget his lines.

His presentation was basically in three parts: (1) the problems the audience members needed to face, (2) a new set of goals and strategies for moving forward, and (3) a method for organizing to implement the strategy. When he was done, the lights went up and he answered questions for thirty minutes. The questions fell into three categories: clarifications ("Are you saying . . . ?"); very polite disagreements with the data or the logic connecting the data (polite in the sense that no one came close to saying, "Your facts are wrong"); and nonquestions that were mostly endorsements of his conclusions and action plan ("The point about" such and such "makes sense to me, and let me explain why").

Manager number two was noticeably more nervous in his presentation the next morning. He put his notes down and stood beside the podium. Because the lights automatically went down and there was a spotlight only on the podium, he was mostly in the dark along with the audience. He made a joke out of this gaffe. "Kerry [the CFO] keeps telling us we are all in the dark, and I guess he may be right." Then, instead of moving behind the podium and into the spotlight, he asked that all the lights be turned up. When they were, he made another very small joke and received another very mild chuckle from the audience. He then proceeded to talk for an hour with very few PowerPoint slides. He was less articulate than the other manager. He paused at times as if searching for the right words. He made a case for change much like the first speaker's. To back up his assertions, he used only a few statistics, no more than 10 percent as many numbers in the first manager's speech, but data that was all attention grabbing. For nearly half his speech, he told stories: about his father's company that had gone into bankruptcy, leaving his family in difficult circumstances; about a friend of his who worked at a competing firm and who recently, after a few too many drinks at the clubhouse, disclosed information about the competing firm's very aggressive new strategies; about the speaker's great pride in working for his company when he was a young man, during a time when the firm was number one in all its markets; about what a customer had recently told him that left him surprised and upset; about the fact that he and his wife had talked about early retirement but declined because he wanted to retire a winner, which, he said, *he damned well planned on doing.* He ended and received the longest applause heard at the entire meeting.

Whether either man knew consciously what he was doing, I have no idea. I did not have the opportunity to talk to either one at the meeting or afterward. But I do know that what each did, on the same stage, with the same audience, at almost the same time, had a very different effect.

Lights-down signals to our senses that the workday may be over and it's time for sleep. People have a hard time paying careful attention or engaging material if their bodies are wondering whether it is bedtime. An exciting adventure movie, made by Steven Spielberg with a $70 million budget, may be able to overcome this impulse. A speech by the rest of us rarely can.

When we stand behind a big, old wooden podium, it can feel as if someone is putting a shield between us and the audience. Shields tend to push people away, buffer any personal connection, and make an audience wary and less receptive. Most traditional podiums also create a formality that is increasingly out of step with contemporary culture, producing yet more disconnect.

A spotlight on someone can suggest that he or she is a star. If, indeed, the person is a star—in movies, in politics—that probably will feel right to most people. If the person is not a star, it can feel odd. Is the person on the stage being presumptuous? Arrogant? A fraud? For the most part, people like humility and hate arrogance.

PowerPoint slides so dense that they cannot be read in the last seven rows can annoy the audience in the last seven rows. Small print can create all sorts of irrational feelings that do not help the situation. The questions raised unconsciously might include, Does the speaker not care whether I can see because he thinks I cannot understand the information? Is the speaker trying to show off all the detail he has mastered? Has he chosen print too small to read because he is trying to hide something from me?

Humor can have a very powerful opposite effect if it is truly funny and not in any way mean. It can reduce stress, with all the benefits of reduced stress. If people in an audience laugh, it can feel as if the speaker understands them. The sense is, He is one of us. If audiences feel a speaker is one of them, they will tend to treat him or her with less suspicion. Skepticism does not necessarily block communication. Suspicion does.

Neurologists say that our brains are programmed much more for stories than for PowerPoint slides and abstract ideas. Stories with a little drama seem to be enjoyed by our feelings and, more importantly, are remembered far longer than any dry slide filled with analytics. Personal stories also create a more intimate atmosphere. Intimacy suggests friends. Friends suggest people who are not trying to take advantage of one another.

Our logical minds worry about awkwardness in a presentation. But up to a point, most people seem to feel more comfortable with less-than-superman speaking qualities. It makes the speaker more human. It makes the speaker look more vulnerable. Vulnerable means he is less likely to aggressively attack our decisions or beliefs, and that makes us more comfortable. A little awkwardness also feels real, not slick or phony. When we feel someone is being slick and phony, we are much more likely to reject the message.

Our rational minds tell us that none of these issues should be so important. What is important is content: is this a solid analysis and plan, or not? But the best plan may raise little urgency in a company whose very successes have left it so complacent that most people are not looking for, and are not inclined to listen to, a new plan.

Within the company in which those two managers made speeches, six months after the yearly meeting many people were moving with a new sense of urgency to deal with their considerable challenges. The second man's speech was only one of many actions that lowered a sleepy contentment with the status quo. But it was an important action. The sequence of events seems to have been, first, an emotionally compelling speech is given at a very important meeting to a very important audience; then urgency rises among many of those in the meeting, including the speaker's boss; the increased urgency is one factor in helping form a better and more committed team to deal with the challenges; the committed team energetically works with others to create a new, sensible vision and strategy, with the first speaker's ideas having a significant effect at that point; the energized team spends hours carefully and cleverly communicating the strategies, visions, and plans with both their minds and their hearts—and onward from there.

Most of what is taught repeatedly in management education and in most organizations suggests that I have overstated the case here. People are emotional creatures, yes, but they are educated to allow their minds to guide their actions in sounder ways than with frightened or angry impulses that might have guided cavemen. Look at a good management meeting, one might say. For the most part, it is thoughtful, smart, and rigorous. People find the facts and try to deal with them logically. People strive to identify problems and plan actions that are rational. Yet an ever-increasing body of research from neurologists and psychologists affirms that below the calm, logical veneer rages another world. Strategizers and number crunchers long conditioned to discount and discard feelings may disagree with a theory of raging emotions, or may choose to ignore it. But they do so at their peril. After three decades of studying great leaders who mobilize people to unexpected achievement by winning over hearts and minds, I can say with some confidence that the leaders would side with the neurologists and psychologists.

Great leaders understand, or at least sense correctly, that historical success tends to produce stable and inwardly focused organizations, and they, in turn, reinforce a feeling of contentment with the status quo. Recent failures to produce short-term results or to adapt to change can produce a great deal of activity, but it's often unproductive activity driven by anxiety about one's own future (not the organization's future) or anger at others. In an increasingly competitive, fast-moving world, all this is not

strategies for increasing true urgency

— giving people important facts —

Excellent information by itself, with the
best data and logic, that may define new needs
and new (probably ambitious) goals

Can win over the minds and thoughts of others,
but will rarely win over the hearts and feelings
sufficiently to increase needed urgency
(*and this happens all the time*).

— winning hearts and minds —

A logical case that is a part of a heart-engaging
experience, using tactics that communicate not only
needs but emotionally compelling needs,
that communicate not only new stretch goals,
but goals that excite and arouse determination

Can win over the hearts and minds of others
and sufficiently increase needed urgency.

only a problem, but it can be deadly. And none of this can be fixed by a mind-only strategy.

the tactics

The most successful tactics people use to increase urgency with heart-head strategies fall into four categories.

In the first, people dramatically bring outside reality into groups that are too inwardly focused. They *do not* just collect data and dump it on individuals or massage valid information into goals and present them on Power-Point slides, which is mostly what the first speaker at the annual management meeting did. Instead, they create emotionally compelling experiences involving other people, information, and even the right kind of business cases, which is much of what the other speaker did.

Second, they behave with true urgency themselves *every single day*. They *do not* just say the right words daily, but, more importantly, they make their deeds consistent with their words. They do so as visibly as possible, to as many people as possible, all in ways designed to reduce contentment with the status quo and the anxiety or anger that comes so easily with failures.

Third, they look for the upside possibilities in crises, but very selectively and with great care. They *do not* view a crisis as only a threat but also as a potential opportunity to destabilize an overly stable organization. Destabilization can hit people emotionally and, if done correctly, reduces complacency among the management and staff. If done poorly, it creates the sort of running-around behavior associated with a false sense of urgency.

Fourth, they confront the problem of "NoNos" and do so effectively. They *do not* accept, as inevitable, that an organization must put up with people who relentlessly create experiences that kill urgency, people whose reaction to any new idea is "No, no, you see . . ." They defang these individuals with three methods that work— methods used far less often than two other methods that tend to be ineffective.

All four sets of tactics can have an effect that is visceral, and not only intellectual. And when they are used well, they influence attitudes, thoughts, feelings, hopes, dreams, and behavior. You turn a complacent contentment with the status quo, or the anger and anxiety associated with a perceived mess, into a determination to move, and win, *now*.

These tactics are a part of what virtually all great leaders do, but using them does not require the genes, charisma, or astonishing skills of a great leader. The use of some tactics may require a powerful position in an organization, but many can be employed by people at any level in an enterprise. All need to be used much, much more often. And they *can* be.

increasing a true sense of urgency

the strategy

Create action that is exceptionally alert, externally oriented, relentlessly aimed at winning, making some progress each and every day, and constantly purging low value-added activities—all by always focusing on the *heart* and not just the mind.

the tactics

1. **Bring the Outside In**

   - Reconnect internal reality with external opportunities and hazards.

   - Bring in emotionally compelling data, people, video, sites, and sounds.

2. **Behave with Urgency Every Day**

   - Never act content, anxious, or angry.

- Demonstrate your own sense of urgency
  always in meetings, one-on-one interactions,
  memos, and e-mail and do so as visibly as
  possible to as many people as possible.

3. **Find Opportunity in Crises**

- Always be alert to see if crises can be a friend,
  not just a dreadful enemy, in order to destroy
  complacency.

- Proceed with caution, and never be naïve,
  since crises can be deadly.

4. **Deal with the NoNos**

- Remove or neutralize all the relentless
  urgency-killers, people who are not skeptics
  but are determined to keep a group complacent or, if needed, to create destructive
  urgency.

tactic one

bring the outside in

Tactic One is based on the observation that organizations of any size or age tend to be too internally oriented. Even people who know this fact often underestimate the size of the problem and its consequences. The disconnect between what insiders see, feel, and think, on the one hand, and external opportunities and hazards, on the other, can be astonishing at times—even in organizations that are producing very good short-term results. An inside-outside disconnect always reduces an organization's sense of urgency. When people do not see external opportunities or hazards, complacency grows.

Because of the natural tendency toward internal focus and the complacency that follows, one powerful way to increase urgency is by reducing the gap between what is happening on the outside and what people see and feel on the inside. There are seven very practical methods that will do so, any of which you can use effectively when you clearly understand the basics: the inside-outside problem; the need and power of reducing the gap; the difference between a real and a false sense of urgency; and what a heart-head strategy really means.

recognize the pervasive problem of internal focus

Most organizations fail. In the automotive industry, well over 90 percent of the car companies that existed in the early 1900s were gone by the 1940s. The vast majority of new restaurants don't survive two years. Organizations that do survive have to succeed in pleasing some combination of investors, clients, or the world at large. Satisfied groups tend to desire more of whatever an organization provides. Providing more goods or services requires growth. With growth, the need increases for coordination across more and larger departments and geographical areas. With growth, more plants and offices must be managed. Because of how complex organizations become, these communication, coordination, and facility management demands draw eyes inward, eyes that once were focused on external contingencies.

Enterprises that grow over a sustained period of time are seen as successful. With success, a "we know best" culture easily develops. And why not? The evidence seems to suggest that managers and employees do know best. Over time, pride easily shifts to overconfidence or arrogance. When people think they have the answers and others don't, they tend not to pay much attention to those others—especially outsiders—because it seems like a waste of time.

An inwardly focused organization inevitably misses new opportunities and hazards coming from competitors, customers, or changes in the regulatory environment. When you don't see opportunities or hazards, your sense of urgency drops. With less urgency, you are even less inclined to look outside for the new possibilities and problems. Complacency grows. Yet if success has given an organization a strong enough position through a globally recognized brand, huge economies of scale, a monopoly charter, or patents, it is amazing how much people can ignore the outside and still survive, even prosper, possibly for decades.

Examples abound of how success creates size, market power, and an entitlement culture, all of which, in turn, create an inward focus, a lack of understanding of external reality, and a total lack of urgency to correct the problem. In the United States, IBM and GM in the 1980s are very visible examples. At least a few of today's most successful enterprises appear to be going down the same path.

In the supermarket business, one regional chain was the very first in its geographical area to offer a broad selection of packaged goods, meat, and produce, all with a level of service found only in its best smaller competitors. Customers loved it. As a result, over forty years the chain grew from two stores to sixty-two. The size of each new facility increased, economies of scale grew, margins were kept exceptionally high, the firm's brand became the most respected in its territories, and national supermarket chains chose to stay away from a difficult competitive situation. For years, the owners constantly praised the actions of management and employees, and rightly so. But over time, with great success, pride turned into a subtle arrogance. The external focus of a two-unit organization turned into the internal focus of a much larger and more complex company. With weak competition, the negative consequences of an inward focus and a lack of urgency were small. Then a younger and more innovative competitor encroached upon the firm's territory with stores that were brighter, with wider aisles, a broader selection of fresher produce, and easier checkout. Amazingly, the successful chain practically ignored those developments!

Sitting in on management meetings, as did this observer, you would rarely hear any discussion about the

how success creates an inward focus, which kills a sense of urgency

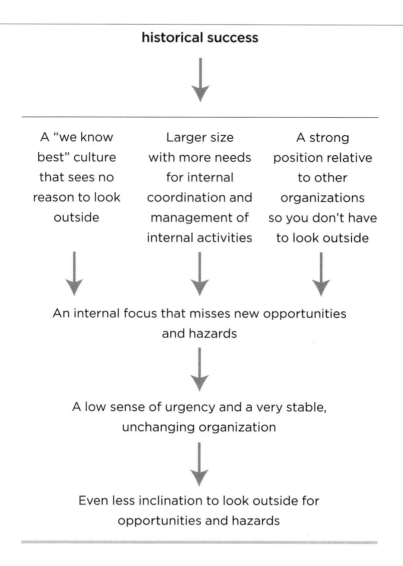

historical success

A "we know best" culture that sees no reason to look outside

Larger size with more needs for internal coordination and management of internal activities

A strong position relative to other organizations so you don't have to look outside

An internal focus that misses new opportunities and hazards

A low sense of urgency and a very stable, unchanging organization

Even less inclination to look outside for opportunities and hazards new competitor. The talk was all about the firm itself: margins in store 42 were off budget, renovations at one of the locations were coming along fine, and a new performance appraisal process for middle management was almost ready for implementation. More astonishing, if you had asked elementary questions about the new competitor—how big it had become, what its competitive strategy was, what its current growth rate was—most executives did not know, nor, again astonishingly, did they show any great concern that they did not know.

Variations on this story are much more common than most people seem to realize, and yet the scenario is far from inevitable. When people see the external world clearly, it can increase their sense of urgency. Seeing problems that threaten jobs, career opportunities, or pride can decrease complacency and increase urgency. Seeing new possibilities that might greatly expand job security, open up new promotion options, make bigger bonuses feasible, increase job satisfaction, and contribute to customers and investors and communities—all this can help managers successfully create a call to action, even in enterprises that have been totally content with the status quo.

Over time, you can change an organization's culture to make it externally focused. People will then naturally look to the outside. They will see relevant information about threats and new possibilities. The disconnect between the outside and the inside will shrink. Complacency will be reduced. I'll have more to say about all that later. But cultural change often requires many years. When you don't have many years, in a much shorter period of time people can build formal mechanisms and structures that can systematically bring in the outside. There are even all sorts of actions that can be taken this week or this month that will make a difference—actions that will help you, over time, move toward the right systems and ultimately the right culture.

listen to customer-interfacing employees

In terms of shrinking the disconnect between the inside and the outside of an organization, one method used today by some of the world's most successful corporations is to listen very carefully, and often, to the lower-level personnel who interface with customers.

Whether customer service employees at an auto dealership, clerks at a bank, or sales representatives for large computer systems, certain types of people, if encouraged, can collect masses of external information simply as a part of doing their jobs well. If this information finds its way to decision makers, an organization can become more externally oriented and a sense of urgency will tend to grow.

Some of the world's most successful entrepreneurs rely on this method, and with great success. They regularly visit groups of frontline employees during trips to offices, stores, and factories. They ask questions about customers and customer reaction to their products or services. They listen carefully to what they are told. They demonstrate respect for the people with whom they are talking. Employees sense this and go out of their way to pay more attention to customers and to share this information honestly with the boss. Successful entrepreneurs then look for patterns. They encourage other mangers to do the same. They encourage or require that frontline supervisors engage in some form of this activity as a regular, ongoing part of their jobs.

Sam Walton was a prominent example of someone who used this practice. And Wal-Mart, during his years, was the most successful organization of its kind in the world. The same was true for Herb Kelleher at Southwest Airlines, where customers, employees, and investors came to find joy in an industry with almost no joy.

One apparent trend today is that more enterprises actually are listening more to frontline personnel. The method typically requires the following:

- A small leap of faith at the beginning. That means believing that frontline people are intelligent and motivated enough to be a source of useful cus-

tomer information, even if past evidence suggests
they are not.

- Treating these employees accordingly. Very few
  people will help, regardless of what you say, if you
  treat them without respect.

- Asking questions, listening closely to answers,
  and not giving up if employees don't respond
  immediately.

A newly promoted district manager in a retail chain
tried this simple formula with great success. Because he
visited stores regularly, the cost of using this method was
small. Eventually, most employees began to respond in
the way he wanted. One pattern he noticed in their responses: some of his people noted that customers sometimes commented negatively on the piped-in music that
was a staple in all stores. He began to ask all his employees about music. When he heard no one say that customers commented favorably and that occasionally they
commented negatively, he began asking customers himself. In this unscientific vote, 50 percent did not like the
music, often comparing it to the annoying "blah" heard
in elevators, 40 percent didn't even notice there was
music or didn't care one way or the other, and fewer than
10 percent commented favorably. The firm was already
doing an annual survey that sampled customer opinions.

Music was not on the survey. The new district manager presented this information to his boss in a face-to-face meeting, not in a memo. He presented the facts not as data per se but as a story, and one that was interesting, surprising, and a bit dramatic. He left his boss to ask the obvious questions. What else might be left off the customer questionnaire? Do we really know all the details about the customer experience that we should know? Urgency around these questions went up, and, after this first step, some useful action followed.

This music story did not lead immediately to big results, but much of bringing-the-outside-in comes in small packages that stack up over time to make a significant difference. The music story did, however, alert managers to the fact that their customer survey was a problem. So they changed it. It also told them they might need other systematic methods to make sure there was not a disconnect between their offerings and customer responses. Within six months, they created one such mechanism: a frontline employee survey that solicited their ideas.

There is nothing revolutionary about reducing the outside-inside gap with the help of frontline employees. But very few organizations use this method well. Ways of running a business better fitting twenty to forty years ago live on. This helps no one.

use the power of video

Another effective way to better connect insiders with the outside world is to use video.

A firm manufactured large, made-to-order containers for customer use in transporting its products. The company made "high-quality" containers in the usual way we think of quality: the steel and rivets were always according to specifications, the tolerances were right, the product did not break down or require unusual maintenance. But some of the detailing did not fit the specific needs of a major customer. As soon as a shipment was received, the customer had to make changes in the product to fit its requirements. The modifications were not expensive, but, in light of a made-to-order contract, they were irritating, especially since switching to another suppler would be expensive. The customer had told some people at the plant about this problem. The plant personnel listened politely but didn't alter what they were doing. If you had confronted them, they would probably have pointed out that they had set the standard for their industry, that they knew what the product should be, and that if the customer wanted to make modifications on its end, that was its choice.

The firm's CEO convinced the customer's president to be filmed while explaining his needs and showing his growing frustrations. The video was shot inexpensively and edited to fifteen minutes. Included were relevant facts and the clear angst evident in the customer's voice and facial expressions. Groups of twenty to thirty plant employees were then brought into a conference room at the factory. The boss said he wanted to show them a short video that he found very disturbing. Then he played the tape. Because most plant personnel never talked to customers, they were shocked, first, by the facts of the case and, I suspect, even more so by the emotion pouring out of the TV screen. Some employees became defensive: this is not a typical customer; we make a quality product; is this his way of negotiating a lower price? But a core group of employees said, in effect, we need to do something about this, and *fast*. And they did. As a result, a tradition-bound factory was reinvigorated. And customers loved it.*

One lesson I have learned again and again over the past few decades is about the power of video when it is honest and human and deals with a topic of importance to individual or organizational performance. What we derisively call "PR material" brings out the cynicism in

---

*The entire story, told in the words of the key executive involved, is reported in John P. Kotter and Dan S. Cohen, *The Heart of Change: Real-Life Stories of How People Change Their Organizations* (Boston: Harvard Business School Press, 2002), 18–20.

people and can reinforce complacency or increase anger. In contrast, material that is emotionally and intellectually honest, shown at the right time to the right group, can be surprisingly influential. It is much more than a replacement for a person who for practical reasons cannot be in the room. Because of the control possible with shooting, editing, and showing the material, it can sometimes be more powerful than a live person.

There is another lesson here, and one that applies broadly, not only in the use of video. The idea is called, "Show them, don't tell them." For the most part, we have been taught to tell people the facts, and as logically as possible. But there is another method and one that is arguably more powerful. Show them. Let them see with their own eyes, and not only through aggregated, abstract data. The latter might be much more rational, because you can summarize in aggregate far more situations than anyone could possibly have the time to see. But "rational" misses the exceptionally important point here about the effect of thinking on behavior versus the effect of emotions on behavior.

As with the case of importing information through frontline employees, you can systematize the use of video as an urgency-raising mechanism. The most obvious way is to make, as a part of the job of any communication department, finding and creating and displaying powerful video on a regular basis a priority. The task may be difficult, but it is not beyond the capabilities of a competent communication group.

don't always shield people from troubling data

The boss in the made-to-order containers company shared what he had learned from a customer with every single individual who worked in the plant. He judged that the behavior of plant personnel would not change unless most people became less complacent. His actions, I think, were very smart. They were also unusual.

People resist sharing outside information broadly with managers or employees either because (1) they believe most people are not smart enough or experienced enough to understand it, (2) they worry about being unfairly blamed when the information does not make them look good, (3) they fear that leaks to analysts and brokers will cause a drop in stock price, and (4) they worry that a broader distribution of troubling information will hurt morale, increase turnover, and, in general, turn damaging contentment into even more damaging anxiety and anger. These concerns can block action, even when some executives understand that they need much more external information, presented to many more employees, more often.

The head of human resources in a division of a packaged goods company lobbied strongly for giving a consultant's report to everyone in a management position within his division. The two most powerful people on the executive team lobbied strongly for not doing so. The report showed that customers in the highest-growing segment of the market did not much like the company's new line of ready-mix products. Its brand was good enough to keep shelf space in supermarkets and keep revenues running at a reasonable rate. Nevertheless, the consultants were very critical of the entire product development effort and painted a disturbing future if broad changes were not made. The two executives arguing against distribution of the report had two concerns: first, that the consultant's analysis could be seen as bleak enough that the firm might lose a few of its most talented people, and, second, that a disgruntled manager might give the report to someone outside the company, and it would make its way to the financial community, a major retail customer, or both, through the trade press. The head of HR lost the debate.

The top team members scrambled to solve the immediate problem with focus groups, a round-the-clock effort in product development, and carefully calculated responses to any press inquiries. To a remarkable degree, they succeeded. Sales dipped for a quarter, but many explanations about inevitable new product challenges were, for the most part, accepted, even though some employees were deeply disappointed by the new product line's lack of expected success.

With a potential crisis averted, the division CEO decided that the consultants were to a large degree right and that much change was needed in his organization. At the annual top management meeting, he made a strong speech about building for the future and keeping the company's leadership despite increasing competition. Three other executive committee members made similar talks. During the morning of the last day of the meeting, the consultants' analysis and recommendations, *modified to sound much less harsh*, were introduced as "a bold step forward to maintain our leadership position in a changing world." During the final afternoon, the agenda focused on execution.

The audience divided into four camps. The smallest by far was made up of people who were already the most externally focused, who already had a strong sense of urgency, who thought the bold steps were obviously needed, and who were delighted to see top management leading. The largest group was made up of people who thought that, in light of the division's historical track record and the lack of any crises, the strategy was either unnecessary or potentially reckless. The two other groups agreed some change was needed but strongly disagreed with the specific recommendations that directly affected them. Both groups thought the big problems were not in their departments but elsewhere. If the challenges are elsewhere, one feels little urgency to act, and neither of those groups did.

Twelve months later, a highly frustrated CEO hired yet another consulting company. The task? Help him implement the new product development strategy that was needed more than ever and yet was not being executed within his organization.

This story, in varying forms, is not unusual. Information from outside the firm offers disquieting news. Top management shields people from the news due to legitimate worries. At some point, top managers try to initiate significant changes based on data they have but many others do not have. A sufficiently low sense of urgency within middle management makes execution painfully difficult. The change effort eventually fails or falls far short of top management's aspirations.

There is much evidence showing that with conviction and some sophistication, you can deal with all these issues. The solution starts at the top:

- Top management sees an opportunity and not only a problem.

- Executives clearly see the goal and the error to be avoided—the objective being to move complacency to urgency and not inadvertently to a flurry of anxious or angry behavior that is mistaken for urgency.

- They give as much of the disquieting information to as many people as is practical.

- They make it clear that external data offers an important opportunity to galvanize action to help make changes that are necessary to strengthen the organization.

- They make it clear in word and deed that a blame game will not be tolerated. They make it clear that a prosperous future is the only issue.

- The top managers act with self-confidence and little visible fear, anger, or arrogance.

- They try to anticipate in advance who will react in what ways. For groups that will be inclined to react with anxiety or anger, top management visibly demonstrates passion, self-confidence, and a steely resolve to help channel that fear and anger into a determination to act and win.

The top managers at the packaged goods company did not give the consultant's report to thirty people, much less three hundred. They could have. They could have minimized risks by explaining the opportunity (urgency up, people mobilized, effective action taken). They could have acted in ways that demonstrated their own determination to move, and win, quickly; that communicated their belief that winning was crucial and possible; that showed others that the issue was to succeed in the future and not to punish people for the past (quelling fears and the emergence of false urgency). That is, they could have provided leadership to create urgency instead of retreating totally into damage control. Even then, there would inevitably have been some negative reverberations. But the choice is clear. Do you want to risk short-term problems, or do you want to shield people from relevant external information, allow complacency to remain too high, and ultimately to undermine an organization's future? Stated as such, this question sounds so stark as to be simplistic. A decade ago I would have said "too simplistic." Not today.

redecorate

I can still remember a visit I made to a company ten years ago as if it happened last week. The firm had been exceptionally successful in the middle part of the twentieth century. But by the time of my visit, market share had been steadily eroding for *twenty* years. The company was in a war, badly wounded, some would say bleeding to death. Yet when I opened the door to corporate headquarters, I entered a visual fantasy world.

Nowhere was there a single sign that the company was struggling, had been struggling for two decades, and was continuing to be beaten again and again in the marketplace. Nowhere was there a sign that the technology affecting its products was changing faster, offering it wonderful opportunities to leap ahead of competitors. The huge waiting room was pin-drop quiet and had the air of an antechamber outside the king's throne room.

In total contrast, I once visited a successful firm that seemed to have its entire outside world hung on the walls of its waiting room. There were pictures of customers, of its own products, of its manufacturing plants, office buildings, competitor products, recent articles from industry publications, and comments (mostly good and some bad) from customers. There were a few prototype sketches of products to come. There were two big charts, one showing margins over the previous two years (which made the firm look good) and one that showed stock price (which made the firm look not so good). The entire effect was somewhat like a teenager's room, especially the picture of a competing CEO with a mustache drawn on it!

I asked and learned that the wall hangings continuously changed. Something new was added or subtracted at least once a week. The person in charge of that space organized most of that change, but employees were em-powered, within certain boundaries, to do so themselves, and they did.

The person I had come to visit was delayed at the airport and arrived late by nearly an hour. I couldn't have cared less. The room was fun and, more to the point, unbelievably informative. In one hour I learned more about an industry, its products, the competition, the global expansion, and so on than I might have learned from a much longer (and more boring) briefing from an industry specialist. The underlying message permeating the room was one of excitement, caution, speed, and change.

I was there once. Employees poured through that space at least twice a day. If the wall hangings were informative but visually boring, or if they never changed, they might have had little effect. For new employees, the effect could be big. But for the rest, the walls would have faded away. But the information *wasn't* visually boring. And the information *did* change on an ongoing basis.

The more general point here is that visuals make a difference. They can signal to us what is happening outside the enterprise. Therefore, look and make sure the signals are accurate. Ask some department to look around on a regular basis. Perhaps the communication group again can help. Or marketing. The key is that the people you choose understand the issue, have relevant skills, and know that dealing with the internal-external gap is a part of their job.

send people out

The idea is simple. Send out "scouts" who, when they return, bring new information about the world and a newfound determination to do something with that information.

Based on a suggestion from a midlevel marketing manager, the CEO of a sporting goods company asks his two top IT executives to accompany sales reps on a visit to key retail accounts twice a year. When he first started this practice, he found little enthusiasm for the idea from either the reps or the IT people. But the CEO persisted, making sure the technology managers were paired with sales personnel who did see the point of the exercise.

The first year, both IT executives visited three cities and twelve customers in three days. The face-to-face, live, non-memo conversations, facilitated by the sales reps, were most revealing. The IT people learned what the customers liked or did not like about all the electronic interfaces between the customer and the supplier. The two executives learned more about how customers rated their shipping, billing, and customer service systems and, just as important, why. They learned what people really did not like and, again, specifically why. Systems that looked $B+$ or A to the IT executives, given the measurements they used, looked different from the customer side.

Perhaps most of all, the visiting executives learned about the specific demands placed on the retailers by their customers, about the challenges created by their retail competitors, and in general about life inside the customers' firms. Much of this information was not new. But some was, not only about the technology for which the IT people were responsible but also about the demands of running a retail business and the broader implications that followed from those demands. But even "old" news, or "not-my-problem" news, when heard in face-to-face conversations with outsiders, often affected thoughts and feelings in new ways. With live interaction, questions could be asked spontaneously. Feedback came from more than words—from how the visitors were treated and from all sorts of other nonverbal information. The overall experience was powerful. The two executives brought information and feelings back to their managers and employees. A sense of urgency for improving IT went up.

With a similar rationale, the head of leadership development at that same firm sends two or three senior managers every year to a three-week program at a major university. His goal is less to educate a few executives than to create, through them, a source of information and urgency that can flow back to a much larger number of employees. A marketing manager tries to achieve a similar purpose by taking his entire ten-person team to the yearly American Marketing Association conference. After the meeting, information is brought to many of those who did not attend the conference and is conveyed with an effect far different than it would be if the non-attendees had been mailed papers given out at the meeting.

Urgency can be increased by sending people, judiciously, to any of an organization's constituencies. Insiders learn about the outside and invariably bring some of that back when they return. Information gathered in this way tends, quite naturally, to be given to other insiders not as antiseptic facts but with stories and with an excitement or distress that affects more than thoughts. It affects how insiders feel, which (in a head-heart strategy) is so crucial.

A few years ago, the top thirty people in a billion-dollar, non-U.S. organization made a two-week trip to Europe and the United States. A young staff manager in HR proposed the idea—not unusual since almost all the bring-the-outside-in methods can be initiated by people at nearly any level in the hierarchy. Senior management accepted. Carefully planned in detail by that young manager, the journey took the executives to similar organizations that did not operate in their country. It took them to universities. It took them to companies known for certain relevant best practices, where they would not only read or hear about the practices but see for themselves (with the accompanying influence on emotions, and not only thought). I asked the CEO how the company could afford to have its entire top management away for two weeks. He looked at me as if I had asked a strange question and replied, "We delegate."

bring people in

A sixth way to bring the outside in is by importing people. Everyone does this to some degree, and yet few gain the true power of the method.

At one large manufacturing company, the annual management meeting had a format that had been used for years. A few hundred managers were invited: the executive committee, its direct reports, plus senior corporate staff. The meeting lasted three days. Depending upon how profitable the firm was, the event was held at a luxurious resort or a more modest venue. At least one afternoon was set aside for golf. Over the three days, about fifteen people were at one time or another on stage talking to the audience. All fifteen were always senior managers and executives—100 percent insiders.

Then one year someone in human resources convinced his boss who convinced the CEO to bring in an external expert from a university. Because the talk was well received, the next year an industry analyst was placed on the agenda, along with three very carefully chosen customers.

All three had some credibility because they were large buyers and had no reputation for being difficult. All three were extensively coached before the meeting to be straight-forward and honest about their dealings with the firm: no overstatements, but no pulling punches. The event provoked much interesting discussion. Because of the apparent success of this bringing-people-in strategy, the next year another analyst, another academic, and another group of customers were invited to the meeting, but this time a key supplier was added, the latter again carefully chosen and coached.

Over three years, time on this firm's annual management meeting agenda moved from 100 percent internal speakers and 0 percent external, to 65 percent inside and 35 percent outside. Because the meeting was held only once a year, this was an exceptionally small change in the lives of senior management. But because of the importance of the meeting and the natural tendency for those not on the executive committee to study the event for clues as to what was happening at the top, the shift from 100/0 to 65/35 was very much noticed. When it became known that the CEO signed off on all choices of speakers, the audience paid even more attention to the outsiders and their messages. Since the number one message was that the world was changing and that the company needed to move faster to keep up, urgency increased—not dramatically, but even small jumps helped start some new and badly needed changes.

People can also be imported as new hires. One manager I know pays special attention to any interviewee's possible complacency. Bringing in one person with a high sense of urgency rarely helps, because he or she can be ignored by complacent insiders. But an ongoing stream of the right kinds of people can make a difference.

Consultants are often imported for a period of time, usually with the explicit task of bringing in outside data, ideas, or wisdom. How effectively this is done varies widely. Almost everyone has heard or seen stories in which organizations gain very little from consultants. But there are powerful examples in the opposite direction, where an insider could never have reduced complacency without visits from external advisers.

It is amazing how seldom organizations look for opportunities to cheaply and easily bring in outsiders. A growing company might have people interviewing for jobs constantly. But it is a rare firm in which the HR function has, as a part of its work, the job of systematically using all interviews to learn about the competition when interviewees have worked for competing firms. A hiring firm usually debriefs people who accept jobs but loses potentially interesting information from all the rest. Companies might have many vendors but never invite them to corporate headquarters as an information gathering exercise. These opportunities can often be relatively inexpensive, but they often go unused.

bring "data" in, but in the right way

Gathering data about the external world is the most widely used tactic today for reducing the internal-to-external disconnect. It's also the most common method that is used poorly or at least in ways that waste its potential.

With importing data, no one needs to leave the office unless it is demanded by his or her job (e.g., most salespeople). Here, no outsiders need be brought in. You just rely on the many sources of data available through the press, consulting reports, the Internet, and the like.

The bringing-in-data process can become unduly time consuming and expensive, but an examination of some organizational practices demonstrates that it need not be. It is amazing what one twenty-five-year-old can find on the Internet today, and how quickly and cheaply he or she can pass it on to others. A consultant is not necessarily required to set up a customer-satisfaction measurement system for a $6 million fee. Perfectly valid and useful systems can be purchased for a quarter that price, even much less for small firms. Mounds of incomprehensible information do not have to be dumped on employees, distracting, annoying, and confusing people in the process. Information can be aggregated in ways that are clear, easy, and efficient to absorb. The simplest forms of information, gathered at virtually no cost, can have a surprisingly useful effect if served in the right way at the right time.

Years ago, when organizations first had computers in offices and factories, I watched a lower-level manager in an IT group convince his CEO to put a graph of the firm's stock over the prior two years, as well as the stock price of its six major competitors, on every computer desktop in the firm. One Monday morning, with no prior warning, the graph appeared, with no way to make it go away until the close of the business day. The unexpected event stirred much conversation, not all of it useful, but some of which led people to look for more data, for the first time, that would help explain the information on share prices. It was a bit of a gimmick, obviously, and the CEO did risk having people blame him for the less-than-stellar stock performance, and some did. But the surprising information—put before people's eyes for hours, not minutes, and before everyone, not a selected group of managers—seems to have helped, if only in a small way, increase a sense of urgency.

One of the staff in the communication department of a low-tech manufacturing enterprise convinced his boss, who in turn convinced the executive committee, to try an experiment with a so-called clipping service. An outside vendor was hired to supply the staff person with stories from a large number of media outlets each day. The communication manager and a colleague from the strategic planning staff scanned the large volume of material and picked out one story a day to send to middle and senior managers through the firm's intranet. The criteria they used were (1) the story was clearly relevant, (2) the text or video could been read or viewed in less than ten minutes, (3) the information seemed credible, and (4) the information was interesting enough, eye-catching enough, or dramatic enough that people might be drawn to read or view it. The experiment was judged to be sufficiently successful that the practice was adopted and has, over time, been modified to make it additionally useful. Today, different groups within the firm are sometimes sent different stories. Senior managers who find articles on their own that they deem potentially important are encouraged to notify the people in charge of the clipping-service system. As you might expect, this methodology has at times encountered political problems, as when the staff running the system disagrees with a suggestion from a powerful executive. But, overall, those involved believe (and I would agree) that their clipping-service system has been very successful at importing data to increase a sense of urgency.

Many organizations in the past two decades have found ways to more systematically collect data on customer satisfaction. A few firms, not many, are now extremely sophisticated in importing information that gives a valid picture of their relationships to customers and potential customers: information on why people buy their products or don't buy them, how customers use the firms' offerings, what problems clients experience and how often, and the responsiveness of the organizations' service personnel. A few successful consulting firms have been built on the practice of providing enterprises with detailed data on competitors, including financial information on costs, overhead, margins, cash flow, and so on. Few organizations seem to seek comparable facts about their key suppliers, although there would seem to be an obvious benefit.

No one would disagree with the general point here. Yet few enterprises use the power of the import-data method fully. They bring in antiseptic data that is soon forgotten. They are sporadic, not systematic, in pulling in information. They amass too much for people to absorb or too little to truly inform them.

Those that do a good job with this method adhere to four guidelines.

First, perhaps the most obvious, is that they bring in enough information. Someone makes sure that systems exist to collect data on competitors, customers, technological trends, and the like. Not doing so seems so primitive, and yet you find internally focused firms making this mistake all the time.

Second, at the other extreme, they do not collect and send to people information in such volume that it is simply lost among the deluge of memos, reports, and conversations that crowd people's days. So they send one article per day from a clipping service that can be read in less than ten minutes, not fifteen articles that would require an hour.

Third, they avoid sending information that is so anti-septic that it flows in and out of short-term memory with great speed. Instead, as much as possible, they send data that feels interesting, surprising, or dramatic. This is yet another example where effective urgency-raising tactics work within the context of a heart-head strategy.

Finally, they pass on information that is interesting and useful to as many people as is possible without undue risk. They don't let hierarchy, a status orientation, or a fear of disclosing troubling information paralyze them in ways that limit information flow and limit possibilities for increasing needed urgency.

In terms of importing data, the new source with huge potential is the Internet. Here I mean not just random trolling, but the clever use of Webcasts, bulletin boards, chat rooms, Webinars—the list goes on and on and will grow over time. I'm not sure whether anyone does this really well today. But smart players will learn to use this resource in ways to serve well urgency-raising purposes.

watch out that you don't create a false sense of urgency

One final, very important, point. External reality, mind-lessly dumped into an organization, does not automati-

imagine

We call this a thought experiment.

Imagine, if you will, an organization where people up and down the hierarchy, and systems throughout the organization, help pull the outside in through

- Sending out people

- Bringing in people

- Bringing in relevant data in an eye-catching manner

- Listening to customer-interface employees

- Creating video about the outside

- Widely sharing what is learned instead of shielding others from possibly troubling news

- Changing the visuals

Nearly anyone in an organization can use these tactics to create more urgency among peers or their bosses. Imagine what would happen to complacency if many people at many levels did so.

cally create real urgency. It can create the anxiety, anger, and dysfunctional flurry of behavior associated with false urgency. It's usually best to avoid this problem in the first place. But if that is impossible, the challenge is always to convert the false into the true, and with speed.

Avoiding the problem of creating false urgency—with the outside-in tactics or any of the other tactics described later in this book—requires judgment. Given whom the people are, and given their current emotional state, will importing a specific set of people, at a specific time, to a specific place, in a specific way build a gut-level determination to move, and win, now? Or will it mostly create anger, frustration, and anxiety?

There are times when the only way to break through cement-like complacency is to blast people's emotions. Blasted emotions usually turn negative. Then the task is to convert negative to positive as quickly as possible.

The key to converting false urgency to real urgency is any source of real urgency, and as much real urgency as possible. Here I mean behavior that is visible, determined, self-confident, nonblaming, passionate, and competent, behavior that tends to be highly fulfilling to the person who acts that way and that can also help urgency grow within others. This sort of action is so important that it is an entire tactic by itself—one of the four discussed in this book. And that's the topic of the next chapter.

5.

tactic two

behave with
urgency
every day

The conversation goes roughly like this.

"My team is too complacent," he says.

Available evidence suggests he is right. The other person in the room tells him so.

"We have got to get this done within twelve months at the latest. At the rate we are going it might take eighteen, or two years, or never. That is unacceptable. We have to move."

The other person expresses total agreement.

"I have to talk to John and Henry. This is just not acceptable."

Another expression of agreement followed by a question. When will you talk to John and Henry?

"When I see them next. I'll make it the number 1 item on the agenda. Number 1."

Okay. And when will you be with them next?

"Let's see. Today's the twenty-eighth. I'll be at their office in London next in—we have the sessions in New York, then we are back here for the quarterly reviews on the fifteenth, then first to Paris and on to London. So about four weeks from now. Maybe I should switch the order of London and Paris. It will get me to them nearly a week earlier. What do you think?"

Yes, he is told, four weeks is a long time.

"All right, I'll put London first—although that will probably create a problem with Andre. I don't know."

How important is the complacency problem?

"Huge," he says. "You know that. Why do you ask?"

Sigh.

respond fast, move *now*

Scene shift: different company and different person. In this case, the manager understands that a sense of urgency is an increasingly powerful, if not essential, asset in an increasingly fast-moving world. She understands that without urgency, all sorts of needed action is not initiated or becomes bogged down after it is initiated. She sees deadly complacency to her right, and a false sense of urgency to her left. She has learned from experience that reducing or eliminating these toxins demands a strategy aimed not only at people's minds but more so at their hearts. She has started to do just that with a set of actions that fits broadly within a bring-the-outside-in tactic. She is searching for what else she can do. On a business trip in Asia, she encounters Ninan.

Ninan runs three small offices in India, the largest in Hyderabad. The speed with which the high-tech section of the city is growing and changing can give the impression that everyone is being swept along by a strong wind and that urgency is not an issue for anyone. Ninan knows differently. He sees vast opportunities and great hazards, but an alarming degree of complacency in some successful enterprises.

His firm's business is outsourcing. Most of its employees are in Bangalore. The company's competitive advantage in the global marketplace is that it has a relatively inexpensive and yet educated young workforce that speaks English. The firm has been growing at 40 percent per year. Both Ninan's boss and the company's CEO are highly committed to maintaining very high levels of growth. They see new competition emerging constantly, and not only from India. They believe that they must grow quickly to achieve mass, economies of scale, and a reputation at least as good as that of anyone in their business. They believe their labor cost advantage over U.S. workers will continue to shrink. Ninan agrees completely with his bosses on all these points, adding that great vigilance is required if they are to deal with new competitors attacking from different directions with different strategies.

His employees are young, mostly unmarried, and thrilled with their incomes. They have never experienced a downturn in business. They know nothing of layoffs. They are delighted with a standard of living vastly better than their parents'. Some of the older employees worry about the future of the country, but most of the young and old can little imagine their delight being taken away from them. Under these circumstances, Ninan believes that complacency is forever a looming problem. Yet in his three offices, vigilance is the norm, and complacency is rare. Watch him and at least one reason is quickly clear.

In conversations, meetings, and e-mails, Ninan constantly demonstrates his own sense of urgency, which, almost inevitably, pumps up his employees' sense of urgency. His attitudes, feelings, and actions are contagious. Someone calls to ask for information on a critical issue, and Ninan says he will send it by the end of the working day tomorrow, even though the other person did not request that speed. At the conclusion of a meeting that seems to fly by, he tells the others what he will be doing over the next seven days to implement their decisions, even if the decisions will require months to fully execute. He is very concrete: "I will talk to Raj when I see him on Tuesday." Then he asks each of the others in the meeting what they will do over the next seven days, "and please be specific." When they answer, he nods as if to say, yes, that makes sense; yes, that will help.

He tags onto e-mail after e-mail some comment, perhaps only a sentence, about how the competition is trying to offer better service, faster service, or less costly service. If someone asks, "When can we talk about" an important subject, more often than not he says, "How about now?" People who dare to open their appointment books and shake their heads, signaling that there is no possibility to meet any time soon, receive a glaring look from the boss. Anyone who does not respond to one of his e-mails in a timely manner will receive the same e-mail quickly sent a second time.

There is very little that is overtly punishing in any of Ninan's actions. He is not mean. He praises, speaks of opportunities, and emphasizes pride. He smiles, laughs, and shows excitement in a manner that seems, and undoubtedly is, genuine. His behavior encourages others to smile, laugh, and be excited. He is not a stressed-out man who creates stress all around him. Nevertheless, seen by all, in encounter after encounter, is a tough message that comes through words and actions. "We have to be constantly vigilant. Past success tells us nothing about the future." It's a message that affects how people think, but more so how they feel and then how they behave.

But maintaining schedules and efficiencies each day while also changing to stay ahead of the competition is difficult to do well. How does he do all this without hundred-hour workweeks and eventual burnout? His boss says that one part of the answer is that Ninan delegates well. Another part: he constantly eliminates activity that no longer adds high value. A customer-visit methodology that gave great results for two years and then greatly diminishing returns is purged. It took too much time relative to what was learned. The same with the monthly XL report. It was essential when Ninan's offices had only twenty-five people, but not now. So it's gone. His supervisors see this attitude and behavior daily, and most of them have learned to act in the same way. They delegate and purge.

Ninan's boss strongly believes that Ninan's small part of the company displays the least complacency and the most urgency within the firm, and that this attitude and behavior are directly related to the astonishing economic results in those three small but rapidly growing offices. So what exactly does Ninan do?

- Certainly his words about competition and markets and change play a role in creating the sense of urgency.

- More so, it's the constant flow of those words, pouring forth all the time.

- But most of all, it's the deeds, and not only the words, that his people see hour after hour, day after day.

In meetings, hallway conversations, e-mails, everywhere, it's Ninan's passionate, eye-catching, relentless action to spot opportunities and hazards, and to embrace the former while ducking the latter. It's behavior that teaches, encourages, pushes, and rewards others to act in the same way. It's a lack of mixed signals, where you say one thing but behave differently. Ninan is a congruent, nonstop, urgency-creating machine.

What propels him to act this way? His boss says it's hard to make an argument that the man has special genes or a rocket scientist's brain. Ninan has, for whatever reason, learned this behavior. How complex is the formula he has learned? The boss shakes his head. Once you understand it, it's not that complex. How common is this behavior among the people he knows? The boss shakes his head again and says, "It's not what my generation was taught to do."

the norm: un-urgent behavior

All of us send messages constantly. What we say is obviously important. How, when, and where we speak can be even more revealing. People watch how quickly we move on various issues. They notice tone of voice, facial and body movements. They notice details, if only unconsciously, like whether we start meetings on time. The implications for creating a sense of urgency, or not, follow directly. Ninan has learned this and uses it to his advantage. But Ninan is far from the norm today.

Tony Crandell is the president of two large hospitals in the midwestern United States. He is a well-educated, thoughtful, and committed man. One day, in his office, he met with the chief of surgery of one of the hospitals, his vice president of finance, the head of a task force focused on cost reduction, a senior physician on that task force, and a guest. The president had called the meeting to review their efforts to consolidate overlapping services and reduce expenses. Little had been achieved over the prior twelve months. The president was frustrated but saw nothing to be gained in a finger-pointing exercise. The 9:00 meeting started at 9:10. The president offered the others coffee or tea. All but one declined. He then graciously asked the head of the task force for a report.

The task force head talked for twenty minutes. The president asked for the opinions of all those in the room. The head of finance stated clearly that the hospital was under considerable pressure to reduce costs and that the pressure would only grow. The head of surgery explained, as he had before, some of the problems that would be caused by consolidating certain services. The president would nod and often say, "That's true, but . . . " always with thoughtful comments or facts, always with a tone that was collegial. He was well aware of the head of surgery's concern that unhappy doctors could move to competing hospitals.

The discussion was lively at times, but the liveliness was almost always due to somewhat sharp comments from the head of finance. When an assistant knocked on the door and said a board member wished to speak to the president, he looked plaintively at the others, with the unstated message, "I'm sorry, but you know as well as I that I must take this call." He assured all that he would return within a few moments, and he did. At 10:04, the assistant interrupted again, stating that it was time for his next meeting. The president ended the session by saying that he appreciated the others' help on this project and that the board was, frankly, becoming increasingly frustrated by its slow pace. All stood. One set of people left his office, followed by another set coming in. Overall, it was a meeting that must have looked like many thousands of others occurring that same day around the world—a pattern of interaction that, though so common, is increasingly dangerous in a more rapidly changing world.

Hospitals, or health care in general, are a perfect example. In the United States, the percentage of GDP going to health care has increased from 4 percent to over

15 percent in only a few decades. Yet this huge flow of funds seems to have done little or nothing to increase the U.S. health care rating on key dimensions compared to other industrialized nations. This huge flow of funds has not increased the average doctor's income; in many cases, the opposite is true, with physicians saying that their salaries just don't make up for the expensive education, mounds of daily paperwork, and restrictions on how they can practice. Given the facts, most people outside the health care sector say the system is in a major crisis. Yet a true sense of urgency to deal with this crisis was astonishingly low inside the two hospitals overseen by the man within whose office that meeting had been held. Instead there was a mixture of resigned contentment, frustration, and anger. The boss's behavior in that meeting did nothing to help change that reality.

The meeting started late. Ten minutes seems trivial. The Indian manager would disagree. The action sends a signal. The coffee ritual was observed and the beverage was served on china—another signal. Ninan would have skipped drinks and, had some seemed necessary, served them in Styrofoam cups. There was no clear statement at the beginning of the meeting that the cost level at the hospitals was unacceptably high. There was no clear reminder of the obvious: that high costs could eliminate projects in the future that would contribute to the quality of medicine offered at the hospitals, an outcome that would be unacceptable to the doctors. Another signal. The board member could have been called back when the *important* meeting was over. That did not happen— another signal. The president could have asked the task force head to prepare before the meeting a short report estimating the costs incurred because the project was moving so slowly. He did not. The president could have shown from the first minute of the meeting until the last his total determination to deal successfully with the cost issue for the sake of the hospital, its patients, and its staff. He could have shown a sense of urgency that the group had to move faster. He did neither. The executive could have ended the meeting as did the Indian manager with all his meetings: with clarity about what he, and then the others, would actually do within the next seven days (seven, not forty-seven). If this gathering was important to the future of the hospital and too little time was scheduled for the session, he may not have ended on time, instead canceling the next, less-important meeting. He would have explained to his finance chief, task force head, and the others that they too *must* delay or eliminate other appointments until this *important* work was done. He would have ended the session when progress was clearly made. He would later have explained to those who had been in his waiting room why he had gone overtime. And he would have offered the explanation with a sense of urgency.

These comments might seem true but of less consequence than I suggest here. The successful Indian manager would, again, disagree. The issue, as he sees it, is simple. Increasingly changing environments create a need for alertness and agility, which demands a sense of urgency that must be modeled by the boss *all the time.*

clear the decks

Q: What is one particularly important enemy of urgency?

A: A crowded appointment diary.

Almost everyone is too busy today. We are too busy with dozens of different, often unrelated activities. The hospital manager certainly was. We sometimes live in meetings where the pace is thirty miles an hour because the pace has always been thirty miles an hour and that sets everyone's expectations. When you are going from one meeting to the next, all on different topics, all run inefficiently, attitudes and feelings about urgency drain out through sheer exhaustion. Clutter *undermines* true urgency. Fatigue *undermines* true urgency.

If you watch the Indian manager's behavior carefully and contrast it with the hospital executive's, you find that the former relentlessly eliminates low-priority items from his appointment diary. He eliminates clutter on the agenda of the meetings that do make it into his diary. The space that is freed up allows him to move faster. It allows him to follow up quickly on the action items that come out of meetings. The time freed up allows him to hold impromptu interactions that push along important projects faster. The open space allows him to talk more about issues he thinks are crucial, about what is happening with customers and competitors, and about the technological change affecting his business. His actions also serve as a model that people see every day, even if they are not entirely aware of it. His actions, in a sense, give other people permission to delegate and purge, even if tradition and social forces do not.

In stark contrast, the head of the hospital often allows others to delegate problems up to him, crowding an already full calendar. He also rarely challenges a tradition—the monthly such-and-such meeting—that absorbs time and yet no longer produces appropriate benefit.

The Indian manager's behavior gives credibility to his words when he tells his people that they cannot wait twelve months, or that they must finish a project in half the time. The hospital executive's actions give him little or no credibility when he says the group must achieve a goal much more quickly. His behavior undercuts his words.

An overcrowded appointment diary easily creates this words-deeds mismatch, which can be lethal. Verbally, people say what is true and so important in an increasingly turbulent world. Nonverbally, they give out a very different message. The disconnect does nothing to increase urgency. Mostly, the words-deeds mismatch creates cynicism.

So why would an experienced, thoughtful man behave in a way that undercuts his words? He certainly does not want to fail. The very opposite is true. But . . .

- He is trapped in a set of habits that helped him earlier in his career.

- He is pushed in the wrong direction by his organization's culture—also the product of the past and not today's reality.

- Certainly little in his decades-old education prepared him for a twenty-first-century world.

- The delegation up to him is a strong force.

- And no one confronts him with this problem. People don't see it themselves, or they feel very uncomfortable in confronting the boss.

Could he change? People do. But overcoming habits or going against the culture is not easy. And it is surely impossible if you do not see the problem clearly. That's where it all seems to start: seeing clearly your own behavior, seeing how it is undercutting a sense of urgency, and seeing how dangerous this is in a twenty-first-century world. The hospital manager—a good man—didn't see the problem. Most around him did not either. The few that did were not trying very hard to change the situation.

The hospital story would drive Ninan crazy.

be visibly urgent

Study people like Ninan and you also learn that they go out of their way to be visible. They conduct themselves so as to let as many others as possible hear their words and see their actions. This strategy is also far from the norm today, when so many of us become trapped in our offices and conference rooms, seen and heard by very small numbers of people.

David Bauman is the plant manager for a factory that makes high-tech components for use in the technologically sophisticated products of his customers. He has about one thousand employees, with all except management belonging to a national union. He has a degree from a local college, an even temperament, a dry sense of humor, and no signs of charisma. His plant is a great economic success story, despite all sorts of factors that should put it at a competitive disadvantage. Each year the story grows better as the management constantly makes changes that improve productivity, reliability, on-time deliveries, and safety. The changes are both small and large. With great pride, a manager at this facility once showed me how the entire factory floor had been redesigned over the prior two years and how a part of the floor had been redesigned twice. None of the other plants run by David's corporation has a comparable record, and not one has more employees with an equivalent sense of urgency to keep improving. The urgency is undoubtedly driven by a number of factors, none more obvious than the visible daily behavior of the factory's management.

David spends at least one hour a day out on the factory floor, as do all his direct reports, even his chief accountant. A part of this meandering up and down aisles is relationship building or maintenance, bolstered by much talk of sports and families. But most of the conversation is about productivity, quality, safety, delivery commitments, customers, and competition. The management does not interrogate the workforce. There is no sense of hysteria, where one or more of the managers talks shrilly or runs in circles warning of this and that. There are very few confrontations. Any condescending lecturing was hard for this observer to find. But the talk has an intensity to it. It is also consistent and relentless.

The oh-so-visible message is oh so clear. "There can be no letting up. The only way we can guarantee job security, keep raises higher than inflation, and maintain a clean, attractive, safe workplace is if we move faster, smarter, and better than the competition. Because the competition does not sit still, this task is very challenging. Yes, we have been successful and should be proud. But our success in meeting the challenges of the past tells us little about a future that constantly throws new problems and opportunities at us."

Each and every day people see the managers (and not just because they pass them momentarily in the parking lot). Each and every day people see the managers showing their own urgency (and not just sending memos about the need to improve productivity). The style with which conversations are conducted varies with the personalities of the managers. The plant manager has genuine humility. Yet his mild voice has an intensity that makes you feel he wants to be on the team winning the World Series. The accountant's conversations tend to be filled with numbers. But the data is usually presented in an understandable way, with a goal of praising or cautioning. One manager seems to move at seventy miles an hour. He can be annoying at times but rarely is, because he doesn't push people or run over them. Another manager has a hilarious sense of humor that sends those on the factory floor into howls of laughter. But underneath the jokes is a very clear seriousness of purpose and message.

This message is broadcast to every single employee, every single day, every workday in the fifty-two-week year, with words and deeds. Having everyone at one facility helps make this easier than if David, the plant manager, were in charge of ten factories in six countries. But the principle would still apply. He would just have to have ten Davids running the other plants—more difficult, yes, but certainly possible.

Some simple math can help put this story in perspective in another way. At least one hour a day, every day, David's ten department managers are on the floor. Five hours times ten managers equals fifty hours. Subtract nonwork banter and you might have forty. Multiply forty hours by fifty-two weeks and you have two thousand eighty urgency-raising hours. Over two thousand hours a year is a hefty number. And this counts *only* the top managers of the plant during their special daily one-hour trip to the factory floor.

None of what they do requires an MBA degree from a prestigious institution. It requires only insight, which leads to action, which, in this case, keeps a factory winning—all despite the competitive disadvantages.

urgency begets urgency

In David Bauman's plant, it started with him. With a bit of nudging and role modeling, his direct reports then developed more urgency themselves and started behaving accordingly. That, in turn, provided multiple, visible role models for first-line supervisors and others in the plant. A sense of urgency can be like that. It can begin with a single person and then expand outward.

A growing wave of urgency can overcome or minimize the damage from one of the most difficult management problems today: the hard-core cynicism that comes from a history of flavor-of-the month change efforts, from other massive initiatives that have failed, or from a long string of enthusiastic but ineffective top management teams. Importing more (and more accurate) information about opportunities can also be useful in dealing with this problem. Real possibilities—if they appeal to ideals inside the heart, and not only the logic of the mind—can build positive feelings and erode negative ones. Eliminating NoNos—those people who hate change and are very clever at fanning the flames of cynicism—can help (more on this later). Disarming honesty can help: "Let's be honest with ourselves. We have gone through this string of silver-bullet ideas for so long it has made us wary if not cynical, and we must stop that today. Today! From now on . . ." But ultimately, it is often only a steadily growing wave of people behaving with real urgency *each and every day* that can conquer built-up cynicism and negativity—a real urgency that can start with one person, then two, then ten, and on.

behave with true urgency

purge and delegate

Stop an over-crowded appointment
diary from making it impossible
to behave with urgency.

Purge low-priority items.

Cancel distracting projects.

Delegate, delegate, delegate.

Do not allow subordinates to delegate up to you.

move with speed

Use freed-up time to respond
immediately to calls, requests
for meetings, e-mails on high-
priority issues.

Never end meetings without
clarity about who will
quickly do what and when.

speak with passion

Relentlessly talk about the need to
behave urgently: move, adapt,
and stay ahead of the competition.

Talk with feeling.

Make the feeling infective.

match words and deeds

Don't just talk about the external
world, look at it constantly.

Don't just talk about exploiting
new opportunities, do it always.

let them all see *it*

Do all of the above and more as
visibly as possible to as many
people as is possible. Let them
see your sense of urgency.

urgent patience

Behaving urgently does not mean constantly running
around, screaming "Faster-faster," creating too much
stress for others, and then becoming frustrated when no
one else completes every goal tomorrow. That is false urgency. People who understand the basics—a faster-
moving world, the need for more urgency—fall into the
false-urgency trap far too often.

Because true urgency has this strong element of *now*,
it can be easy to forget the time frame into which large
changes and achievements fit. Behaving urgently to help
create great twenty-first-century organizations demands

patience, too, because great accomplishments—not just the activity associated with false urgency—can require years. The right attitude might be called "urgent patience." That might sound like a self-contradictory term. It's not. It means acting each day with a sense of urgency but having a realistic view of time. It means recognizing that five years may be needed to attain important and ambitious goals, and yet coming to work each day committed to finding every opportunity to make progress toward those goals. "Urgent patience" captures in two words a feeling and set of actions that are never seen with a false sense of urgency.

Ninan uses the term "urgent patience." I rather like it.

Once you understand the basic idea of how people act to increase a sense of urgency in others, it's relatively easy to see how the method can be applied in any situation. The tactic is simple. Look at all you do. Ask a trusted aide or colleague to look at all you do. Does your behavior make others feel a true sense of urgency around key issues? Are your actions modeling what you need from others? Do your words match your deeds? The odds are high that you have not been taught to behave the way you now need to behave. Why can't you learn? Why not start—today?

tactic three

find opportunity
in crises

Most people hold one of two perspectives on the nature of crises. The first group, by far the larger, sees crises as rather horrid events, and for obvious reasons. Crises can hurt people, disrupt plans, or even cripple an organization or community beyond repair. Within organizations, a key component of what is considered good management is crisis avoidance or, if necessary, crisis management and damage control. Budgets, budget reviews, and financial control systems are designed to minimize the probability of a sudden financial crisis. Quality control systems are designed to avoid product failures that create a crisis of customer confidence or a legal battle. Damage control systems—run by lawyers, public relations experts, and others—seek to minimize the financial and other costs of any crisis that does erupt.

A very different perspective on the nature of crises is described with the metaphor of a "burning platform." In this view, crises are not necessarily bad and may, under certain conditions, actually be required to succeed in an increasingly changing world. Within this burning-platform logic, complacent organizations are seen to be the real danger, and yet they are exceptionally difficult to change. But even people who are most solidly content with the status quo will begin to act differently if a fire starts on the floor beneath their feet. With fire spreading around them, everyone moves, the status quo is then eliminated, and a new beginning is possible.

> **Q.** Which perspective is correct: avoidance systems and damage control, or burning platforms?

> **A.** Neither.

> **Q.** What does this tell us about how to create a true sense of urgency?

> **A.** A great deal, actually.

Let me explain.

avoid and control crises, but watch out . . .

As I write this page, a lower-level employee in a financial institution has been reported to have allegedly lost $7 billion of his firm's capital. The press is saying, in a monumental understatement, that the bank lacked adequate controls.

There are two ways that organizations control behavior to avoid minor problems or huge crises. The first is formal and hard: structures, processes, systems, and rules. The second is informal and soft: peer influence, bosses' attention, and, most of all, organizational culture. Enterprises, especially large enterprises, tend to rely overwhelmingly on the first, because formal mechanisms are more concrete and measurable and can be designed and implemented with some reasonable probability that they will succeed. Only small and young enterprises tend to rely more on the latter—informal and soft—because of a distaste for the former or a lack of knowledge of how to create good formal controls.

Without sufficient formal and informal mechanisms, you run the risk of the $7 billion crisis. But the problem with all control systems, especially the formal, is that they can over time become so heavy handed that they kill any entrepreneurial spirit and make change difficult or impossible. They also draw eyes inward—to make sure the laws and rules are being followed—thereby creating a lack of external focus and generating complacency, which leads to more inward focus and so on.

If a crisis does break out, most people with an avoid-and-control mind-set immediately bring in the damage control specialists, sometimes explicitly called damage control experts, more often public relations professionals, communication experts, or lawyers. Some of these people are highly skilled in minimizing negative consequences.

Damage control experts know how to (1) hide a crisis from public view so that it does not scare or enrage others in ways that produce a bigger crisis, (2) convince others that a crisis is not really a crisis or that it has already been solved, again to prevent events from spiraling out of control, or (3) take actions that mollify enraged others, but at a minimum cost to an organization. In cases where the potential negative consequences of a crisis might devastate an organization, these advisers can be invaluable. They can stop a good group from going out of business or from being tarred so badly that it can never fully recover. They can salvage careers or projects that are important in serving the public.

But the problem with a damage control mind-set is that it is too often applied by people to protect their own careers, and not the reputations of their organizations. Worse still, it eliminates an opportunity, and one that is increasingly important: the opportunity to create a sense of urgency, mobilize needed action, and help an organization prosper in an increasingly challenging world.

use a crisis to create urgency, but watch out . . .

When the cold war ended, a Russian enterprise flooded the U.S. market with a commodity product. Supply of the product increased nearly 25 percent, and prices dropped dramatically. For the number one U.S. domestic enterprise in that industry, revenues decreased, profits disappeared, and financial analysts called for immediate reductions in employment. Great effort failed to convince Washington to save the firm with stiff tariffs. A constant stream of articles in the business press made the company's troubles very visible. Inside the firm, complacency did drop, but it was replaced by anxiety over jobs, anger at the government, bitter arguments about who was to blame for the untenable position the company was in, and a flurry of activity, little of which helped the situation much (i.e., a false sense of urgency).

The press reports grew even worse. Some commentators warned of large layoffs in the face of unfair but unstoppable competition. No one talked about urgency. Everyone seemed to think that was a nonissue. If asked, people would point to increasingly frantic behavior, which they mistakenly saw as real urgency.

With bickering on the increase, a small group of mid-level managers began to meet informally and to talk about how it was essential to use the crisis as an opportunity. The managers spoke of who was reacting how and for what reasons. They agreed that one of the executive vice presidents seemed to see the situation as they did, and that led to a meeting with the man, and that subsequently led to a meeting with the CEO. That, in turn, led to more discussion with additional people. The communication was passionate. The message was simple: "We have to act, and quickly. Blaming others will get us nowhere. If we are smart, we can not only solve the immediate crisis but position ourselves to deal with stronger competition and turbulent events in the future."

The clear sense of urgency in all of this communication, the strong feeling of determination to *move-win-now*, and the positive tone of the message began turning anger, anxiety, and the flurry of unhelpful activity within management and the workforce into a sense that all of them must move swiftly, boldly, and with intelligence. With true urgency increasing in the firm, a long list of actions that should have been taken years before was finally initiated. The union allowed some work to be reorganized in the plants, creating broader job categories. Top management took out a layer in the hierarchy and offered buyout packages to avoid layoffs. A few exceptionally talented managers were given more responsibility, even though in traditional terms they were too young and had too little seniority for their new jobs. The compensation system for the sales force was changed to align it more with market realities. Taken with care and competence, these and other actions not only helped stop the crisis by increasing productivity, reducing costs, and increasing revenues, but also helped reposition the firm to compete better in an increasingly globalized industry.

Situations like this one, where people do use sudden crises to their advantage, all appear to share a number of characteristics.

Most fundamentally, some people not only see a terrible problem but actively look for a *potential opportunity*. They don't panic and make the situation worse. They don't automatically go into crisis management mode and hand the reins over to damage control experts. But they also never assume that an opportunity is guaranteed. Their attitude is not, "Please give me a burning platform, any burning platform." They clearly realize that angry, panic-stricken, or fearful people may create the frenzy of activity associated with false urgency, which can make a situation even worse. Hence the word *potential*, but a potential that is actively sought.

The people who see an opportunity in a crisis may be anywhere in an organization. But if they are not at the top of the unit that is being damaged, they locate and approach someone higher in the hierarchy who is most likely to also understand the opportunity. In this way, they gain the more powerful footing that they will eventually need to mobilize others.

The key players in these sorts of situations either intuitively or consciously realize that the big challenge is almost always more a heart problem than a mind problem. They see that generic facts, figures, and logic, mechanically designed to change people's analysis of a situation, simply miss the central target. They see that the single biggest problem is all in the heart, where fear and anger can kill hope and stop the growth of a true sense of urgency.

Because they recognize that the heart needs hope, they tend to act with passion, with conviction, with optimism, and with a steely resolve. Analytically correct but unmoving lectures do not succeed, so they don't waste time offering them.

Possibly most important of all, they do not mistake false urgency for real urgency. They don't look at sudden energy and movement as conclusive signs that real urgency has been developed. They do not believe that a high level of anxiety is actually good and should be maintained as long as possible. They take carefully considered action to convert initial anxiety and anger into a determination to act now and win. In this case, *carefully considered action* means anticipating how others will behave. It means crafting plans that sequence actions for maximum useful effect in generating true urgency.

Irene's crisis offers a good example of all of these points working in concert.

Irene Goodwin is forty-two years old, has been with her firm for ten years, and is in charge of marketing at the corporate level. Late one Friday afternoon, she was told by her boss that all staff budgets for the upcoming year, including hers, would be cut 20 percent. The primary reason, she was told, was that new revenue forecasts were down significantly and the executive committee was especially worried about the company's very volatile stock price. Irene pointed out the obvious: cutting the corporate marketing budget could make the revenue problem worse. Her boss was firm, showing no signs of a willingness to negotiate. He said the executive committee was not going to take the time to redo, on a case-by-case basis, dozens of staff budgets at corporate headquarters, in the divisions, and in sales offices. Irene could have argued the point—there was a sensible argument that the overall approach the committee was taking was a mistake— but sensing that any discussion would be a waste of time, she did not.

After recovering from the initial shock and frustration of the conversation with her boss, Irene began thinking about how she could turn this very unpleasant problem to her advantage.

She had inherited a marketing department that thought in terms of work quality but very little in terms of the financials. Her attempts to introduce almost any discussion of fiscal discipline had been rebuffed by a group of long-term employees, who loudly argued that service quality was the department's mission and "an obsession with trivial contributions to short-term income" would undermine quality. In contrast, Irene strongly felt that the group wasted money all the time that could better be used to produce more innovative marketing.

She canceled plans for the weekend and spent hours with pencil and pad thinking through her situation. How would various individuals and groups within her department react to the news of cuts? She made lists. Some people, she decided, would, at least at first, be dumbfounded. Some would become very angry, especially those who had been with the firm the longest. A few would take the budget reduction as a sign that Irene, personally, may have lost the confidence of top management. One key employee, already considering an attractive job offer elsewhere, might simply resign. Only three of her direct reports, she thought, would quickly see the same opportunity that she saw.

For each group or individual, Irene considered what she might do. What were the options? Which seemed best? Where should she start? Would a phone call or meeting during the weekend be helpful? Or should she start implementing a plan early Monday morning?

Ultimately she chose to start Monday with the thirty-five-year-old manager who was considering the outside job offer. She judged that he felt the need for more challenge, more career opportunities, and more power to implement his (good) ideas, and that these feelings were exacerbated by the 10 percent increase in salary he was being offered by a competitor. She also thought that winning him over would have a large effect on subsequent conversations with other individuals in her group.

Irene began the meeting with the man by describing what had happened on Friday, how she was caught by surprise, and how frustrated she was. She held nothing back. She then talked with an intensity that went beyond simple, cold logic. She said that this tough blow could be used as an invaluable opportunity to shake things up. She was honest in stating that this would be a significant challenge. But she also made a clear argument about what could change and how that could improve the department's standing in the eyes of senior management, with the increased career possibilities that might follow. She answered his questions clearly, because she had already identified the most likely inquiries ("Will we be laying off people, or will we cut purchases and subcontractors?") and had formulated sensible responses that she delivered with conviction ("The numbers won't add up unless we let a few people go, but we can produce a minimum of pain by focusing on the obvious people who are not pulling their weight"). She made no promises about increased salary or responsibilities, but she made it clear that if the department could make the needed changes, she would fight for the employees' interests. She ended the discussion by telling the man that no one else in the group had yet heard the news. She told him that she had come to him first because she believed he could be the essential element in helping her turn the crisis into a very successful episode. Within an hour, he had tentatively agreed to stay and help.

For step 2, Irene chose to talk with the three subordinates who she judged to be the most likely to see the opportunity. She believed that their support would come quickly, especially after hearing, to their surprise, that their well-liked colleague was turning down the attractive job offer elsewhere. She also believed a team of five could do much more in a shorter period of time than she could alone. The fact that others in her department would see a real sense of urgency coming from five of them, she believed, would be most useful in converting anxiety and anger into still more urgency. She turned out to be right in all of these judgments.

Her initial plan went through four more steps, implemented with back-to-back closed-door meetings all day on Monday, from 7:00 a.m. through dinner. Although the talks varied in important details depending upon the person involved, they all ultimately conveyed the same message: a blunt statement that the department had been hit hard and that there was no way to cope by making a few small adjustments; a clear statement that her boss and higher management were aligned on their decision and had made it clear that negotiations were not an option; a surprising statement that five of them (then six, then seven) saw an opportunity here, and not only a big disappointment, not a horrible situation requiring maximum damage control—all statements made with words and feelings that were filled much less with anger or anxiety than with a visible determination to move quickly.

Most discussions worked as she had hoped. One session did not. The story of the following month is a long one, but the summary is this: (1) unexpected crisis; (2) a reaction from Irene that was neither panic nor damage control; (3) careful but swift thinking on her part about how people would feel and then act; (4) careful but swift implementation of a plan based on that assessment; (5) no attempt to soften the blow; (6) visible urgency and conviction on her part; (7) a message given that she and the others could deal with this and that *they would*; (8) an increase in true urgency in her department; (9) the emergence of new possibilities for action that would have been resisted before; and (10) in Irene's case, a boss watching all this activity unfold and being rightly impressed.

Two years later, while most staff groups in the firm were still struggling to operate under reduced budgets, while many were caught up in anger and anxiety and ineffective activities, Irene and her people were doing more innovative and effective work. The company benefited, as did people who had a financial or employment stake in the company. Top management was pleased, as it certainly should have been. Irene's marketing group was filled with people who were very proud of their achievements, and justifiably so.

create a crisis—maybe

Within the logic of burning platforms, if natural events do not create a crisis, you must. You don't wait. You don't hope. You develop a strategy and act. Employed with blind enthusiasm, this idea is not sensible. Used in a judicious way, it can be exceptionally important.

When needed change seemed impossible, a new CFO cleaned up an airline's balance sheet, taking numerous write-downs that should have been taken over the years but were not. This single action led to a reported loss of income that was the largest by far in the company's history. The loss was so unprecedented and dramatic that it caught everyone's attention. A charismatic CEO then successfully redirected astonishment, anger, and fear into a sense of true urgency. With a larger-than-life personality, he was able to lead people off the fiery platform with a minimum of panic or fights and lead them in the right direction. In the process, dozens of initiatives were launched over the next three years that made the firm more customer oriented, more productive, and more profitable. By the standards of some industries, the airline's efficiency and customer service left much to be desired, but the changes precipitated by a manufactured crisis created a vastly different and better organization.

A new CEO announced that every division within his firm would have to become first or second in its industry. Where they were unsuccessful, he told his management, the divisions would be sold or shut down. The CEO offered compelling evidence that this new corporate strategy had been proven to be effective within a few highly regarded firms and that the reason it was effective made perfect sense in an increasingly competitive world where anyone but an industry leader was vulnerable. With this single decision, announced with an intensity that suggested that nothing would stop him in a quest to make a truly outstanding organization, "one that we can all be proud of," the CEO created what was certainly seen as a crisis for those running businesses that were not the leaders in their markets. Some division managers were able to use the crisis to develop the urgency needed to create much better organizations. Without exception, they set high goals, but ones that their management teams found challenging and exciting, not punishing. The failing divisions were sold or shut down. All of the latter may have had unfixable businesses, but in almost all cases the division managers made the situation worse. They couldn't get over their own anger or anxieties. They autocratically set objectives that their managers thought were impossible to meet, creating self-fulfilling prophecies of failure. The strengthening of some divisions, plus the selling or shutting of others, repositioned the company's overall portfolio of businesses, increased profits as a percentage of sales, and significantly improved its stock price.

In a similar way, I have seen any number of people create crises through stretch goals. As a good friend of mine says, the goals need to be high enough that they cannot possibly be accomplished through business as usual. The goals also need to make people say "Wow"—but not create a mutiny. The "Wow" must eventually become "Wow, this is a tough but meaningful challenge," and not "Wow, this is stupid."

I have known people who create crises through bringing-the-outside-in, usually by helping insiders see (and feel) explosive situations that exist outside corporate walls, where tremendous hazards (and wonderful opportunities) exist in an entire industry, or because of new technologies, or through new legislation. It is amazing, but certainly true, that inwardly focused organizations can have bombs going off in the street next door and not hear the noise without assistance.

People who successfully create crises to increase urgency use all the same approaches as those who have crises thrust upon them. They think in terms of opportunity. They find more powerful partners, if needed. They move proactively, making no assumptions that a crisis by itself will reduce complacency and create needed action. They see the central role of emotions, and not only thoughts, and act accordingly.

Further, in creating a useful crisis, and not only reacting to one, people take actions that are visible and unambiguous: the unexpected and mind-boggling loss; the statement that if you cannot be number one or two you'll be sold or shut down. These actions are not subtle. They are not known to only a few people. They create situations that cannot be dealt with only by an incremental change. The fire is big. There is much smoke. There is no chance that the problem can be solved with a bucket of water. People who try but fail to create urgency by developing crises sometimes engineer situations that others think are not that serious or can be handled with small adjustments.

And perhaps most of all, successfully created crises are associated with real business problems. They are not ploys detached from the real challenges facing a business. Ploys are sometimes used because they are easier to create, but they misdirect newfound energy and they can undercut a manager's reputation for acting with integrity.

135

know (and avoid) four dangerous mistakes

The problem with using crises to reduce complacency and create urgency is that the tactic is a potential diamond sitting on a rock surrounded by quicksand and very nasty beasts. Any naiveté about the downside risks can cause disaster.

BIG MISTAKE NUMBER 1: Assuming that crises inevitably will create the sense of urgency needed to perform better.

An example. At a major European retailer, margins were shrinking year after year because fashionable boutiques were taking its top-of-the-line business, and discounters were taking away its low-end business. Then the European edition of the *Wall Street Journal* published an explosive article spelling out many of the firm's problems. The CEO had two weeks' warning, but instead of alerting others or working to kill the story, he deliberatively chose to do nothing. Not only did he not warn others, except one close confidant, but he also did little to analyze in advance exactly what would happen the day the article came out and what precisely he should do to channel fear, anger, and confusion into a determination to act fast and succeed.

The day came. A full-blown crisis was created. The CEO waited for a great wind to start pushing his organization off its complacent platform and into a good direction. But it didn't happen. Instead of mobilizing people into action, the crisis led many managers into making fewer decisions because they didn't want to be accused of mistakes with the press and public watching. Many other managers were genuinely afraid that if they rushed into action their decisions might accidentally create harm. So they held back just at a time when the CEO most needed their help to get the organization moving swiftly into a better future.

A burning platform, yes. But without needed planning and action to leverage the crisis, the situation grew worse, not better.

BIG MISTAKE NUMBER 2: Going over the line with a strategy that creates an angry backlash because people feel manipulated.

No one wants to feel manipulated. If people sense that someone has created a crisis that deliberately puts them in harm's way, especially if it is not strongly connected to real business problems, they may suspect sabotage or lunacy, both of which can create anger and not a steely determination to act fast and win. The crisis-creating strategy not only fails but makes matters worse.

Because his managers and employees would not change to meet new market demands, the head of the largest division of a Midwestern manufacturing company reluctantly drew the conclusion that his only alternative was to engineer a crisis. His enterprise was the leading producer of a component used in making automobiles. He had traditionally sold only to the Detroit automakers but was now trying to expand sales, with little success, to non-U.S car companies, especially Toyota. His new market was demanding a level of precision and quality that his plants could not meet. Because of huge historical success, especially in the mid-twentieth century, his factories had cultures that were astonishingly arrogant and inwardly focused. Though his sales were stagnant and the future looked troubling, his change initiatives were met with apathy and resistance, especially from his union.

Over a twelve-month period, instead of cracking down when deadlines were missed on a variety of projects, this man sympathized with the many excuses people made. When warned by a young engineer that the company was not keeping up with the ever-increasing number and types of electronics going into all cars, the division manager set up a very bureaucratic (and thus slow) process to examine the issue. In these and other ways, he purposefully created conditions that could precipitate a major problem, and he succeeded. A competitor's new product took away nearly 10 percent of his volume of parts sold to the old U.S. automakers, and close to one-third of his sales to the foreign-owned plants. The resulting dip in total revenue was the first in the company's seventy-five-year history. After four months of press reports praising a competitor's product and speculating about potentially serious problems in his enterprise, the burning platform blazed. But energy within his organization did not emerge as a strong sense of urgency to act. New energy formed more as anger looking for someone to blame for the crisis. Suddenly, a rumor started that the plant manager had purposefully taken steps in the prior year in order to create the severe problems the company faced. Any energy to confront the facts and deal with the real business problems was redirected at the plant manager.

BIG MISTAKE NUMBER 3: Passively sitting and waiting for a crisis (which may never come).

A major problem with passive burning-platform strategies is that nature may not cooperate by providing the right amount of lightning in the right place at the right time. The fire is too small. The fire is too large. The fire never breaks out. A passive, hopeful, wait-and-see strategy fails.

The CEO at an electric utility was actually looking forward to deregulation as a means of unfreezing a tradition-bound monopoly that was not adequately preparing for a more competitive future. But deregulation came slower than he anticipated and with fewer new freedoms. Complex politics stopped bills in Congress and state legislatures. Bills not stopped were rewritten to be more limited in impact. No crisis was thrust upon the firm. The enterprise continued to make money even as it started slowly to lose market share in a post-monopoly world. The positive net income helped greatly in supporting complacency. In frustration, his change agents waited and waited for powerful legislation that they knew must happen in the current year. But it never did, and the crisis never came.

BIG MISTAKE NUMBER 4: Underestimating what the people who would avoid crises at all costs correctly appreciate: that crises can bring disaster.

Example. Using a technology recently made available because of ever-shrinking microchips, a new competitor took away dozens of a firm's key customers. The crisis could have been anticipated. But because the management believed that only an unexpected burning platform could help push a complacent organization out of its comfort zone, it didn't pay attention to the danger signs. Revenues collapsed, losses mounted, the stock tanked, people were laid off, and some good employees jumped ship. The platform burned for all but the most complacent. Yet the economic collapse meant there was little or no funding left for new plant equipment, a new

IT system, and a new R&D effort, all of which were required if the firm was to leap into the future. Even the few employees who were mobilized into action found that the firm's needs were overwhelming. Morale sank. Losses continued to grow. Then the firm was bought by someone at a bargain price, someone who sliced and diced the company out of existence. In summary, a burning platform, yes; a changed organization equipped to meet the needs of the future, not even close.

Of all the risks associated with crises, this last one is obviously the biggest. Instead of creating a sense of urgency, you end up out of business. You don't find this happening often, because people sense the danger and work very hard to avoid it. But crises sometimes do cripple or destroy organizations. Here is the strongest demonstration yet that crises, though they can be highly useful, are not necessarily your friend when urgency is needed.

the bottom line

Don't be naïve. Management control systems and damage control experts serve a critical purpose. But don't let that blind you to an increasingly important reality. Controls can support complacency in an era when complacency can be deadly. Handled properly—and we know the rules for proper handling—a crisis can offer an opportunity to increase needed urgency, an opportunity that cannot be disregarded.

Best evidence available today tells us that crises can be used to create true urgency if these principles are followed:

- Always *think of crises as potential opportunities*, and not only dreadful problems that automatically must be delegated to the damage control specialists. A crisis can be your friend.

- *Never forget that crises do not automatically reduce complacency*. If not monitored and handled well, burning platforms can be disastrous, leading to fear, anger, blame, and the energetic yet dysfunctional behavior associated with false urgency.

- To use a crisis to reduce complacency, *make sure it is visible, unambiguous, related to real business problems, and significant enough that it cannot be solved with small, simple actions*. Fight the impulse to minimize or hide bad news.

- To use a crisis to reduce complacency, *be exceptionally proactive* in assessing how people will react, in developing specific plans for action, and in implementing the plans swiftly.

- *Plans and actions should always focus on others' hearts as much or more than their minds*. Behaving with

passion, conviction, optimism, urgency, and a
steely determination will trump an analytically
brilliant memo every time.

- If urgency is low, *never patiently wait for a crisis*
  (which may never come) *to solve your problems.*
  Bring the outside in. Act with urgency every day.

- If you are considering creating an urgency-raising
  crisis, *take great care* both because of the danger of
  losing control and *because if people see you as manip-*
  ulative and putting them at risk, they will (quite rea-
  sonably) react very badly.

- *If you are at a middle or lower level* in an organization and see how a crisis can be used as an opportunity, *identify and then work with an open-minded and*
  approachable person in a more powerful position who
  can take the lead.

Certainly we need to be prudent. But in a more rapidly changing world, finding opportunities in crises probably reduces your overall risk.

tactic four

deal with NoNos

A few years ago I wrote a fable with Holger Rathgeber about an emperor penguin colony in Antarctica. We called it *Our Iceberg Is Melting*. The book is about life in a changing and turbulent world. It tells a story in which a colony of emperor penguins encounters the frustrations, fears, and problems nearly all of us face today. But unlike 90 percent of real-life human colonies, our penguins find solutions to their problems that are similar to those used only in the very best twenty-first-century organizations.

One of the main characters in the book is named NoNo. It requires little imagination to predict how he reacts to any new idea. And he not only talks, he acts, often with great effectiveness.

NoNos are highly skilled urgency killers. If they cannot undermine attempts at diminishing a contentment with the status quo, they create anxiety or anger and the flurry of useless activity associated with a false sense of urgency.

All organizations have a least one NoNo. More often, there are many NoNos. We can experience them as aggravating or extremely aggravating, but they are, in fact, far worse. For those who do see the dangers and want to act, NoNos at times can seem like hopelessly powerful barriers to progress. They aren't—as long as you know the two methods for dealing with them that don't work, and the three that do.

the NoNo problem

A NoNo is more than a skeptic. He's always ready with ten reasons why the current situation is fine, why the problems and challenges others see don't exist, or why you need more data before acting. In *Our Iceberg Is Melting*, when a middle-management bird tells the Leadership Council of a potentially disastrous problem, NoNo reacts in a way that is typical:

> This *junior* bird says that melting ice has opened that canal. *But maybe it hasn't.* He says the canal will freeze during the winter and trap water in the big cave. *But maybe it won't!* He says the water in the

cave will freeze. *But maybe it will not!* He says freezing water always expands in volume. *But maybe he's wrong!* And even if all he says turns out to be true, is our iceberg really so fragile that freezing water in a cave can break it into dangerously small pieces? *How do we know what he says is not just—a theory? Wild speculation? Fearmongering?!!! Can he guarantee that his data and conclusions are 100 percent accurate?* *

Drum roll and kaboom.

We may have a small piece of a NoNo in all of us. More likely, we have a bit of the skeptic. But even minor league NoNos are *not* skeptics. Skeptics, if you don't have too many of them, can usefully keep enthusiastic, but naïve, impulses in check. Skeptics, once they have been convinced their opinions are wrong, can become an initiative's biggest champions. NoNos are very different. They will often do nearly anything to discredit people who are trying to create a sense of urgency. They will do nearly anything to derail processes that attempt to create change.

NoNos are much more dangerous than we are inclined to believe, and that is one of the main reasons we make mistakes in trying to deal with them.

---

*From John Kotter and Holger Rathgeber, *Our Iceberg Is Melting: Changing and Succeeding Under Any Conditions* (New York: St. Martin's Press, 2006), 30–31.

---

skeptics versus NoNos

	A Skeptic	A NoNo
Past experiences	Has never seen instances in which the current relevant issue was a danger or opportunity, or has never seen the issue dealt with particularly well.	Is not concerned with the past except as ammunition to shoot down the need for nearly any change today.
Desired data	Wants enough information to convince him or her that new action, or some specific course of action, is needed and feasible. Is not willing to take leaps of faith.	Doesn't really want data but hides this fact. In public, keeps demanding more and more "proof" that any new action is needed.

---

don't waste time trying to co-opt a NoNo

There are two methods that people typically employ to deal with powerful NoNos. Unfortunately, both methods work very poorly.

The first is co-optation.

Jerry Blackburn was the managing director of a successful midsize consulting firm. For years the enterprise

	A Skeptic	A NoNo
Use of data	For the most part, treats data logically, but often wants a great deal of information. Is usually risk averse.	Very selectively chooses information that suggests no action is needed. Is never open minded.
How active or passive	Can be either active or passive but is often the latter. Has an attitude of "show me."	Usually is very active out in the open or behind the scenes. Can be highly disruptive.
Bottom line	Can be annoying. Can slow down movement. But also can be very helpful in keeping naïve enthusiasts from creating damage.	Reinforces any contentment with the status quo. Raises anxiety. Always kills urgency, stopping needed action. Can be very dangerous.

had grown rapidly under his leadership by focusing almost entirely on six sigma. By gaining more and more experience, through shrewdly investing in refining its tools, and by aggressively selling its services, the firm had become one of the top three players in a highly fragmented market.

One of Blackburn's most trusted senior partners came to him with disturbing data suggesting that the six sigma movement may have peaked and was declining, even though the firm had yet to see a decrease in revenues. The partner urged that he and Blackburn go talk to potential clients that recently had not accepted the consulting firm's proposals for work. He also strongly suggested that the two of them visit current customers that were not increasing their billings as had been expected. Blackburn agreed to both ideas, and off they went.

After a dozen interviews, the two consultants concluded that, indeed, interest in their six sigma product seemed to be sagging as interest in other management techniques was growing. Blackburn immediately pulled together his most senior management team and told the members about what he had learned. He explained that, in his opinion, they should move quickly to confirm or disconfirm his findings. If the findings were confirmed, they should move without delay to identify new arenas with growth potential that would leverage capabilities they already had. He pointed out that it would require time to develop a deep expertise in new arenas, to sell services, and to gain more experience than competitors. He expressed a belief that if they did not move quickly they risked (1) in the short term, a stagnation in revenues that would decrease bonuses and increase turnover among some of their best staff and (2) in the longer term, being left behind by more aggressive consulting companies.

Most members of the executive committee were surprised not only by what they were hearing but, even more so, by the conviction in Blackburn's voice. In the discussion that ensued, the eleven-person group broke more or less evenly into two camps: one leaning toward Blackburn, and another leaning against.

With ten minutes left in the meeting, one of the more experienced consultants pointed out, accurately, that at least a few people had said nearly five years ago that their market had peaked, and yet the firm had continued to grow. He pointed out, accurately, that at least two strategy consulting companies had for some time been claiming that six sigma tools were not as useful anymore, and yet Blackburn and his colleagues received outstanding reviews from most of their clients. He pointed out, again accurately, that what Blackburn had learned was based only on a limited number of interviews, which was far from proof of anything. Because the firm was extremely busy, the senior consultant advised strongly that it fulfill its current contracts and not waste time on speculation. He also made it clear that sharing this information with middle management or junior consultants would be a terrible mistake. Worrying others, he said firmly, would detract from their engagements, and that was dangerous.

The meeting ran out of time shortly after this man spoke, with the majority now leaning away from Blackburn.

Later that same day, an unhappy Blackburn pulled together a close confidant plus the trusted partner who had originally brought the problem to his attention. The three of them talked about how to proceed, eventually deciding that their NoNo could be a powerful loose cannon. After exploring a few alternatives, they chose to set up a "study committee" of five people that would include the three of them, one colleague who always seemed to be open minded, and their NoNo colleague. Better to keep him inside the tent, they reasoned, than outside creating problems.

Blackburn had hoped to meet at least a half-dozen times in two months in order to explore whether there really was a serious problem and, if so, to create a heightened commitment within the group to move forward quickly. Instead, because NoNo was "extremely busy," the study group met six times over six months, arriving at no consensus at the end. Their NoNo was gentlemanly but relentless in his piercing logic, poking holes in any qualitative analysis. He agreed to do interviews with selected clients that were not giving the firm more business, but he kept canceling meetings due to crises, immediate needs, scheduling mistakes, and so on. Meanwhile, he insistently raised questions about any hard data the others gathered. "This is limited in its scope," he would say. "This assumes X and Y and Z. How do we know these facts are absolutely true?" He continued to contend that the study group was taking attention away from serving current clients.

After a particularly galling meeting, Blackburn suggested to his closest confidant that they must consider pushing their NoNo out of the firm—fire him in the gentlest of terms, present the firing to the world as a resignation for some legitimate purpose, and get on with it. His colleague pointed out the inherent risk in that course of action. NoNo ran the firm's biggest project and ran it well: on time, on budget, and with a happy customer.

With short-term business pressures drawing his attention elsewhere, Blackburn reluctantly continued with the co-optation strategy, continued with the five-person study group, and continued to have infrequent study-group meetings. One and a half years after Blackburn and his colleague first visited clients and became alarmed, the firm's future billings flattened for the first time in the company's history. *BusinessWeek* magazine ran a story about a smaller consulting enterprise that was using a different management technique and was growing at 50 percent a year. Although the article never said so directly, the implication was clear that Blackburn's firm had seen its best days in the past. The strategy of co-opting the NoNo had only caused delay and frustration. The firm has never entirely recovered.

NoNos can kill urgency, kill action, and wound firms, sometimes with tragic results. Co-opting these sorts of people can seem like either the best or the only realistic strategy. But as with Blackburn's firm, it is not easy to make NoNos behave usefully inside the tent. Their capacity to disrupt conversations and delay action is formidable. At some point, it can become obvious that co-optation is not working. That raises the obvious question. Should you move the NoNo not only out of the tent but out of the firm? Often the Blackburns of the world want to take decisive action but feel paralyzed for any number of reasons. The disrupter is powerful. The disrupter produces important short-term results, and it is unclear that anyone else can do as good a job. So the boss does not act. More often than not, the story ends poorly, as in the consulting case.

Co-opting NoNos can seem like such a logical strategy, particularly because they are so often incorrectly seen as only serious skeptics and because it is seldom obvious how to keep them off the team. So why not use the power of the group's majority to pull them toward a consensus opinion that a problem must be addressed or an opportunity must be exploited? At a minimum, neutralize the troublemakers.

Unfortunately, *co-opting NoNos almost never works well* because the fundamental requirements for co-optation are missing. Regardless of what they say, NoNos are not skeptical but still willing to examine the data. They are not at all inclined to listen to others with an open mind. They won't accept a majority opinion. They have usually learned all sorts of methods to delay action, to make "study groups" not function well, and to aggressively use other disruptive tactics, often unconsciously. As a result, time is lost. Urgency does not grow high enough and fast enough. Needed action does not happen fast enough and smart enough. At some point, those who try to co-opt a NoNo almost always come to regret it.

never ignore the NoNos

Another approach one finds in these sorts of situations is to leave a NoNo outside the tent. Isolate and ignore him. The idea is to get on with the work. The belief is that the NoNo will be a distraction, but so what? He's only one person. And, again, it sometimes seems as if this is the only realistic alternative.

But an ignored NoNo can create much mischief. He will often relentlessly talk to others, especially the open minded (ironically), the anxious, and anyone who has a grudge against those trying to find new opportunities or avoid new hazards. The talk always contains observations or arguments that could be true. "Those people are worrying too much." "They are overstating the problems." "They are not doing their real jobs." "They are putting us at risk."

A smart NoNo can always find reasons why the only intelligent course of action is to do what has been done before or, at the most, to take only incremental action. A smart NoNo can find weak spots in any argument but, unlike a skeptic, locates weak points not to make better decisions but to stop action. A smart NoNo is expert at creating anxiety and undermining any new determination to exploit opportunities and avoid hazards.

NoNos can, and often do, organize an active resistance movement. Avoiding large-scale confrontations, they tend to work at the margins. They insert doubts and anxiety-raising arguments into one-on-one meetings, at sessions with their staffs, or over drinks away from the office. A NoNo can do this endlessly. Endless small acts add up.

Working constantly—as many NoNos do—they can create a small civil war in an organization. As a result, any urgency that rises is channeled into winning the war, and not into serving the customer better, incorporating new technologies, or becoming more externally focused.

That is precisely what happened at a division of a well-known manufacturing company a few years ago. The president of the division was convinced that the company had to face the fact that its industry was globalizing, and yet nearly 90 percent of the division's sales came from U.S markets. Because there was no visible crisis—revenue rose very slowly, but it did go up year after year—he decided that he first had to address a complacent management. But he knew from the beginning that his vice president of manufacturing believed that the firm was a winner and that "globalization" was totally unnecessary at that point in the firm's history. So the president brought together five of his officers and pointedly left out his manufacturing executive.

The team of five began holding informal meetings with groups of twenty other managers at a time. Facts and figures about the competitor's rapid expansion into Asia were presented. An argument was given about how those actions were going to put the firm in a difficult position when it eventually began a similar reach outside the United States. The message was clear: "We cannot delay." The initial meetings seemed to go well. But soon the team of five began to see and feel the new sense of urgency dropping rapidly. Surprised, and concerned, they looked into the problem and found the manufacturing vice president's fingerprints everywhere.

This executive left outside the tent and ignored turned out to be a very busy and very clever participant in the globalization discussion. Whenever he was with people who were not as committed to action as was the president, he brought up the topic. He slid selective data into the conversations. "An industry magazine says competitor A is losing $50 million a year in its India strategy." "Did you see the article in the *New York Times* about the tensions growing between India's new super-rich and the wretchedly poor? The implications for anyone trying to do business in India could be vastly important. And what of . . . ?" He constantly warned about the risks of precipitous action. "Yes, we will obviously grow outside the United States. The issue is timing." He pointed to the company's good and steady track record. He came up with scenarios for achieving additional growth in existing markets. "There is no need to spend resources now in a highly uncertain venture."

The manufacturing VP was smart and sophisticated enough to carefully qualify his statements so that he did not seem to be an irrational source of unrelenting negativity. "They make a good point," he might say before pounding away with his urgency-killing message. "No, those facts are accurate, but they are not relevant. Just think this through for a moment. Run the numbers and compare our margins in the United States to what they will probably be in Asia for the next five years if we . . . " With the president and his five-person team absent from these conversations, and with their point of view missing, anxiety among some of the staff rose and urgency among others fell.

Even relatively junior NoNos can distract their peers, but powerful senior NoNos can disrupt a whole organization. Rationally, this behavior usually does not seem in their own best interests. Rationally, a NoNo should be listening to data and thinking carefully, or else his employer, and his career, could be in jeopardy. But the force behind the behavior of NoNos is rarely rational. It's usually based on insecurities: change means risk means anxiety. Or it's based on anger: "In a just world, I should be in charge and I am not going to let those who are in charge succeed." Most NoNos are totally unaware of these feelings, although some highly ambitious ones recognize the I-should-be-in-charge drive.

The bottom line is that ignoring NoNos can be tempting. You think, "There is too much to do to waste time trying to follow up on all their conversations. If we don't watch out, our main task will become managing the NoNos instead of running the business. So let them be." But all the evidence says that this is a very bad approach.

distract the NoNos

There are three effective solutions for dealing with NoNos. The first is to keep them from creating mischief by actively distracting these distracters. The second is to push them out of the organization. The third is to expose their behavior in ways that allow natural social forces to reduce or stop it.

Active distraction comes in a number of forms. Send your NoNos on a special assignment far away from where urgency needs to be increased. Pair them with

the danger of NoNos

You take actions to increase a sense of urgency (e.g., bring the outside in, act urgently every day, find opportunity in crises).

NoNos' antics: "We have always succeeded." "Can they guarantee their conclusions are 100% accurate?" "They are scaring our people, morale will drop . . ." "They are no longer paying sufficient attention to the quarterly dividend." "Are they saying we are doing a poor job?!"

Contentment with the status quo, anger, or anxiety remain the same or increase.

People do not act more alert, move faster *now*, seize opportunities, help your initiatives, and provide leadership themselves—all to make your organization succeed.

people who understand that their number one job is to keep NoNos from creating problems. Give NoNos so much work that there is no time to create too much mischief. Each of these activities has been shown to work.

Stephen O'Malley, CEO of a financial services firm, used all three tactics. He sent his NoNo to Shanghai on an important and time-consuming job far away from corporate headquarters in London. The position in China oversaw a troubled operation in the expanding firm. The office needed discipline, and this NoNo knew much about imposing discipline in a way that could produce superior results. The NoNo was not pleased with his reassignment, but the need was real, his credentials were appropriate, and the boss showed no signs of backing down. In confidence, O'Malley also explained to a trusted aide in China why he had sent this executive to Shanghai. London was becoming too complacent with its recent success, he told his confidant, and this NoNo was undermining any sense of urgency to deal with new problems or opportunities. He didn't in any way demonize his colleague from London, but he made it very clear that stopping the man from generating an arrogant complacency, creating anxiety, or encouraging fights at headquarters was essential. He asked his trusted aide to keep their NoNo focused on the new job by constantly identifying new, and real, personnel, government relations, and client problems in Shanghai.

The confidant did what he was asked to do. The challenges in Shanghai did require long hours of work. Little travel to London was needed or possible. The NoNo still found ways to create mischief when he did interact with his colleagues back in Europe. But the problems he was able to cause were minimal. O'Malley's strategy worked remarkably well.

Effective distraction strategies keep NoNos from undermining a sense of urgency on an ongoing basis, not just occasionally. They have an affect that is not intermittent, but continuous. Effective strategies also focus NoNos' efforts on real business challenges, not made-up problems. Diverting someone's efforts into made-up problems can raise legitimate questions about manipulation and integrity, with all the negative consequences that might follow.

Distraction strategies have been shown to be effective in situations that can seem, at least to some people, hopeless. In O'Malley's firm, a number of young, up-and-coming client-relation managers were either discouraged, angry, or ready to quit. They saw a major opportunity. They saw their efforts to mobilize others to act on the opportunity constantly stifled by the firm's powerful NoNo. They saw that O'Malley's initial strategy of ignoring him was failing. Most were sophisticated enough to realize that putting the man on a committee would not help. Some wanted the boss to fire the NoNo and were unhappy that O'Malley did not do so. A few saw no solution and were, discreetly, talking to competing firms about job offers. When it became clear that O'Malley's distraction strategy seemed to be working, the resume-shopping stopped, anger was converted into a heightened determination to change and succeed, discouraged people found new energy, and, ultimately, the firm did successfully exploit a number of new opportunities.

get rid of them

The push-NoNos-out-the-door strategy is straightforward in concept. You might first confront them. "We have a difference of opinion, and it is hurting the enterprise. You change or go." Almost always, NoNos won't change, even if they say they will. So you fire them. You offer an early retirement package that is attractive. You don't just move them to Shanghai; you send them to a job that is a demotion. If they don't accept the package or new assignment, you force the issue.

If you work in countries where firings, demotions, and forced retirements are not realistic possibilities, you search for options that have the same effect. Managers in some Western European enterprises have, of necessity, devised all sorts of other legal actions, like reorganizing so that NoNo's job no longer exists. If this is done honestly—"You are undermining the business, you must go, we have an obligation to make you go"—then, if there are ethical issues to be raised, they are about NoNo's ethics. What right does he have to keep a specific job if that risks hurting hundreds or thousands of other employees and their families?

Many of us find the push option either distasteful or risky, and therefore it is not seriously considered. The risks are certainly real if the NoNo has many friends and the situation is handled poorly. If an action seems like a cruel way to deal with an employee of long tenure, you will have a very real practical problem. If any action truly is a cruel way to deal with an employee of long tenure, you will have a very real ethical problem. But, ultimately, the choice is clear. Do you allow a person to reduce urgency, undermine needed action, and hurt the future of an organization? Or do you take steps that may be uncomfortable in the short term but that deal with this critical issue? Too often, people refuse to take the uncomfortable steps.

immobilize them with social pressures

A third and final strategy for dealing with lightweight NoNos is to find socially acceptable ways to identify them in public and then let social pressures do the rest.

An example. The head of a company with about three hundred employees had small group discussions with all of his people after they had had a chance to read our *Ice-*

berg book. The light-hearted fable made the discussions less threatening than if he had set up meetings with the stated agenda, "What changes do you need to make to cope with our changing environment?" After a session in which she participated, an administrative assistant went to the toy department at Wal-Mart and bought a two-and-a-half-foot-tall stuffed penguin. She brought it to work, put it on her desk, and hung a sign on its neck: "NoNo is _____." When she came back from lunch that day, she found that someone had written on the small sign the name of one of the firm's managers. Most people who passed her desk that afternoon either rolled their eyes and nodded or laughed out loud. Of course the word got back to the manager, who came to see the sign for himself. The woman held up her hands and said, truthfully, that she didn't write in his name or know who did. The manager had little choice except to laugh himself. The next day a second name appeared, with a similar aftermath, but this time the manager did not laugh much. Nevertheless, in both cases, the problem was now out in the open. People who knew that these men were not skeptics, but were systematically undermining the useful discussions started by the head of the company—these people felt free to say so to their friends, to their bosses, and in a few cases directly to the NoNos.

On the surface, much of this was done with a friendly laugh because the *Iceberg* fable is whimsical—"Someone finally nailed Harry and Jim, ha, ha." But underneath the smiles was a serious message and one that spread everywhere, including to the CEO, and including to Harry and Jim. The two men were, in a sense, put on notice. Their NoNo-like behavior then shrunk greatly. When it reemerged in a management meeting, more often than not one of their peers, always with a smile, would say something like "Now NoNo, I don't . . . " The line would receive a group laugh, and the disruptive behavior would shrink even more.

I doubt if those two men changed much inside, but on the outside their behavior did shift. Had they been heavy-duty NoNos, perhaps one or both would have been clever enough to play the humiliated victim, gain sympathy, and then be able to continue with some variation on the old behavior. But they weren't heavyweights. And no one except a few friends ever, for a second, considered them victims. So they were neutralized. Their destructive behavior, which hurt everyone by hurting the company, was stopped. And the key player in the story was a very clever administrative assistant.

(In an interesting coincidence, as I edit this chapter, I just received an e-mail saying, "By the way, when I returned to Germany I was almost instantly confronted with your Penguins. Our senior management gave all managers a copy and used it as the motto of last year's 'Budget/Business Planning Board.' It is very interesting to see how NoNos get their act together because they do not want to be called NoNos." He is near Frankfurt. The secretary in the earlier story is in New Jersey. The problem, and solution, has nothing to do with culture or nationality.)

An unfortunate but accurate rule: *never* underestimate the damage that a hard-core NoNo can do in undermining efforts to reduce complacency, increase urgency, make smart action happen rapidly, and help an organization to survive and prosper. To repeat, I am not talking about a thoughtful skeptic who can be moved by evidence and who can actually serve a useful purpose by controlling naive enthusiasm. A NoNo is another breed, and an increasingly dangerous breed.

A second, more encouraging rule: a powerful NoNo is not a hopeless barrier to progress, because there are three effective tactics to deal with him or her. When a big, old company like GE achieved what people said was impossible to achieve in the last quarter of the twentieth century, it started with a huge number of NoNos. I know; I was studying the firm at that time. With employment in the hundreds of thousands, if only .5 percent were of this breed, that would have added up to many more than five hundred people. Yet dedicated men and women did successfully deal with those people. Complacency dropped greatly. Urgency rose greatly. The firm went on to invent astonishing machines in its medical products division, quieter and less polluting engines in its aircraft engine group, incredibly innovative tools in its financial services group, wonderfully entertaining shows in its NBC unit, and a return to investors that no one would have thought feasible. In a depressing moment, NoNos can seem to anyone like ten-foot-thick steel walls blocking progress. They're not.

So . . .

1. Identify the NoNos.

2. Don't be naïve about the damage they can do.

3. Use one or more of the three strategies that work, not the two that are usually unsuccessful.

4. Get on with creating the sort of twenty-first-century organization we all want, one that serves well investors, employees, customers, and the public at large.

8.

keeping
urgency
up

An organization that can sustain a high sense of urgency over time has the potential to become a high-performance machine, where results go from good to great and beyond. Financial returns to investors grow past anyone's expectations. Innovation flourishes, leading to new products and services that customers could not have imagined. The sense of pride and excitement, and the economic rewards flowing to employees, grows and grows still more. But sustaining urgency over time requires that it not only be created, and created well, but that it be *re-created* again and again.

Urgency does not, and cannot, remain high without conscious effort unless it is very firmly ingrained in an organization's culture, something that today is exceptionally rare. Even when one has a strong culture of true urgency, unless there are crises that are impossible to ignore, natural forces tend to push toward stability and contentment. The basic pattern is simple: urgency leads to success leads to complacency.

At no time are these natural forces stronger than after people have worked very hard and have been rewarded by a visible, unambiguous win. A win can signal in people's minds that any crisis is over and any sacrifices are no longer necessary; that if mistakes or bad luck had plagued the recent past, they will now be absent in the foreseeable future. After a big win, urgency can slide with remarkable speed into a new complacency—a problem under any circumstances, but a much more significant problem in an era of change.

urgency up, success; urgency down, a mess

When he was made a division manager, the net losses within his group were growing. A cutback in residential construction had hit his home furniture business hard. Although many of his more senior employees rationalized that the company's situation simply reflected the dif-

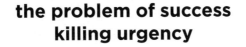

the problem of success killing urgency

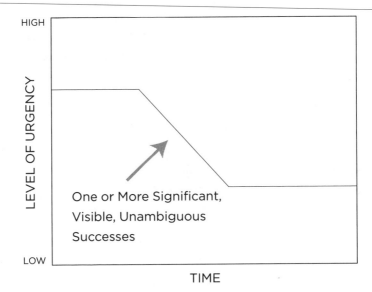

One or More Significant, Visible, Unambiguous Successes

ficulties experienced by the entire industry, he successfully used the near-crisis conditions as a way to help increase urgency, create a highly motivated top team, clarify a new vision and strategy for the division, and convince nearly all of the managers that they must implement the new strategy. Over three years, a combination of actions— shedding a product line, rebuilding strained relationships with a few key retailers, reorganizing to focus less on products and more on markets, and cutting unneeded bureaucracy—turned losses into profits. The work was hard, but with many people helping provide some critical leadership and many more making the appropriate sacrifices, they did the job well. Over a year and a half, the improvement in economic results was impressive.

When third-quarter numbers confirmed what people already knew, the tired but happy managers and employees declared victory. Those who felt overworked, relative to their pay, expected to be rewarded. They looked to the yearly performance appraisal and bonus-setting process with high expectations. Many people were simply relieved that the division was no longer in peril. They started spending more time at home. In their actions, nearly everyone was implicitly saying that the war was over and the company had won. The firm was now a great success story within an industry that was still struggling. All sense of urgency took a swift and deep decline.

The CEO and the division general manager were also proud and relieved. But urged on by a dynamic young woman in a corporate strategic planning role, they developed aspirations for the division that went far beyond a turnaround. They saw their successes—which, in terms of margins, cash flow, and net income, just kept looking better and better—as the conclusion to the first phase in a journey that would have many phases. Next on the agenda was a very ambitious push into higher-price, and higher-margin, lines and an expansion into all forty-eight states in the continental United States.

The division manager called the new thrust phase 2. At a series of meetings with his managers and staff, he explained the basic idea, the logic behind it, and what he wanted to achieve in the next fiscal year. His words were neither understood nor well received.

Many people clearly did not listen carefully, sometimes did not show up at the meetings, and did not, as a result, see the sweeping scope of phase 2. Some people treated the meetings as routine, probably unnecessary, boring management sessions. The call to arms was seen as an unnecessary pep talk. All is well now, they seemed to believe. And why not think that way? The numbers kept going up and up. Some people at these meetings listened carefully but did not understand the point of the new strategy. "Doesn't it involve risks? Didn't we just make sacrifices to eliminate risks? Aren't we now a great success story?" Still others were incredulous that the bosses wanted more from them. "Will they never let up?! Don't they see what we are accomplishing?! Have they made ridiculous commitments to the corporate head office?! *What is their problem?!*"

The red flags were all there. But the complacency problem was downplayed or ignored by the division general manager and his boss who were focused on strategy. Once into the details, the two executives found the plans for a geographic expansion and product line extension more and more exciting. "The best time to pursue an ambitious agenda," they told a visitor, "is not when you are crippled but when you are on top and have the financial resources to overcome inevitable obstacles, to offer management lucrative economic incentives, and to stay the course despite competitive countermoves." With increasing determination to make phase 2 a success, the executives used the levers at their disposal to push their agenda. Budgets were readjusted to fit the strategy. Some people were promoted or moved.

After eighteen months, phase 2 stalled, even though more evidence began to emerge that the new strategy was potentially very clever and even though some on the top team responded with great energy in light of bonus possibilities. But among the vast majority of the management and workforce, contentment with the status quo or outright angry resistance to new ideas became anchors that slowed and then stopped needed initiatives. The division general manager became frustrated, pushed harder, and became still more frustrated. Eventually, he took a job elsewhere, leaving the CEO without his best executive and strongest ally. And although neither of these men would have known it at the time, their case was far from unique.

the problem with short-term successes

It is impossible to execute bold new strategies, become much more innovative, smoothly bring in upgraded information technology, revamp factories with the latest management techniques, and leap forward as a result without producing wins in the short term. Successes that come quickly, as long as they are unambiguous and visible, demonstrate that a vision of the future has credibility. Quick successes can turn skeptics into supporters while reducing the power of cynics and NoNos. Celebrating successes can also make the hard-working feel vindicated and appreciated. When people see no wins within a sensible time frame, those who are making sacrifices can become discouraged, skeptics will ask more questions, and the NoNos inevitably gain power.

But with success comes a major problem: keeping up the sense of urgency needed to accomplish a bigger goal or to sustain a high level of performance over time. Some people will see that a vision has yet to be achieved and that there is still much work to do. Some people will see more opportunities that should be exploited. Some will see the hazards of not continuing to leap ahead and grow stronger. Usually, however, those managers and employees will be a small minority. The majority, perhaps the overwhelming majority, becomes complacent and, still worse, will not even see the complacency. If only unconsciously, these people will view their successes as a seemingly rational reason to let up. They want to, and do, stop talking about new opportunities or hazards, continued change, and any sacrifices for the greater good.

If urgency drops sufficiently and momentum is lost, pushing complacency away a second time can be much more difficult than it was the first. It is somewhat like having a bus with a stalled engine sitting on the side of the road in the pouring rain. Convincing passengers to step out into the rain and help the driver solve the problem is not an easy sell. Those who are warm, comfortable, listening to their iPods, and in no hurry may think it is the driver's problem, not theirs. Others may think that someone from the bus line should be able to come in a short period of time and fix the problem or, worst case, that a replacement bus can be called to take them on their journey. Still others may be furious because they will be late for an appointment, but they focus their fury on the driver and the bus line. Imagine the driver somehow using pleas (one of the passengers needs to arrive at a hospital before her mother goes into surgery), pragmatic logic (it could take hours for another bus to arrive), and a generally dynamic personality ("We can do this!") to create among the riders a determination to find the problem and solve it. Imagine many passengers getting off the bus into the pouring rain and then one of them alertly noticing that the crisis can be solved if they can just get the vehicle moving, perhaps to only five miles an hour, so the driver can pop the clutch and start the engine. Now everyone comes off the bus. With great pushing and sweating and groaning, they succeed. The bus rolls, the clutch pops, and the motor starts. Everyone gets back on the bus. They now have quite a story to tell their friends. Some may not know it, but they are actually rather proud of their achievement. A particularly funny passenger starts them all laughing about the ridiculous situation that they have been put through. Now imagine the bus going ten miles and stalling again. How hard, compared to the first time, will it be to create a determined group who will get off the vehicle in the rain and risk straining a muscle or hurting a back?

anticipate the problem, use the strategy, and choose the right tactics

The problem of urgency dropping after successes is difficult but solvable. Step 1 is being aware of it. Step 2 is knowing the tools available to stop it. Step 3 is using the right tools.

The tactical tools have already been described in this book. It's a matter of bringing the outside in. Behave with true urgency yourself. Go beyond yet another business case. Deal with the NoNos. See if you can use a crisis wisely and effectively. The difference is that after short-term wins, these actions must be taken again and perhaps again after that, but in each case with a keen awareness to what's already been done.

If bringing in customers to the annual meeting no longer has much effect, to successfully keep urgency up you find new ways to achieve the same objective. You might bring customers into a divisional management meeting. You might invite a customer's technicians, and not senior managers, to sessions held at lower levels in the organization. You might find a customer who has experienced the negative effects of a drop in the organization's urgency and have him talk to managers or employees. You might try an unprecedented and thus attention-catching action: perhaps a customer attends a product planning review meeting?

If your organization has had a policy of never sending people to long educational programs at universities, you might change the policy. That shift by itself may catch people's attention and lead them to listen more carefully to any explanation of why it is being done.

Of the several mechanisms that can help bring data in from the outside, if five were used initially, you try some of the other techniques. Or you creatively bring in a different sort of data, in a newly dramatic fashion. If importing data on market share is no longer useful because the information is not shockingly low, you look for other information that is surprising, that suggests clearly that employee perceptions of $A+$ performance are not accurate, or that $A+$ is not sustainable without change.

If visibly demonstrating a sense of urgency starts to feel grating to others, those who keep complacency down identify what is annoying and stop it. Too much repetition of the exact same line? "We cannot delay!" Say it differently. Too many e-mails sent twice and too quickly? Start sending only one e-mail with a polite note saying, "I would appreciate a reply tomorrow."

If a new sort of crisis might help, consider creating one, but with all the many caveats and principles discussed earlier. Release a new product developed by an increasingly complacent engineering group, even though you think it will likely not be very successful in the marketplace? If the financial and reputational risks are acceptable, at least consider the idea.

If NoNos still exist after some short-term successes, deal with them in a manner that makes sense then. This might mean facing up to the NoNo issue for the first time. Don't automatically draw the conclusion that you should leave those sorts of people alone because they did not stop you from raising urgency the first time. They may have been caught off guard. They won't be caught off guard the second time around.

If one aspect of your behaving-with-urgency role modeling seems to be particularly powerful, push it even harder. At the end of meetings, if pinning down short-term commitments has been helpful but you don't always do it, start disciplining yourself to use the tactic more consistently. If your own *look-move-lead-now* attitudes and feelings have been made visible regularly at corporate headquarters but not in other offices, get on the plane. Or start experimenting with teleconferences.

And as before, never use the tactics in a way that creates and then sustains the anger, anxiety, and flurry of activity associated with false urgency. Don't let your own frustration grow into anger and then into behavior that may shake things up but does not create the thoughts, feelings, and actions needed for long-term success.

The possibilities here, if not endless, certainly will create a long list. Make the list. Choose. Get moving.

keeping urgency up: a success case

Here's an example, told in the words of the executive involved:

> When we began, nearly everyone in the company
> was motivated to change because of the threat of
> being closed down. Then, as we started to turn our-
> selves around, there was a lot of excitement through-
> out the organization. People were motivated by our
> recent success and challenged by the new challenges.
> As we made more and more changes, we kept the
> momentum from slowing by comparing ourselves
> to similar healthcare companies. We explored our

strengths and weaknesses along a number of dimensions in each of our business divisions. On top of that,
I was out there talking face to face with all the people
in our organization once a month. I would try to explain why we were making the changes and talk
about the metrics that we were trying to achieve and
the competitors we faced. There was Q&A. As we
grew larger, we used teleconferencing once a month
to get the same messages out.

When we started to lead the field, comparing ourselves to our competitors became a piece of cake. If
anything, we kept reconfirming the fact that we were
miles ahead of everyone. In light of this success, we
were faced with the tendency to fall into complacency. After all, things were good; we were at the top
of the mountain. What was the reason to keep on re-
newing ourselves, to keep on building the stronger
organization that would inevitably be needed in the
future? People began to say, "But we *are* number
one." Even worse for me, "Why won't the boss just
let up?"

This was no good. But what could I do?

Now we've started using the idea of looking at
ourselves "from the investor's point of view." What
that means is that we've started to compare where we
are in relation to other investment opportunities
within the broad healthcare field. The real message
now is: We're in competition not just with firms like
us but also for investors' dollars. This is no longer
about just us and how well we run our business. This
is no longer just about our success in relation to the

competition out there creating the exact same products and services as we do. This is about recognizing the fact that other people out there in the healthcare industry are doing some pretty amazing things. Those people are getting a lot of attention and a lot of money from investors. So we may be the best at what we do, but if another company can create a price to earnings [PE] ratio of 50 and our PE is 12, boy, we've got trouble.

The reaction to this new focus has been very interesting. With some effort at helping the management and professional staff understand this idea, a lot of them got a renewed sense of urgency pretty quickly. They started to see the loss of potential investors as a threat and they started thinking about ways we can improve our own position. They began recognizing that there are a lot of newer companies who are beginning to offer some [of] the same services we do.

There are some people, however, who still say, "Company X is in the business of doing Net-based software, so it's not a good comparison. People are investing in those companies for different reasons. They're attracted to the technology, or to the newness of the company. We can't compare ourselves to them." Maybe it's just human to want to think this way: They aren't relevant, so we're fine. I've been learning that you can never over-communicate in helping people deal with these sorts of things. You have to be there talking with them as much as possible.

To keep you moving, in many situations it's going to be essential to have an external problem. If you are just going to beat up on people and say we have to do better, it doesn't work. People don't really believe you and it's not at all productive. Making more money doesn't do it either. There has to be something real that they can see outside that leads them to say, "We haven't made ourselves into the organization we should be. We need to do more. We need to try harder. I'm willing to try harder."*

A crisis helped this executive bring up urgency in the beginning of his story. Then with the crisis over, and with complacency growing, the executive imported certain information that compared his company to the best of its competitors. The tactic worked. Urgency again rose. When the firm succeeded in beating the best of its competitors, urgency dipped, but much more so than the first time. So he brought the outside in again, but in a different way. He also communicated-communicated-communicated, probably even more so than before. He may also have spoken more directly, face-to-face, showing his concerns, beliefs, excitement, commitment, and determination. Urgency rose once more. As a result, he and his people have helped create a more dynamic company in a health care industry that desperately needs more dynamic companies.

---

*Quoted in John P. Kotter and Dan S. Cohen, *The Heart of Change: Real-Life Stories of How People Change Their Organizations* (Boston: Harvard Business School Publishing, 2002), 144–146.

When I first encountered this story, before I did the research for this book, I certainly did not appreciate the significance of this executive's passing reference to communication at the end of the narrative. Today I would bet that "communication" is his simple, summary word to refer to his aggressive use of tactic number 1 (bringing the outside in), tactic number 2 (acting urgent every day), and tactic number 3 (finding opportunity in crises). Communication is obviously central to behaving urgently every day. But much of bringing-the-outside-in is all about communication. The difference between using and not using a crisis successfully is often highly dependent on the nature and frequency of communication. The same is true for dealing with NoNos: to help others see the importance of not hiring or promoting them; to help others see what could be viewed as harsh treatment of them.

You have a success. Urgency starts to go down. Before you're overwhelmed with complacency, you find a new way to bring urgency back up. Complacency retreats. Action continues. Your successes grow. Then urgency starts to drop again. As quickly as possible, you find still another way to bring it back up. Ultimately, successes that the pessimistic say are impossible become a reality, with benefits flowing to many. In some ways it is a simple formula after you understand the material in this book. It's a simple formula that can make a difference for many, many people.

drive it into the culture

The ultimate solution to the problem of urgency dropping after successes is to create the right culture. This is especially true as we move from a world in which change is mostly episodic to a world in which change is continuous.

With a culture of urgency, people deeply value the capacity to grab new opportunities, avoid new hazards, and continually find ways to win. Behaviors that are the norm include being constantly alert, focusing externally, moving fast, stopping low-value-added activities that absorb time and effort, relentlessly pushing for change when it is needed, and providing the leadership to produce smart change no matter where you are in the hierarchy.

The fundamental process by which cultures are created applies here, too, just as it does everywhere else. Create the behaviors you want. Make sure those behaviors actually help a group to succeed. Make sure success does not undermine urgency and allow the powerful winds of tradition to pull new behaviors back to historical norms. Use whatever managerial mechanisms are available— who is promoted, how people are compensated, how the group is formally organized—to make sure new actions are not driven away by short-term operating pressures that encourage expedient decisions that hurt you in the long term. Always treat new cultures as fragile, where a

keeping urgency up after a success

1. Anticipate, in advance, a possible downturn in the sense of urgency.

2. Plan for a solution.

3. Whether or not it is anticipated and planned for, as soon as urgency starts to dip use an appropriate combination of urgency-raising tactics within the framework of a heart-head strategy.

   a. Bring more of the outside in.

   b. Act urgently in new and fresh ways.

   c. Use (or create) a new crisis.

   d. Deal with the remaining NoNos.

Most of all, work, over time, to drive a sense of urgency into the culture.

single action—like promoting the number-one change champion to headquarters and replacing him with someone who does not believe or understand the new way of operating—can hurt greatly. Be patient, because it takes time for new behaviors to sink in and become organizational norms based on supporting shared values. The new behaviors then have roots.

Today, I don't think many organizations anywhere have cultures that truly reflect a sense of urgency. This will change. Some people will find that to prosper and maintain that prosperity in a turbulent, fast-moving world, a culture of urgency is a huge asset. Through time, effort, and perhaps a bit of luck, they will create that culture. And it will provide immense benefits to many people.

9.

the future

begin today

The ideas in this book will, in all probability, become more relevant in the foreseeable future because of the change swirling around us. Not only is the world hitting us with new opportunities and hazards, but it is doing so in many arenas at an accelerating rate. Intensity of competition, technological breakthroughs, continuing globalization, and the increasing need for innovation all feed this rate acceleration. The specifics will vary from industry to industry, across different levels of government, and in different countries. But the implications are always the same. Those who feel content with the status quo—*feel* being the key word, and not what they necessarily say—

put themselves in a more and more dangerous position. The anxious and angry focus on the wrong issues, often waste time in a flurry of unneeded activities, all with the same consequence—a growing vulnerability. Those with the compulsive drive to move, and win, now—feelings associated with a true sense of urgency—position themselves to achieve more than seems logical or reasonable for themselves, their employers, and the world in which we all live.

focus on quick and easy

With time and thought, anyone can generate dozens of ideas from this book that are relevant to a specific situation. My advice: don't try. A long list can be overwhelming. A sense of being overwhelmed stops action instead of encouraging it, just as a hopelessly cluttered calendar can kill urgency around a key issue. A better strategy is to identify three or four ideas that will be easy to implement, and start doing so immediately.

Most of us have been taught to think in a very linear fashion. The relevant question becomes, What logically must be done first, then second, and then third? In many cases, you must use this approach. But in terms of selecting a few items to help increase urgency, a linear strategy is not the best way to proceed. The problem is that item number 2 may be very difficult to implement well. Action slows, perhaps stops, and that is precisely what you are trying to overcome by reducing complacency.

An alternative to struggling with fifty items or limiting yourself to the logically linear is to focus first on what is quick and easy. Be opportunistic. Try something. Every situation is different and it is difficult to know what is the absolutely best way to start. Whatever you do, look for feedback. If an action does not help, abandon it. If it works well, consider doing more. Make something happen. Develop a bit of momentum. Then move on to bigger items, actions that do require planning or scarce resources.

start now

Quick-and-easy actions usually do not require the creation of a new project. They fit into your existing calendar for the upcoming week or month. They do not require new resources. Quick-and-easy usually means using existing plans, budgets, and activities in a new and different way. So if evidence suggests that an organization's culture is a terrible problem, instead of only trying to create a culture-change task force—easily a three- to six-month project just to set it up—you might simply raise the culture question in most of your meetings starting tomorrow: "Is the way we do things around here a barrier to _____?" where the blank space is the topic of the meeting.

Acting Urgently is the tactic that creates results quickly. The other three tactics can all be started immediately, but results will take time. So you make sure that people not only hear the question about culture in meetings tomorrow, but that they see your genuinely urgent concern that the organization's culture may be stopping them from succeeding. You don't want to be frantic and lose credibility or raise questions about hidden agendas. You simply let others see some newfound energy within you on the issue of culture, a seeming belief that they must deal with the question, and soon.

Instead of waiting to secure a major consulting report before taking action—a year of work to find the budget, identify possible advisers, ask for proposals, and so on—you or your staff might start dipping more into the Internet now. You could more systematically search for information on markets, products, competitors, technologies, and then see what actions would be appropriate based on the informal research. The consultant might still be a great idea, and you can start the process tomorrow that will bring the outside in via a consultant. But with the Internet, you might start finding useful results this week.

Instead of deciding to give a NoNo a reduced performance rating at the annual review next year, you might make the man the topic of conversation with a close friend and colleague at an already scheduled lunch today. You still might, or might not, use the next performance review as a part of a strategy for dealing with the NoNo. But you start acting immediately, and without having to modify your appointment calendar at all.

With actions implemented easily, you can also start developing additional skills, as soon as possible, that will be increasingly important in the years ahead. Most of us will need new skills because of the most basic trends that shape the world around us.

we must . . .

Speed will only increase. A sense of urgency will only become more essential.

It can be helpful to think in terms of the biggest issues of all, because to do so adds clarity. Think nationally and globally: climate change, terrorism, the monumental effects of China and India becoming developed nations, the ethical issues to be raised by the biosciences, the need for better K–12 education, or the reform of Social Security in the United States. Do we have a strong sense of urgency to deal with these issues? Remember, words are not the test. Action is the test. Never forget, furious activity and running and meeting and slick presentation are not a sign of true urgency. Alertness, movement, and leadership, *now*—and from many people, not a few—are the signs of true urgency.

So where do we stand today? Is this where we need to stand for the sake of the next generation?

We can do better.

About the Author

JOHN P. KOTTER, Konosuke Matsushita Professor of Leadership, Emeritus, at Harvard Business School, is widely regarded as the world's foremost authority on leadership and change. His is the premier voice on how the best organizations actually "do" change.

Kotter's international bestseller, *Leading Change*—which outlines an actionable, eight-step process for implementing successful transformations—has become the change bible for managers around the world. *Our Iceberg Is Melting,* the *New York Times* bestseller, puts the eight-step process within an allegory, making it accessible to the broad range of people needed to effect major organizational transformations. In October 2001, *BusinessWeek* magazine rated Kotter the number-one "leadership guru" in America.

Kotter has published sixteen books, twelve of which have been business bestsellers and six of which have won awards or honors. With millions of copies sold, his books have been translated into more than one hundred foreign-language editions. He is also the author of several seminal articles in the *Harvard Business Review*.

Professor Kotter's honors include an Exxon Award for innovation in graduate business school curriculum design and a Johnson, Smith & Knisely Award for new perspectives in business leadership. In 1996, *Leading Change* was named the number-one management book of the year by *Management General.* In 1998, his book *Matsushita Leadership* won first place in the *Financial Times*/Booz-Allen Global Business Book competition for biography/autobiography. In 2003, a video version of a story from his book *The Heart of Change* won a Telly Award. In 2006, Kotter received the prestigious McFeely Award for "outstanding contributions to leadership and management development." In 2007, his video "Succeeding in a Changing World" was named best video training product of the year by *Training Media Review*.

Dr. Kotter is a graduate of MIT and Harvard. He joined the Harvard Business School faculty in 1972. In 1980, at the age of thirty-three, he was given tenure and a full professorship.

For additional information, see www.johnkotter.com.

BURN

a novel by Suzanne Phillips

LITTLE, BROWN AND COMPANY
NEW YORK   BOSTON

Little, Brown and Company

Hachette Book Group USA
237 Park Avenue, New York, NY 10017
Visit our Web site at www.lb-teens.com

First Edition: November 2008

Library of Congress Cataloging-in-Publication Data

Phillips, Suzanne.
  Burn / by Suzanne Phillips.—1st ed.
    p. cm.
  Summary: Bullied constantly during his freshman year in high school, Cameron's anger and isolation grow, leading to deadly consequences.
  ISBN 978-0-316-00165-6
  [1. Bullying—Fiction. 2. Emotional problems—Fiction. 3. Post-traumatic stress disorder—Fiction. 4. High schools—Fiction. 5. Schools—Fiction.] I. Title.
  PZ7.P54647Bu 2008
  [Fic]—dc22   2007043520

10 9 8 7 6 5 4 3 2 1

Book design by Alison Impey

RRD-C

Printed in the United States of America

ACKNOWLEDGMENTS

I am blessed with the world's best editors.
Thank you to Nancy Conescu and Harriet Wilson
for their unrelenting support.

*

Thank you, also, to Jerri Borkert and Tamra Winchell,
my first readers, for their thoughtful criticism.

PART I

SUNDAY

3:20PM

Cameron's mother's new *family* thing is that you have to tell her everything you did with your day. Last night at dinner he made up an entire Scout meeting. *That* wasn't hard. He knew they were going to work on slipknots and plan community service. He told his mother he thought he would put in some volunteer hours with Parks and Recreation. He likes being outside. He thought his mother would buy it, not suggest he work at the old folks' home.

✳

"They really need someone to come in and talk to the seniors. Read them books. That kind of thing," his mother pressed.

"Or change their diapers," his younger brother, Robbie, said, and would have laughed until he choked on his chicken, but Randy, their mother's boyfriend, gave him something to think about: "You want to help him, Robbie? You're going to need some volunteer hours for Boy Scouts."

Robbie stuffed his mouth full so he didn't have to answer.

Their mother leaned closer, tapped the table to get Cameron's attention.

"What do you think?" she asked.

She smiled, but when Cameron didn't return it, the corners of her lips fell flat. She'd looked like that a lot, when she was still married to Cameron's father. Unhappy. Disappointed. Afraid.

Cameron's stomach twisted into a fierce knot, and he hated that. She was counting on him to come through for her. She didn't want to worry about him. If it was possible, she'd tuck him into one of her envelopes — bills, coupons, Cameron — and then flit around the house, her office, the grocery store, thinking everything was okay. But it wasn't.

He was mad all the time. Felt it burning beneath his skin. He probably had a higher body temperature just thinking about school, Rich Patterson and his jock punks, and his father, whom Cameron still wanted to hate but couldn't.

"Well?"

His mother's fingers drummed on his forearm. Cameron shook himself out of his thoughts, tried to push down the fire smoldering inside him.

"We're supposed to look for something that'll be a good fit," he told her. Really, the key word was challenging. At the last Scout meeting Cameron actually had attended, they were told to find a new interest, something that would make them think and test their abilities. But talking was something Cameron wasn't good at. At all. Even talking to his mom was getting hard.

"Cameron, I want you to do something that puts you with people," his mom said. "You spend too much time alone."

"I'm never alone," Cameron protested. "I go to school with a thousand other kids." None of them were friends. None of them were anything like Cameron. They all belonged. They were players or gamers or geeks. And Cameron didn't fit with any of them. He was a runner. Too bad sports were ruined for him. His grades weren't good enough now to even try out for the track team. "I don't even have my own bedroom," he finished.

"You had more friends last year," she pointed out.

That was before ninth grade happened to him. The first week wasn't so bad; he blended in. He and his buddy Steve had two classes together (science and Spanish); they ate lunch, checking out each table in the cafeteria for the hottest girl. Steve went for legs; Cameron liked the girls who wore too-small T-shirts and put lip gloss on, even in the middle of class.

But everything changed when he went to sports orientation. His whole body clenched like a fist just thinking about it. They held the orientation at night and his mom was late getting home from work, so they were late — just a minute or two — getting to the gym. Cameron didn't like walking into a meeting already in progress, didn't like being the only thing for people to look at, but he didn't have a choice. He was almost to the empty spot in the bleachers, his mom right behind him, when the coach with the microphone tried to direct them to the girls' gym. Cameron felt his whole body explode with fire. Spontaneous combustion.

He wanted to blame his mom (most of the boys had their fathers with them), but he knew it was his hair, which he had grown out over the summer and was streaked blond by the sun, and his body, which was too small and thin for a guy in high school.

Cameron turned and faced the coach, his whole body stunned and refusing to find cover. The coach stuttered an apology, making the whole thing worse. Then Cameron scrambled into the bleachers and tried to hide.

But it didn't end there. The next day, Rich Patterson, a junior and an offensive lineman on the varsity football team, found him. Cameron was walking upstairs for first period when an arm, all bunched-up muscle, curled around his neck and pulled him to a stop.

"Looky here, guys — it's Cameron Diaz."

And that's what everyone called him now.

The third week of school, Cameron found his name carved

into the bathroom wall: CAMERON DIAZ LOVES STEVE FINELLI. Cameron stared at it while his stomach crawled up his throat. He stared at it until everything turned red, like he had looked at the sun until his eyes fried. He didn't try to scratch it out; he couldn't move. The tardy bell rang but didn't shatter his paralysis. It was the first time he had skipped class. For three days he worried about other guys seeing it — seeing it and laughing and thinking he was gay.

He didn't tell Steve about it, but someone did. Steve stopped having lunch with him — stopped going to the cafeteria, period. And he found somewhere else to sit in class, clear across the room. When Cameron called him at home, Steve hissed, "I'm no fag, Grady. Stay away from me," and hung up.

So Cameron went back into the bathroom, a nail he brought from home in his pocket, and was going to scratch out their names, but someone already had. And in black marker someone else had written FAGS with an arrow pointing toward where the names had been.

Cameron was ruined the first week of school. His mom didn't understand: in high school there were no second chances.

✳

"I told you, high school is different." You could actually turn invisible there, but never when you wanted to.

7

"Not that different. Everyone makes friends the same way. You find someone who likes to do the things you like and, presto, you're friends."

"That's not how it happens. Not now." Not ever.

"You could have joined football with Steven."

"I'm not good at it."

"How do you know?"

"I weigh a hundred pounds. I'd be roadkill before halftime."

His mother's face got that look of concern, where her nose scrunched up and her eyebrows became one big bird of prey. Cameron didn't like the look, mostly because it made him feel bad, heavy in the chest and like his Adam's apple was too big for his throat.

"Then what do you want to do?" she asked.

Cameron shrugged.

"I want you to have something you like to do," she insisted. "And people you like to do it with. Friends are important."

"Because you had a whole bunch of friends in high school?"

"No, because I didn't have any," she said. "Well, I had one friend. One good friend, but that didn't happen until tenth grade. High school can be a lonely place, Cameron."

His mother's fingers swirled around the edge of the salad bowl. She only did that when she was nervous.

Cameron could deal with lonely, but the kids he went to school with, the kids who *ran* the school, were brutal. They roved in packs, flushing the vulnerable out of their shells, cornering them, and taunting or beating on them. Every time he walked through the doors, it was like crossing into enemy camp. He watched his back, spent as little time as he could in the halls, and tried to get through the day without using the bathroom. He stayed away from places where ambush was easy.

"Cameron?" his mom prompted.

"I'm not lonely."

"Well, you have Scouts," she said, picking up her fork. "I guess that's enough. For now. But I want you to do your volunteer hours communing with something other than trees. Seniors are mostly forgotten. I doubt anyone else in the troop will think to volunteer there."

No kidding. "What would we talk about?"

"Laxatives," Robbie suggested, and chuckled.

Randy ignored him. "You could read them the newspaper," he said, dropping his napkin on the table and giving Cameron his full attention.

Cameron didn't look at him; he felt his skin get tight, like he was standing in hot water. It's not that he didn't like Randy Stewart. He just didn't feel comfortable around him. His mother was always breaking up with the guy and Cameron didn't know if he was supposed to like him or not. So he never spent more time with him than he had to. Never talked to him unless Randy started the conversation.

"I don't read the newspaper," Cameron said. He put enough 'mind your own business' into his tone that he hoped Randy would pick up on it.

He did. He smiled at Cameron like any offense was forgiven and suggested, "You can start with the sports page. That'd be painless."

Probably. If he stayed with it. If he started going back to Scouts regularly. It wouldn't be too bad, reading about baseball and March Madness. He shrugged his shoulders and looked at Randy.

"Maybe," Cameron said.

"You'll ask?" his mother pressed.

"Yeah."

SUNDAY

5:00PM

Cameron cuts through the woods on his way home. It's faster and there's enough space between the trees and rocks that he can push his bike through. He knows these woods like he knows his backyard. When he was a little kid he built a fort here, he and his friends. They smuggled chips and sodas from their houses and sat out here telling made-up monster stories and trading baseball cards. But that was a long time ago.

Cameron finds a boulder with a flat surface, lets his bike drop into the grass, and opens the plastic wrap around the package

Mrs. Murdock gave him. Banana-nut muffins. They're still warm and Cameron lowers his face and breathes in the sweet steam. He sits down, plucks the nuts from the tops of each muffin, and tosses them into the brush for the squirrels. Then he eats the muffins, all three.

Mrs. Murdock bakes while Cameron is working in her yard. She moves around her kitchen, slow but determined, and he tries real hard not to look at the window where she sometimes stops and peers out at him. Mrs. Murdock treats him like she would her grandson, if she had one. He wishes she did. Cameron doesn't want to disappoint her, but he knows he will. He doesn't know how to make people happy. He was assigned to Mrs. Murdock by his Scout leader. The project was supposed to last four weeks and end in February; it's March 11th.

Cameron put in his community service hours, but Mrs. Murdock's yard was a jungle and it took weeks just to cut back the overgrown bushes and trim the trees. Today, he put new boards in her fence and mowed her lawn and she spoke to him about turning over a small patch of dirt in the back corner for a garden. So he supposes he'll be back next Sunday, too. And that's how he spent his afternoon.

He doesn't want to tell his mother about it. She doesn't know Cameron is still working on Mrs. Murdock's yard. She'll want to know why, when the job was finished weeks ago, and Cameron has nothing to tell her. Even he isn't sure why he returns, except that whenever he thinks about not going back, he sees Mrs. Murdock's face all bunched up with worry and he thinks about her shuffling around in her house all alone. She once told him that she had outlived all of her friends and Cameron thinks that's a pretty sad place to be. Anyway, if he tells his mom this, she'll get all teary on him. He can do without that.

He finishes the last muffin, stands up and brushes the crumbs from his shirt. He knocks the dirt from his jeans. He looks himself over for any other signs of what he's been up to. Evidence. Randy is a cop and sometimes Cameron feels like the guy can figure him out, know everything that's in his mind, just from looking at him a piece at a time.

Cameron takes the book of matches from his sock and stashes it under a rock. He checks every pocket, twice, then moves through the trees, pushing his bike. From the edge of the woods he looks at his house. There's a light on in the kitchen window, his mother's minivan is parked in front of the garage, and the garbage cans have been moved to the curb. That's his job. His mother must have had Robbie do it because it was getting dark. That means he has to load the dishwasher, unless his mother is going out with Randy tonight. Then Cameron will make Robbie do it, and give him enough grief that he won't tell.

Cameron stands a moment longer, looking at his house like he doesn't live there. It seems normal, like all the other houses in his neighborhood, with bikes in the driveway and the windows lit up. Maybe it's just he who's different. He doesn't feel like he belongs in this house; he doesn't even feel comfortable inside his own skin. Most of the time, he feels like he could swallow a stone and it'd keep on going. Bottomless. Empty.

His mother is in the kitchen, washing lettuce in the sink, when Cameron walks in.

"You're home," Cameron says, wishing he could say something more. He used to hug her when he came home. But he's fourteen now, a freshman in high school. And anyway, he doesn't feel like something more.

"Home for a quick dinner." Cameron's mother looks over her shoulder at him. "I have to fill in for a few hours tonight — make up for my time off."

His mother went with Randy to Philadelphia last weekend. A friend of hers stayed overnight with Cameron and Robbie.

"You've been gone awhile," she says. "What have you been up to?" She places the lettuce on paper towel to drain, then catches him again with her gaze.

Cameron shrugs his shoulders. "Nothing. What's for dinner?"

"Salad for me and Randy. You and Robbie are having mac and cheese and ham sandwiches." She presses the lettuce between the pieces of paper towel. Her eyes never leave him and he feels like he's pinned to the wall. "You okay?"

"Yeah."

"Really?"

He doesn't like his mother looking at him like maybe he needs shock therapy.

"Really."

He walks past her, scuffing his shoes on the tile floor because she hates when he does that and he hates that she worries so much about him but doesn't have a clue. He notices that she waits a full five seconds longer than usual to tell him to pick up his feet.

"They are up," he calls back to her, letting his foot streak across the floor one last time.

SUNDAY

7:00PM

Robbie is lying on his bed with the TV remote on his stomach. Cameron snatches it as he passes, changes the channel from Animal Planet to ESPN, and then reaches under his pillow for his stash of candy bars.

"Hey! I was watching that." Robbie lunges toward the remote, but Cameron holds it out of reach.

"You're too old for Mr. Rogers," Cameron says.

"Sharks, dufus," Robbie says. "I was watching a program about sharks."

"Don't you get enough of that at school?"

"This is homework."

Robbie makes another move for the remote and Cameron raises his leg, plants his foot square in Robbie's chest, and pushes him backward. Not hard. Just enough to put his brother on his butt, in the center of his bed.

Robbie's hands curl into fists.

"Turn it back on," Robbie says.

"Or what? You gonna tell Mom?"

"No."

Robbie's face turns pink, even his ears.

"Nice blush," Cameron says, knowing it'll make Robbie angrier and that he won't do anything about it. "Don't forget your lipstick."

Robbie is in the seventh grade and is an inch taller than Cameron. He weighs more, too. Robbie takes after their father — he has shoulders to grow into. But he's not a bully. He doesn't lose his temper. Robbie is Cameron's opposite: no matter how many times Cameron plucks at his Achilles heel, his brother doesn't respond. Cameron hates that. Hates his brother's self-control.

He hates that he doesn't have more of it himself.

"I might tell her that you never made it to Scouts," Robbie says. "That was a nice story you made up last night."

"How do you know I wasn't at Scouts?"

"I was at Danny's, working on our science project in his garage. I saw you ride by. Where did you go?"

Cameron thinks about this. He was on his way to Keegan's. He likes hanging out in front of the liquor store. Sometimes, if he's there long enough, some guy will toss him a can of beer from his six-pack. Once, an old guy let him drink from his bottle of Jim Beam. Cameron drank so much that he couldn't feel the ground under his feet the whole way home. But he had to hide in the garage until he could feel his feet again, and then swallow enough mouthwash so his mother wouldn't know what he was up to. She never even guessed, just looked at him a long time across the dinner table, then said, "Did you get your homework done?"

So much for parental control.

"Where did you go?" Robbie repeats.

"'Where did you go?'" Cameron parrots.

Cameron shakes his head, begins unwrapping a candy bar like it's a banana. He takes a bite and rolls it around in his mouth.

"You ever heard of fun, Robbie?" Cameron asks. "It's something that has nothing to do with school. Nope, you can't find it anywhere near a place full of books and peckerheads."

Robbie's mouth, a lot like their mother's, dips like a half-moon.

"They still picking on you at school?"

Cameron feels his skin burn and all over again he hates that his brother will never know anything about being the underdog. Robbie is too big to ever be messed with like Cameron is.

Cameron pushes himself up until he's sitting on the edge of his bed. He rolls his shoulders back, feels his chest lift, his arms grow, and looks at Robbie to see if he understands.

No. Robbie's face is soft, full of concern. Most of the time when Cameron looks at his brother he sees his father. Then Robbie ruins it; he puts a look on his face so different from anything his father ever shot their way that Cameron can't mistake them. He feels his body loosen. Just like that. He can go from pure fight to nothing in ten seconds.

"What do you know about it?" Cameron asks.

"Just what Danny's brother told me. He said you must have a hard time getting up in the morning when you know you're going to get a beating."

"Arthur is an ass. He got his ass kicked just last week."

"He says that's why he knows life must suck for you. It only happened to him once. He says it's every day for you."

Cameron sits up, holds out his arms, turns his face so Robbie can see both sides.

"You see any bruises?"

Robbie looks him over, his brown eyes slow and full of doubt. "No."

"I guess Arthur doesn't know everything then."

Robbie shrugs and lets the conversation go. "You gonna turn my show back on?"

"Well, since you asked so nice . . ."

Cameron aims the remote at the TV and turns back to Animal Planet and the great white shark that's devouring a seal.

In his mind, Cameron plucks the seal from the mouth of Jaws and shoves a squirming Rich Patterson down the great white's throat. It's more Patterson than anyone else beating on him. And not every day. Sometimes it's a hit and run, or Patterson puts him in a headlock and drags him down the hall talking crap. Sometimes Patterson is already pissed and his fists are heavier and he tells Cameron, "I want you to feel this tomorrow, girly-boy."

Anyway, he doesn't know what to do about it.

Robbie turns back to the TV and Cameron rolls over, rummaging deep between the mattress and box spring for his Ziploc bag of matches. Most of them he got from restaurants — IHOP, Friendly's, The Green Café. He has one from 7-Eleven, another from a gas station, and an entire box of souvenir matches he bought on a class trip to a museum in Philadelphia. He takes the book from 7-Eleven and rips off a stick, then strikes it against the flint. It flares to life.

Cameron loves watching the flame jump as it sucks up pure, clean air and spreads down the cardboard. When the flame touches his fingertips, Cameron closes his mouth and breathes evenly through his nose. He watches his thumbnail turn black and smells the acid burn of human flesh as the flame ignites the tip of his nail. When he feels the first lick of fire against the pad of his thumb, he raises it to his mouth and squashes it against his tongue. He loves that. The burn. The smell and the burn.

The pain screams out of him like a tornado; he feels alive and happy to be. Lately, the only thing that makes him feel like one of the living is fire, and what it does to his body.

"You're not supposed to play with matches," Robbie says without turning to look at Cameron. He has a spiral notebook perched on his knees and is writing down facts from his show.

Cameron pulls another match from the book and strikes it into life. "You gonna add that to your rat list?"

"I don't have a list."

"Well you better start writing some of this down," Cameron suggests, lofting the match through the air, aiming for Robbie's back. "You'll forget something."

The match falls onto the mattress, snuffing out. Cameron lights another one.

"Did you hear me?" Cameron says.

He puts more wind behind this match, but it falls short of the mark. When Robbie shifts on the bed, the match slips under his leg.

"I'm not interested in the things you do."

Strike.

"Yes you are. You worship me."

Robbie looks at him over his shoulder. "You're crazy."

"That's the way it works," Cameron tells him, holding up the lit match, letting Robbie watch the flame glide down the paper and melt his thumbnail. "All little brothers worship their older brothers."

"Someone forgot to tell me." The flame grows larger and Robbie leans close and blows it out. "You're dangerous," he says.

"Ah. The respect I was looking for."

Cameron smiles, watches the way his brother's face puckers into a frown, and likes it. He worries Robbie — scares him just a little. Exactly what a big brother's supposed to do.

Cameron lights another match and lobs it. It catches on Robbie's flannel shirt. He waits until a swirl of gray smoke rises up from Robbie's back and then says, "Little brother, you're on fire."

MONDAY

8:45AM

Cameron's mother stops the van two blocks from the high school. The windshield wipers are on full blast and still all he can see are the brake lights from the cars ahead of them. Spring. In Erie, that means sudden thunderstorms and whitecaps on the lake. Before his parents broke up, they lived in Syracuse.

Cameron likes snow better than rain; he liked his other school more than this one. It's been three years and he still doesn't fit in here. His only friends were through Scouts, and most of them left the troop when they started high school. He sees them in the halls with new buddies. Some of them have gone completely to the other side and have become sport punks who line the halls during free period and pass the small kids between them like they're volleyballs. Some of them call him Cameron Diaz or fag — even though he cut his hair months ago.

He does his math homework; it's the one thing he's really good at. Most of the problems he can do in his head, and if the teacher didn't demand that he show his work, he'd have an A, easy. He pats his pocket, where his homework is folded and stashed along with a packet of beef jerky, a book of matches, and money for a drink later, if he can find a Coke machine where there are no predators lurking in the shadows. That's how he plans his day — mapping out in his mind the fastest route to each class that places him in the least amount of danger.

He zips up his parka and pulls his wool hat over his ears.

"You don't have an umbrella," his mom says.

"I don't need one."

"It's pouring." She frowns. "You want mine?"

"No."

"Then let me drive you all the way."

"I'm fine." Cameron pushes the door open and the wind whips a bucketful of rain through the opening. "I'll see you later."

The school is a two-story squat building with a row of stone steps leading to a wall of glass doors at the main entrance. Every window sits in a cement casing with some gothic-looking scrolls around it. On days like today, with the sky heavy and gray and the rain cutting sideways through the air, it looks pretty cool, from the outside — like some place a scientist might be cooking up the next Frankenstein monster.

There aren't many kids grouped around the door. Just the Trench Coats. Goths or emos. Cameron can't tell them apart. He thinks of them as the walking wounded, because the black makeup and nail polish, black clothes, and multiple piercings scream pain. They look kind of like he feels, and for a while he thought they might be it: the place he could belong.

But Cameron doesn't want people knowing he's hurting. He doesn't think wearing it on the outside will help him any. He hasn't noticed any of the Trench Coats feeling better and suddenly showing up at school in a pair of blue jeans, or even smiling, just once. And maybe it's the way they're stuck in their situations that makes him almost the same as them.

And like they know it, like they're just waiting for Cameron to make up his mind for himself, they call out to him as he passes.

"Hey, Cameron."

"Hey." Cameron doesn't know any of their names. What's the point? He'll never be one of them. *Different philosophies,* he thinks. Cameron was raised by a man who screamed at him if he cried. But there's more than that of his father in him. Every time he sees one of them, wrapped in all their black, he thinks, *Crybabies.* He wonders, *If life is so bad for them, then why don't they end it?* He wants to know if they ever thought about it. Fading to black.

Cameron jogs past them, takes the steps two at a time, and pushes through the doors. It's standing room only. All the kids who are usually outside, chatting or cramming last minute homework into notebooks, are knotted in the halls. Their laughter sounds like breaking glass.

He weaves through them, his head up, his eyes scanning faces. He doesn't run. If he sees Patterson or his chump friends, he keeps his pace and looks for a hall or a door he can turn into. That's not running; it's dodging bullets.

He catches pieces of conversation. The girls talk about clothes, phone calls, and what they want to do over the weekend. The boys talk about the game the night before, whose pants they want to get into, and jokes they heard from their fathers.

He could talk about those things, too. He likes baseball and never misses a Pirates game. But he doesn't look like a player. Unless you look the part, no one listens to you.

No one respects you.

There isn't a girl he's interested in. Not yet. But he could make that part up; most of the guys do anyway. Cameron is sure of this because some of the stories he's heard are too fantastic to be true. Like Jumbo Harris making it with two girls at the same time. He doesn't believe that. Girls giving head in the boys' bathroom, he heard that a few weeks ago, and believes it. He's been in there and heard giggling. It wouldn't take much to create a story someone would believe. The jokes, maybe he could get a few from Randy.

But none of this really matters, because he has no one to tell a story to.

Cameron turns the corner and just his luck, Rich Patterson is there, leaning against a locker, hovering over a girl. *Probably a cheerleader.* Cameron can't see her; Patterson's body blocks hers, but he's playing with her hair, a long ponytail the color of a caramel apple.

The girl laughs, her voice bubbling up from her throat, and Cameron thinks she sounds like one of those garden fountains. It's beautiful and he gets lost in it for a minute, forgetting where he is and who he's looking at. Who made her laugh like that.

Patterson is good at just about everything. And that really sucks.

A group of kids passes between them, breaking Cameron's paralysis. He pivots on his heel and heads back the way he came. Fast enough. Patterson couldn't have seen him. He walks the long way through the crowded halls, sliding between warm bodies made musty with rain and absorbing the sounds of life as though through a filter.

Sometimes words are so close he feels them on his skin; sometimes he reaches for them and they slip between his fingers. It's like living painfully aware of everything around you, and the next minute knowing you're drawing your last breath. There is no middle ground, no comfort, no escape.

He skirts a group of kids talking, laughing, and turns down freshman hall and runs right into two Red Coats — jock jackets. Patterson and his sidekick, Murphy.

"It's Cameron Diaz," Rich says, like he's happy to see him.

"You're all wet," Murphy says. "You on your way to a wet T-shirt contest?"

Cameron leads with his shoulder, planning to walk around them. He never ducks his head — he won't give them that. But he doesn't look them in the eye, either.

They shift, blocking him.

"Now, don't be stuck-up, Cameron," Patterson says. "Talk to us. You trying out for next year's cheerleading squad? That's after school today."

"You don't want to miss that," Murphy says.

"You want to show us what you have?"

"Yeah. We'll give you some tips," Murphy offers. "We've seen them up close and personal."

"Yeah. We know their moves real good."

"Piss off," Cameron says, which he knows is a mistake. They never like what he has to say and mostly Cameron just keeps his mouth shut and concentrates on pushing the anger back. Biting down on it so it doesn't become all he is.

He can feel it taking over. Feel it burning up from his fingertips, from his toes, so his hands and feet are on fire. He wants to let it take over — is afraid of what will happen when he does.

Not *if* anymore, but *when*. Soon. He's going to let go and become a windmill of swinging arms and fists that'll put them into next Tuesday. He likes that thought so much he smiles a little. Another mistake.

"What's so funny about being a boy-girl?" Patterson asks.

"Nothing. Nothing at all," Murphy says.

Cameron feels their hands under his armpits, then his feet leave the floor. They walk with him to an open classroom and drop him inside the door, then shut it behind them. Cameron looks around him. Empty.

"No rescue," Patterson says. "But we're willing to let you outta here. Of course, you have to do something for us first."

Murphy snickers. "Give us a cheer, Cameron Diaz."

"You know you're not leaving until you do."

"You know if you don't we're going to have to make you."

Cameron gets that feeling again, where his stomach is pushing up his throat, choking off his air. He knows what they'll do to him if he doesn't play cheerleader. They're not creative; they never change their routine. Murphy will hold him and Patterson will use him as a punching bag. He'll hit Cameron in the stomach until he pukes. It doesn't leave bruises. Not that anyone can see. No evidence.

Cameron prepares himself, because there's no way he's going to act the fag and give them what they want. He pulls his stomach in, makes it tense. Sometimes that helps. He starts that whole believing thing; *my stomach is as hard as rock.* If he buys into it

29

he doesn't feel the pain until later. Much later, when no one is around to see him folded over himself and an even sorrier sight than he is usually.

"Oh, come on, Cameron." Murphy circles him. "What if we ask you nice?" He puts his arm around his neck until Cameron's chin is above the guy's elbow. "Cameron, will you please do a cheer for us?" He reaches for Cameron's wrist, twists it up behind him and makes his voice thin and high. "How about 'two-four-six-eight, who do we appreciate?' We like that one."

"Go to hell," Cameron says. At least he doesn't give in. He has that. He never does any of the things they tell him to. Not the time they wanted him to drink toilet water, on his own or with their help, or the time they stole his clothes when he was in the shower and they offered him a choice: run naked through the girls' gym or go naked the rest of the day. Cameron waited them out, past the tardy bell, then pulled a set of loaner PE clothes from the bin and got through the day.

"Last chance, Diaz." Patterson rolls up his fists.

Cameron feels every one of Patterson's knuckles in the soft part of his stomach, below the arch of his ribs. The breath shoots out of his lungs; his heart stops, then kicks against his chest. His body tries to curl over itself.

"Hold him up," Patterson orders.

Murphy yanks him up, pulling back on his shoulders so that his stomach is easily accessible. He says, "You're a real girl, Diaz. You never put out. A guy's gotta take it."

"I don't mind working for it." Patterson has his hands up again, fists like a boxer. "You gonna dance, Cameron?"

Cameron keeps his mouth shut this time. It'll end sooner if he says nothing. If he stands as still as a post and sucks up what they have for him.

This time, the punch lands on his rib bones. He hears Patterson's knuckles crack and knows he'll have a bruise.

"Damn! You want to hold him still? I gotta pitch with this hand tomorrow."

But before Patterson can swing again, Cameron hears the metallic click of keys in the door knob. They hear it, too, and fall back, Patterson taking a casual stance with his hands stuffed into his front pockets. Slowly, Cameron's body loosens up. He wants to rub his stomach, ease the burn there, but won't do it. Not here. Not in front of them.

The door opens and Mrs. Cowan, Cameron's English teacher, strides into the room. And stops. Her eyebrows lift, but she's fast to recover.

"What's going on here?" She puts a hand on her hip in her I-mean-business pose.

"Just a private conversation," Patterson says.

"Really?" She doesn't believe him.

"Cameron helps us with our math," Murphy says. "He's a genius, you know?"

She thinks about this, looks him up and down. Her lips pucker a little.

"That true, Cameron?"

Cameron tries to stand up a little straighter, feels his stomach muscles tug, but he keeps his face from showing it.

"Yeah. Every word."

"I'm not convinced," she says.

She moves toward her desk, turns and stares at them, probably wondering what she should do with them. Cameron knows it's his job to make her believe. He knows what will happen if he doesn't. He'll spend the next couple of days waiting to be jumped, pulled into a bathroom, and creamed.

"It's true," he says. "We had a conversation." When she continues to look at him with doubt making her face all soft and inviting, Cameron puts a little anger in his voice. "I don't have to like what we were talking about, do I?"

"No," she agrees. "So long as it was talk." Her shoulders give and she tells Cameron to leave first. "You two stay a few minutes."

Cameron makes sure his walk to the door is slow, then he stands there, trying to pour cement into his shaking knees as he waits for a break in the crowds flooding to class. He enters the heavy stream after a group of girls and watches their faces, their bright, sunny faces, and open mouths talking and laughing. But all he can think about is how much he hates this school. His hate is a steady roar that fills his ears. He can't think beyond it, and so he just moves with everyone else.

"Hey! Grady!"

Cameron feels his name tug at his consciousness and turns toward it. And looks down. Pinon, the only guy smaller than Cameron at Madison High. The only guy lower on the food chain. Even Cameron doesn't like him — stands as far away from him as possible in PE class, hoping they won't be paired up for play. Same thing in Spanish class. Even when the teacher does group them together, Cameron refuses to move his desk, to look at Pinon, or even speak to him. And it's not just because Pinon is a crybaby, tearing up every time the Red Coats pick on him. It's because Pinon is the real boy-girl on campus. Or maybe all girl.

"What did they do to you?" Pinon asks.

The little guy is bouncing on his toes, like one of those yippy lap dogs.

"Did they hit you?" he asks.

Cameron wants to swat him. He gets a picture in his mind of Pinon, smashed against the wall, oozing blood and guts, and smiles. He used to feel bad for the guy, with the two of them being the favorite targets of the jock squad. But that's all they have in common. Pinon tucks himself into a tight little ball when the Red Coats fall on him. They bat him around a little bit and he cries.

Cameron stops and looks at Pinon, his thin face, his white-white skin and nervous fingers picking at his shirt buttons. He digs around inside himself for a little compassion and comes up empty.

"I was just the warm-up. You're the real show, Pinon."

Cameron pushes away from him and starts looking at room numbers. Another tardy will lower his grade; he can't afford that.

MONDAY

9:05AM

The only part of history Cameron likes is the battles. Not just the ones on the pages of their textbook, but the daily scrimmages Mr. Hart, their teacher, has with Eddie Fain. The boy is disturbed and is in a special room for the rest of the school day. Cameron takes his chair, two rows over from Eddie, and watches him drill a straightened paperclip into the desktop. Mr. Hart is watching, too. When the bell rings, he asks, "Mr. Fain, do you plan to pay for that desk?"

"My father could. He could buy and sell you, too."

He keeps drilling. Last week, Eddie tore the pages out of his textbook, one at a time, for about ten minutes before Mr. Hart asked him if he was going to buy that, too. You have to pace yourself with Eddie. Let him burn off some steam before you pounce on him. Otherwise, he's scary.

Cameron watched him pin a senior to a wall and keep him there with his elbow pressed over the guy's throat while he turned red, then blue, and squirmed like a mouse in the mouth of a cat. And that was Eddie's reaction to being told he didn't belong in senior hall — to get out before they moved him out. Eddie wasn't ready to move.

Mr. Hart is still working on his timing. He doesn't have it down yet, just how long Eddie needs before he can be approached. Hart pulls out the tab he keeps on Eddie. He reads it aloud.

"One plastic student chair — make sure your father gets that in blue; a dry eraser; two dozen dry erase markers; the window we replaced in October; two textbooks; a yardstick; and now a desktop. That brings your total to about four hundred dollars."

While Mr. Hart is reading the list, Eddie blows the mound of sawdust from his desktop and begins twisting the piece of metal into the palm of his hand. He draws blood quickly and lets it pool on the desk.

"You'll own this school before long," Mr. Hart says and looks up from his list. "Damn."

Cameron thinks, *What did Hart expect?* Eddie's father is in prison and any time anyone mentions him Eddie self-destructs. But this is the first time Cameron sees Eddie inflict physical pain on himself.

"You're going to the nurse, young man, and then straight to the vice principal."

Mr. Hart pulls a pass out of a desk drawer and begins writing on it, changes his mind, and reaches for the phone.

"It's Fain," he says into the receiver. "Destroying school property and himself. Yes. Yes." He nods. "Come and get him."

He hangs up and turns back to Eddie. "Drop that."

Eddie looks at Hart, looks at Cameron, and smiles crazily. He digs the paperclip into his palm until Cameron is sure muscle and bone are involved, his eyes wide and burning. No pain, but deep rage the color of fire.

Cameron feels himself pulled into that, feels the heat from the inside out. He knows he's a lot more like Eddie than he wants to be.

The seat between Cameron and Eddie is empty. Mr. Hart gives Eddie a wide berth, a safety zone for others. Cameron leans over, rolls his arm out over the empty desk, palm up, and says, "Give it to me."

Eddie thinks about it, the red glow in his eyes cooling, then he shrugs and drops the paperclip into Cameron's hand. He presses a finger to the hole in his palm and the blood slows, seeps around his fingertip, and drips on the desk.

Cameron looks at the strip of metal, stained with Eddie's blood, and feels his Adam's apple grow until it hurts to swallow. His eyes dry out so that when he blinks he's sure they're full of sand, and his hands sweat. All over a paperclip and a little blood. He wants to tell Eddie, *You should see what I can do with a book of matches*.

"See ya later."

Eddie says it, laughing, then he shrugs his backpack on and meets security at the door.

"He's crazy," says a girl.

"He's going to hurt someone," says another.

Mr. Hart makes sure the door closes all the way. He pulls the shade down for extra measure, then turns to the class.

"He's a danger to himself," Hart says. "Mr. Grady, throw that in the trash, will you? Then go wash your hands."

1:10PM

"We're going to have to adjust the axle. The wheelbase is off."

Cameron looks over his shoulder at SciFi, his tech partner. The guy is a foot taller than your average bear and about as friendly. Well, he isn't unfriendly. Just not easy to be with. Mostly, the guy talks in a language Cameron doesn't understand. Big, scientific words you don't hear in high school. The second day into their project — building a car with a computer graphics program, then transferring the knowledge into physical form, using a mini wood kit — Cameron asked SciFi to dumb it down a little for him.

Cameron clicks the mouse to save the changes he just made and turns back to the table where SciFi is trying to force the axle into the chassis.

"That's not going to work," Cameron says. "It won't fit, and even if you do get it to go in, the wheels won't turn."

SciFi blows a stream of air from his mouth, fogging his glasses, then starts speaking scienceese.

"SciFi." Cameron snags his attention and gives him the flat face, which is their signal that SciFi is speaking in terms above Cameron's head. "English."

"The axle is too big for the hole we drilled. If we try to drill the hole larger, the wood will splinter and we'll have to start over. Again."

Cameron laughs. SciFi isn't used to failing at anything scientific. The problem is, the guy is book smart. He's good with a microscope and a petri dish, as he told Cameron a week into their partnership.

"I'm going to give you a new nickname," Cameron says. "Maybe Axle Rose."

"I like SciFi."

Cameron looks up at him, surprised. "Really?"

"Really." He hands Cameron the axle and car chassis. "Now, will you fix this please? We only have two labs left before this project is due."

"You ever been late with an assignment?"

"Never."

"You ever get anything less than an A?"

SciFi shrugs. "I got an F in PE last year. That's why I'm taking band."

"Learning an instrument is easier?"

"Safer. I broke a toe and three teeth last year," SciFi explains and taps his front teeth. "Porcelain veneers. My parents are still paying for them. So now I play the clarinet."

Cameron laughs the kind of laugh that gets into your belly and zings through your blood. The kind that makes the incident from this morning seem like a long time ago.

"You're good for me, SciFi."

"I amuse you."

"You are a little like that Vulcan dude from Star Trek," Cameron admits. "You watch Nick At Nite?"

SciFi nods. "Spock. There are similarities."

"It's not a bad thing, you know," Cameron says. "Maybe you'll cure a disease or something. Invent time travel."

"I'm better equipped for disease." He picks up the car and offers it to Cameron. "That is, if I pass this class."

"Okay. It's a fair trade," Cameron decides. "I'll be your A and you can keep me laughing."

"I'm not a funny guy."

"Not on purpose," Cameron agrees.

MONDAY

6:30PM

"You have to use math," Cameron explains. He picks up the graph paper with the scale drawing of the rocket Robbie and his friend Danny are trying to build. The figures are wrong.

"That's the problem," Robbie says. "Neither one of us can do math."

"You do math every day. Time, money, shape . . ." Cameron balls the paper and tosses it into an empty box. "You need to start over."

Danny groans and pantomimes stuffing his head inside an oven. "We're done," he says. "We present Monday."

"There's time." Cameron sits down on a sawhorse drawn up to the workbench in Danny's garage. "You have to use absolute measurement. Meaning, two boxes in your drawing need to equal one inch on the real thing. That can't change."

Cameron begins to draw, using a ruler to mark a straight edge, and then fills in the lines and angles around it. "You're going to need to shave off a few inches from the model. The rudder is too long. Same with the fuselage. And the cockpit is too short. You need a new block of wood for that, unless you think you can get away with using clay. It can work like a joint compound. See if you can sell it to your teacher like that."

"You're a genius," Danny says.

"Einstein," Robbie agrees.

"Can you mark where we need to make the new cuts?"

"You can do it yourself." Cameron stands up and slides the ruler to Robbie. "Remember, two blocks on the paper equals one inch on here." He taps the rocket.

Cameron watches them measure and cut, using a plane. They sand the rough edges and the pieces slip into place, all but the cockpit.

"I'll pick up some Roger's Glue. The astronauts use it to bond things in space," Danny says.

"Where are you going to get that?"

"I saw it at Home Depot. I think if we can show we went out of our way to use the stuff NASA uses, it'll get us some points."

"Yeah," Robbie agrees. "Maybe Stubbs won't think we're idiots."

"Well, my work here is done," Cameron says. He pushes off the sawhorse and walks toward the front of the garage. "You ladies call me if you need more help."

"Wait up." Robbie tells Danny he'll see him tomorrow, then scoots after his brother.

Cameron doesn't wait. His mom sent him to get Robbie, but he's not his brother's keeper. Besides, Robbie is too old and too big for a babysitter.

Cameron picks up his bike, slides onto the seat, and starts pedaling. Dusk disappeared a long time ago. The sky is black and wet, dripping with mist. The streetlights are on and in their cone-shaped light moths flutter their wings and bake.

"You're in a good mood," Robbie says.

"What do you mean?"

"You're not pissed off."

"I'm always pissed off."

"Lately," Robbie agrees.

TUESDAY

10:20AM

Cameron's sneakers hit the hardwood floor. His knees absorb the impact, stay strong, propel him forward. This is where he belongs. Too bad his grades stink. He wanted to go out for track. He's a pretty good sprinter, better at middle distances. He'd have done okay. He'd be a winner, no doubt about it. No one can get close to him. There are a lot of jocks in his PE class, some even on the track team, but Cameron is so far ahead of them he can't even feel them. And when he turns the next corner, he can see he's closing in on the last of the pack, and the middle's not out of reach. Rich

Patterson, loping like a giraffe, and his sidekick Murphy lead the group of stragglers. Patterson may be good at holding the line in football, but he's slow and awkward. Bulky. All that muscle weighs him down. In a pool, he'd sink to the bottom.

Cameron smiles at his thoughts. He wouldn't jump in to save the guy and not just because he's the enemy. Patterson picks on a lot of kids. None as much as Cameron. Still, his death would be a public service.

Cameron finds this so funny he snorts a little as the breath leaves his nose.

He's losing focus. He's not supposed to hear his breathing. He's not supposed to recognize faces in the crowd. When Cameron runs, everything becomes a blur, except the goal. It's called tunnel vision. The best athletes have it. It's how they win the gold. When Cameron runs the lake path, the water, the trees, the birds become just splotches of background color.

Running is good for him. Cleans out his mind. Flushes the anger from his body. Breathing hard, his chest feels almost transparent. And his lungs, past burning, sing with accomplishment. It's a good thirty or forty minutes before memory comes rushing in and he's *that* Cameron again. Patterson's favorite target, the failing student, the difficult son.

Cameron feels his pace slow. His joints grow sticky and he realizes his focus is on Patterson. His square head bobbing on his thick neck. The guy's beefy arms bowed and stiff. A patch of sweat darkens his red T-shirt. Cameron stares at the guy's back, at that patch of sweat, like it's a bull's-eye. If he had aim, if his hands didn't shake, he could put a bullet right through that patch of sweat and into Patterson's heart. Game over, just like that.

He was doing just fine until Patterson happened to him. He used to wake up in the morning, roll out of bed, think about the things he wanted to talk to Steve about. Imagine the shirt Helen Gosset, his lab partner in his physical science class, would wear that day; try to guess the color. Eat breakfast. Make sure his homework was in his backpack.

He doesn't do any of that anymore.

He wakes up with an elephant on his chest.

He wakes up gasping for air. Like he's doing now.

His legs feel heavy.

Don't do this, Cameron tells himself. *Don't let him take this from you, too.*

He lifts his knees, putting enough of his mind behind the motion that his body loses the flow.

He never thinks about running.

To think about running is death.

Focus. FOCUS. *FOCUS.*

Cameron tears his eyes away from Patterson. Sifts through the crowd of runners. A dark head, some kid Cameron doesn't really know. He lets his eyes fall on him; he's just far enough ahead that Cameron has a slim chance of pulling even with him, of overtaking him. And that's what this is about. Running the fastest he can; outrunning the fear, the anger that would eat him up and spit out his bones if he let it.

This is about control.

Cameron clenches his fists. He picks up speed. The sound of his feet hitting the gym floor gains distance. The rush of his breath in and out of his lungs becomes all he can hear, and that comes from the inside. He's back inside himself. No sharp edges, just rhythm and speed.

Cameron rounds the next corner and hears the coach call out, "Five!"

He's run five laps. He has three to go. A half mile today.

He knows it's best to wait until there's two laps to go before he bursts out of his current pace, puts all he has into the finish, but he's suddenly gained the back of the pack, is weaving around kids, pulling to the outside, away from swinging elbows.

"Six, Cameron!"

His thighs burn. He's lightheaded, like he's standing at the top of Mount Kilimanjaro with the air so thin it whistles in his chest. He digs deeper. There's always more. Every time he looks for it, works it, stretches himself until he thinks he's going to snap, it rises up inside him, carries him through. He's never left empty-handed.

The kid with the dark hair is either slowing down or Cameron has more in him today than he's had before, because he's pulling alongside him.

"Eight! That's it, Cameron."

It takes a moment for Cameron to absorb the coach's voice, his words. Eight laps. Half a mile. He wants to know his time. He knows he did better today, much better. Did he break three minutes? For sure. Two-thirty? Probably. Cameron stopped clocking himself months ago, when he realized there was no point. He stopped running for time and just ran when he needed to. When it was life or death if he didn't.

Cameron slows, stops, and leans back to expand his chest. Gulps air. His face is probably as red as his shirt; it's definitely covered in sweat. He wipes at it with his shoulder.

"Two-ten."

"What?" Cameron turns and looks up at the coach, who is peering at his stopwatch.

"Damn, but that's exactly what it reads. Two-ten." The coach turns the watch for Cameron to see. "Why aren't you on the track team?"

Two-ten. Cameron feels like he's breathing helium.

"Well, Cameron?"

"Grades," Cameron admits, and pulls in another breath, this one a little deeper as his lungs begin to ease. "I couldn't get my grades up in time."

The coach shakes his head. "That's a damn shame. Are you training on your own? You must be."

"I run some." Not as much as he used to.

"Diaz gets plenty of practice."

Patterson's voice falls on Cameron like a grenade. He feels the cut of a thousand pieces of shrapnel, especially when Patterson's words are followed by laughter — Patterson's and his sidekick's and a couple other kids walking past who heard and know exactly what Patterson means.

Even the coach picks up on Patterson's meaning and dismisses the guy. "He lapped you, Patterson. And about twenty others." The coach turns back to Cameron. "You keep your runs strong and you won't have to worry about your grade in here."

Cameron rides the sound of pride in the coach's voice, feels a smile opening his chest, until reality snags him. He's going to pay for Patterson's public humiliation. No doubt about it. He may be standing still, but he is officially on the run now.

"And get a tutor if you need one," the coach advises. "I want to see you on the track team next year."

Cameron nods, starts toward the locker room, and then checks himself. Going down there now will mean certain death. Patterson will jump him the minute the door closes behind him. Maybe drag him into the showers fully clothed and drench him. Maybe dunk his head in the toilet bowl. For starters.

Cameron scans the gym for a way out; his eyes catch on the water fountain and he heads for it. He drinks until he's sure the coach bagged the last of the basketballs they used earlier and picked up the last cone. Then, Cameron follows him down into the locker room.

TUESDAY

12:30PM

"Hey, SciFi! Wait up."

Cameron dodges around a group of kids and catches up with SciFi, who is barreling down the hall.

"This a fire drill?"

SciFi slows down. "I have long legs," he explains, "and I really hate walking into class after, well, after this girl is already there."

"This girl?" Cameron is careful not to laugh at SciFi, but can't keep his lips from pulling into a smile. "You got a thing for this girl?"

"She has a thing for me," SciFi corrects.

Cameron watches a tidal wave of red sweep up SciFi's neck and fill his face.

"Really? How do you know?"

SciFi shrugs. "She leaves me things. Notes. Small things. On my desk if I don't get there first."

"Damn." Cameron never noticed. "Who is it?"

"I can't tell you."

"Why not?"

"It's not polite."

"Am I talking to you or your mom?"

SciFi thinks about this. "Both."

"You know I'll figure it out," Cameron warns and begins a mental viewing of all the girls in their tech class. There are a lot and he probably skipped a few, but he doesn't come up with a single girl he wouldn't want to notice him. "Why do you have a problem with this?"

They turn into the next hall, tech alley, and Cameron jogs ahead and stops in front of SciFi, blocking his way.

"None of the girls in our class are dogs."

"She's too aggressive."

"Really?" Cameron laughs, even though he tries not to. "You're scared."

"No, I'm not. What happened to girls waiting until the guy asks her out?"

"Like you'll ever do that."

"She could give me a chance."

"How long has she been writing you love letters?"

SciFi shrugs. "October."

"October!"

"October twenty-third," SciFi confirms.

"It's March," Cameron informs him. "She's given you a lot of time. And girls don't wait anymore. Don't you keep up with the times?"

SciFi gives him a flat look.

"Okay. Right. You need to start, though. Life isn't all about science."

"I haven't been able to find one thing that doesn't have some connection to science."

Cameron has only a moment's notice — the stiffening of Sci-Fi's face — before he feels a pair of beefy hands on his back, with such force his breath is pushed from his lungs as he falls forward. Straight into SciFi's arms.

"Well, lookee here, Cameron Diaz has a boyfriend."

Patterson's voice, sharp with this morning's humiliation, curls around Cameron's neck as heavy as hands pressing against his throat. As Cameron struggles to catch his breath, his vision begins to bleed red at the edges.

"And it's the Incredible Hulk," Murphy, with no mind of his own, chimes in.

Cameron pushes away from SciFi. Sucks in a breath. Watches his lab partner turn to stone. Everything about SciFi freezes, even the anger in his eyes.

He's taller than Patterson; his shoulders are broader and what he has for muscle is real. Not the pumped-up, weight room variety that makes Patterson look like Godzilla.

"Grady here took advantage of me this morning," Patterson tells his friend. "Showed me up when I was down. I'm coming off this hamstring pull and Grady ran like a scared little girl, thinking he's better than the best."

"You'll pay for that," Patterson's chimp says.

"Yes, you will. You'll definitely pay for that."

Then SciFi begins to move. He plows through Patterson and Murphy, using his body to slam them up against the lockers.

It's that simple. SciFi moves through them and Patterson and Murphy are struggling to keep their feet on the floor, rubbing at their heads where they hit metal.

The whole thing is comical to Cameron, who just stares at the jocks and laughs.

"You're going to die today, Grady," Patterson warns, breaking Cameron's trance.

"Yeah," Cameron agrees. "If you can catch me."

He's still laughing, pushing the fear back, keeping it at arm's length, when he walks into the classroom. Cameron's never challenged Patterson before. Never laughed in the other boy's face. It feels good. He likes it. Could get drunk on it. But it could also get him killed.

"That was incredible, man," Cameron says, sliding into his chair next to SciFi.

SciFi turns on him. "Incredible? Oh, yeah, I get it. *Incredible*. Like big and green. The Jolly Green Giant, only meaner. A freak of nature. A failed experiment —"

"Whoa!" Cameron puts his hands up, waving him down. "Poor choice of adjective," he admits. "How about awesome? Really awesome. I hate Patterson and that chimp he has for a friend."

Cameron watches the anger seep out of SciFi's shoulders. His face loosens up, too.

"You just plowed right through them."

"I'm a pacifist at heart," SciFi says and smiles. "But I could fight if I had to."

"I believe you."

"I don't like them, either."

"I wish I had a little of your size," Cameron says.

"It does have its uses," SciFi agrees. "The problem is I don't play sports. Everyone expects me to play football or basketball and they don't believe it when I tell them I'm no good at it."

Cameron nods his understanding.

SciFi opens his notebook and slides a piece of paper toward Cameron.

"I think maybe this is just a big joke for her," SciFi says.

Cameron looks down at the paper. It's an envelope. Blue with small beakers traced over the front and SciFi's real name — Elliott — spelled out in fancy script.

"You can open it," SciFi offers.

"Yeah?"

Cameron picks it up, turns it over. More doodling.

"I don't know how she knows I have a cat. A Burmese, even."

SciFi taps the drawing of a cat with skinny, pointed ears.

"Maybe she doesn't. Maybe she has the same kind of cat."

"They're not that common."

"You know, maybe she's a lot more like you than you think," Cameron says. "Same cat. She's into science, too. Who knows what else." Cameron hands the envelope back to SciFi. "You better open it, though."

SciFi taps the envelope against the table.

"It'll be a mushy card. A lot of them have butterflies or kittens on them."

"What does she write in them?"

"Her phone number."

"You're a fool."

"Yeah."

SciFi tears open the envelope and pulls out the card. The front is a picture of a woman in a bikini holding two furry kittens. A third is tumbling out of her beach bag.

"Wow," Cameron breathes. "No butterflies."

"No," SciFi squeaks and opens the card. A lock of scented hair falls to the table.

Cameron realizes he's not breathing. "Double damn." He leans closer and reads the girl's name at the bottom of the card: Carly.

Call me, and until you do keep this close, Carly.

Cameron slowly rotates on his stool. The bell hasn't rung yet. Not every seat is filled, so it's easy to pick her out. Especially since the hair she tucked into the card is a dark, dark brown and most of the girls in the class are blondes. When Cameron's eyes fall on her she looks away.

Not bad. Small. Half the size of SciFi and even Cameron is bigger than that. But she has great hair; it goes all the way to her waist. And freckles.

"She's cute," Cameron says and turns back to SciFi.

"That's the problem. She's cute. Cuddly cute, you know? She's about the right size for you."

Cameron takes the hit but shrugs it off.

"I'm going to let that slide," he says. "And do you a favor."

Cameron starts to get up but SciFi grabs his arm and when Cameron looks in the guy's eyes the lids are peeled back in horror.

"Sit down."

Cameron does. "Relax. I'm just kidding. But you really need to move on this, man."

"You think this is for real?"

"You know, for a smart guy you're really dumb. It's for real and I think maybe this is your last chance." He looks at the card, lying facedown in front of them. But he remembers the picture and the words the girl wrote. "It doesn't get any more real."

SciFi nods. "Okay. Fine. I'll call her. It won't kill me to call her. Unless she laughs at me. Hangs up on me . . ."

"That's not going to happen."

"Maybe not right away," SciFi agrees. "But at some point she'll decide I'm not what she wants after all. That's how it works with humans. Life is great until it's over."

Cameron laughs; feels it all the way through.

"Now I'm glad I took this home last night," he says, rummaging through his backpack and pulling out the wooden model of their automobile. He pulls out the tires, some paints, and arranges them on the table.

"You got a lot done." SciFi picks up the fully assembled model. "We just need to pop on the tires."

"And paint it," Cameron agrees. "Hey, a deal is a deal. You're definitely amusing."

"And I'm going to pass this class."

Friendships are built on less, Cameron thinks.

TUESDAY

3:05PM

"Cameron? *¿Puedes venir a mi escritorio, por favor?*"

Cameron sits motionless, trying to figure out exactly what Mrs. Marino just said to him. He knows she's asking for something; her voice lifted at the end the way questions do. He tries to remember if there was homework the night before and decides that by now she should know better than to expect him to have it. He looks at the other kids in his group, hoping one of them will translate for him. Nope. He doesn't blame them. He's given them exactly nothing in the forty minutes they've been working on the travel brochure they were assigned.

"I didn't do the homework," he offers and makes sure it sounds like an apology.

Some of the kids laugh. The girl sitting closest to him says, "We didn't have homework last night."

"Cameron, come up to my desk, please."

Cameron is slow to get out of his seat. He doesn't like being called out in front of his classmates. As he moves to the front of the room he feels their eyes on him, knows they're going to be listening. His shoulders get tense, work up until they're at his ears.

"Yeah?"

"You're not working with your group," she says.

"I know. I'll try harder." Cameron is turning away from her when she continues.

"It's not just today. You've turned in two assignments in the last three weeks, which has been pretty much the norm for you this semester. You're failing this class."

This is not news to him. He has a hard enough time in English class, getting by with a D; Spanish is more work and he just doesn't have it in him. His mind drifts in class. Sometimes he thinks about what it would be like if he had never left Syracuse, but then he'd still be living with his dad and that was no good.

"What can I do?"

"Participate. Turn in some work." Her face gets soft. "You had a B the end of the first marking period. A C for your fall semester grade. You've been going downhill. What's up?"

"I'm not good with languages," he offers.

"Stay after school," she says. "I'll help you."

Cameron nods, knowing he won't make it. Even if he wanted to, he doesn't hang around after school. The place is crawling with jocks, with Patterson and his posse.

Mrs. Marino picks up a piece of paper. "This is your progress report. I want you to have your mom or dad look at it and sign it." She folds it and tucks it into an envelope. "I want it back tomorrow," she warns. "Signed. Or I'll have to ask for a parent conference."

"Okay." Cameron folds the envelope and stuffs it into his back pocket. He waits, just in case she has more to say.

"You can go back to your group now."

Cameron turns and notices that just about everyone is so absorbed in their work that they didn't hear Mrs. Marino's broadcast of his grade. Everyone but Steve. He's looking at Cameron with a big frown creasing his forehead. The whole room is between them and Cameron doesn't know what to do. This is the first time since the bathroom wall incident that Steve's let on he knows Cameron is alive. Probably a mistake. Probably someone is standing behind Cameron, someone Steve can see.

Cameron resists the urge to turn and look and just shuffles back to his seat. He leans toward the others in his group, gets the page number they're on, and opens his book.

"Here. You can work on the captions." The girl next to him offers Cameron a folded sheet of construction paper. There are sketches on it of the ocean, a bull fight, a city with tall buildings. "One sentence describing each picture. Write it in pencil, though, okay? I'll check the translation."

She smiles at him and Cameron feels his face burn. He's starting to think he likes it a lot better being invisible. He doesn't like anyone feeling sorry for him. He doesn't like thinking he's someone who needs it.

Cameron takes the paper. He's going to tell her he doesn't have a pencil, that he'll have to do the work in permanent marker, when the seat beside him fills up with a new body.

"Look, I just have one thing to say so you better listen." It's Steve. His voice is low and about as friendly as the roar of a caged lion. Cameron feels his heart rate pick up. His whole body kicks into overdrive. "Patterson is pissed. He's talked to all of us — the football team. You are so dead. Your friend, too. Don't stay after school. If I were you I'd leave now. Try to make it home before he picks up your scent."

That's it. End of message.

Steve gets up and strolls over to the pencil sharpener. Cameron stares at his back, the bright red of his jock jacket, seeing the darkened splotch he saw that morning on Patterson. Seeing it and wishing he could do something about it. Put a silver bullet into the heart of it.

"You okay?"

The girl again.

"You're really pale. Mrs. Marino will probably believe you're sick," she offers.

"I'm not sick," Cameron says. And he's not going to run. Not without finding SciFi first. Even he doesn't stand a chance against the entire football team.

Cameron looks at the girl next to him. Really looks at her, so long she shifts in her seat and then shrugs her shoulders and looks down at her work. Too bad the only reason she's talking to him is because she thinks he needs help.

"Pretend." The advice comes from the only other guy in the group. One of those chess club geeks. Like SciFi. So maybe the guy's not so bad. "Patterson's a dick," he says. "But he's got the whole pack with him. There's no fighting that."

Cameron lets that sink in. The whole football team. They'll tear him apart. SciFi, too. Anger makes Cameron's temperature soar. He feels like he's on fire, without the good stuff. No physical pain, no place for the anger to bleed out of him. He wishes he could strike a match, breathe in the sulphur, let it burn his nose and throat.

Poor SciFi. The guy won't know what hit him.

Everything I touch turns to shit, Cameron thinks. Everything.

"You know Elliott?" Cameron asks.

"Elliott Mercer?" Computer Geek asks.

Cameron doesn't know SciFi's last name. He shrugs. "Big dude?"

"Yeah."

"You going to see him after school?"

"No. Club is Thursdays," he says. "Elliott is at the elementary school, playing with the band."

"He's off campus?"

"They left last period."

So he's safe. Cameron will look for SciFi first thing in the morning and warn him.

That's all he can do.

TUESDAY

4:30PM

Cameron makes it home without breaking a sweat. In the last minutes of Spanish class he decided he wasn't going to run. He wasn't going to hide. He waited until the whole class was moving toward the door, then he got up, told Mrs. Marino he couldn't stay after all, and walked out. He heard her calling after him but kept moving. The halls were crammed with students. Cameron walked the long way to his locker, stuffed his notebook into the small space left, and took his history book. He didn't think he'd get to the questions Hart assigned, but just in case.

All the way home, Cameron thought about Patterson and how this one guy has ruined his life. He looked inside himself for the fire that usually came with thoughts of Patterson, but all he felt was a cold so intense his fingers were numb. His toes, too. Sometimes when he touches fire the same thing happens; he can't feel his fingers or his toes. And he thought about how two different conditions can result in the same thing. How fire and ice can both burn.

His mom is already home, in the kitchen, drinking coffee. Cameron watches her through the window. Her hair is pulled back in a ponytail; she probably ran the lake path, came home, and stuffed laundry into the dryer. She does that, plans things so that she doesn't lose time. Dirty clothes go into the washer before she leaves; they're ready for the dryer when she gets back. She probably mopped the floors, too, so they could dry while she was out.

He doesn't like that he thinks like her. That he maps out his day with survival being the only objective.

His mother believes in prevention. She's all about salads with dinner and berry smoothies for breakfast so they don't get cancer, and Scouts and sports so her boys don't go wild.

She's no good at fixing things.

So where does that leave Cameron?

Who's going to fix him? Because he knows now without a doubt that something is wrong with him. When it was on the inside it was possible he was imagining it. That it wasn't as bad as he thought. Now that it's spreading, there's no denying that he is a carrier.

SciFi wasn't even a blip on Patterson's radar until he spotted him with Cameron.

His gut tightens. SciFi's life is about as over as Cameron's. And when Patterson's through with him, SciFi won't want anything to do with Cameron. Back to being a ghost.

Cameron must have zoned out because suddenly his mother is at the window, tapping it with her index finger, and Cameron's whole body jerks back. His hands fly to his face, the first reaction of a person under attack. She took him by surprise; he doesn't even do that at school anymore. He's always on his guard there.

Cameron tries to cover the action by pushing his hands through his hair.

It doesn't work. His mother's face folds into concern.

"Are you coming in?"

The double-paned glass makes her voice distant. He spent most of this year hearing like this, watching things happen around him like he's not really connected to the world.

"Cameron?"

She disappears and a moment later the kitchen door swings open. She steps out onto the deck.

"What's wrong?"

He shakes his head. "Nothing."

"Are you coming inside?"

He nods. Tries to shake himself out of the land of the lost.

"You run the lake path?" he asks as he climbs the last step and squeezes past her.

"Yes. I just got back."

"I ran the half mile in two-ten today," he says.

"That's great."

"We had to run inside," he explains. "The track was flooded."

"There was a lot of rain on the path, too." She moves toward the refrigerator. "I thought you stopped running."

"Not totally. My PE teacher wants to see me on the track team next year."

"I do, too," she says. She opens the fridge. "You want a snack?"

His mother has every other Tuesday off, which means they'll eat dinner out tonight.

He drops his backpack and moves toward her. "Where are we eating?"

"How about Chinese?"

He takes hold of the refrigerator door and opens it farther, peering in around her. "How about Italian?"

He grabs an apple from the crisper and moves away.

"What else happened at school today?" she asks.

"Why?" He bites into the apple and the juice runs down his throat. He doesn't really remember tasting his food lately; maybe that's why the sweetness of the apple stings his mouth.

She shrugs. "This is the first time in a long time you're talking to me."

"We're talking about food," he says.

"And your running prowess."

He shrugs. "Yeah. PE was good today, I guess. Tech class, too. Me and SciFi finished our project and turned it in. A day early."

His mother's eyebrows shoot up. "That's an improvement."

He nods. "So, you want Italian?"

"My vote is Chinese. We'll let Robbie weigh in, but no swaying his vote," she says.

He reaches into his back pocket and pulls out his progress report. "Spanish wasn't so good." He hands her the paper. "Mrs. Marino wants you to sign this. I need to give it back to her tomorrow or you'll have to come in and talk to her."

"Have you been doing your homework?"

"Not really." No point in lying when she's looking right at the proof. "Spanish is hard."

His mom's eyes move side to side as they scan his grades, or lack of them. Cameron noticed, when Mrs. Marino pulled out his progress report in class, that there were a lot of zeros on it.

"You said the same thing about PE and English."

"I'm doing better in PE."

"How about English?"

"We're reading Hemingway," he says. "Some of his short stories. I like them so far, so I guess I'm doing a little better." Which is true. He does the reading, and that's more than he did with the last book. "I'm participating." Because Mrs. Cowan calls on him. A lot. Probably because he does none of the writing exercises.

"Cameron."

Her voice is flat, weighted by her disappointment, and Cameron feels the pressure build in his jaw until he's grinding his teeth.

"I'm doing better," he says. That should count.

His mother lays the progress report on the counter and lets her eyes fall on him. "You've always been a good student."

"I told you, high school —"

"Is hard. I get it."

Her fingers push the paper back and forth, but she keeps her eyes on him. He hates that, when she tries to look *into* him, like he has a big secret and if she could only figure it out she'd *understand* him. That will never happen. She doesn't have the first clue about what his life is like. Even when he tells her flat out, she's all about making it look pretty and not seeing what it really is: an ugly mess. Her idea to get Patterson off his back: *Tomorrow, I want you to go to the guidance counselor. Tell him what's going on.* Well, Cameron did, and the day after that Patterson gave him a bloody nose.

"Cameron," his mom calls him back to the present. "I almost never see you with a book."

Anger rises up in his throat. It's not his fault. If he could

71

think when he was at school, he'd do better. He always did better than this.

"I do my homework in my room," he says.

"You just told me you're not doing it."

"My math homework and history. I do that at my desk in my room."

"Fine," she says. "But you'll do Spanish at the kitchen table. English, too, until I see your next report card."

"Mom!" Cameron's heart beats so loud it's all he hears. He takes a deep breath, holds it, blows it out through his nose. He has to slow down. Isn't this what he expected? In fact, he thought it'd be worse. He pulls in another breath, feels his lungs expand, his hands loosen.

"One hour to eat a snack and play a video game or watch some TV. Then I want you at the table, where I can see you and give you some help."

Another breath and he feels almost normal. Human anyway, and not a danger to anyone.

"Help? You don't speak Spanish."

"No, but I speak English. I can help you with that. The Spanish we can figure out together."

"Now I'm under house arrest."

"Prisoners don't get privileges," she points out. "I haven't taken any of those away from you. Yet."

TUESDAY

5:00PM

"What are you doing?"

Cameron looks up from his history book. His brother is standing in the door, still suited in his Scout uniform.

"What does it look like?"

"Homework, but it can't be. You don't do homework."

"He does now." Their mother walks in from the laundry room, carrying a basket of folded clothes. Her eyes find and lock on Cameron. "You need help?"

He hates being in the crosshairs. Hates that he's such an easy target.

"No."

"What question are you on?"

"'Was justice ever achieved under the Monroe Doctrine? Cite your evidence.'"

"What number is that?"

"Two."

She nods, but her mouth stays neutral. Clearly, he isn't moving as fast as she'd like.

"I'm going to put this away." She lifts the basket a little higher. "Then I'm coming back and I want to hear your answer."

"It might take a little longer than that," he warns.

"Then we'll bring you home takeout," she says, over her shoulder, as she moves into the living room and beyond.

"Wow, what did you do?" Robbie asks. He sits down across from his brother, pulls off his neckerchief. "Get a report card today?"

He's smiling like a damn pumpkin.

"Shut up."

Robbie's voice changes, gets that deep and serious tone only the unnaturally big can produce. "Something happened at the high school."

Dread thickens the air in Cameron's lungs. "What do you mean?"

"I rode by on my way back from Scouts. A lot of cops there, lights and sirens. What do you think happened?"

Cameron's stomach does a nosedive. He thinks about SciFi and how the football team's going to turn him into hamburger. But not today. SciFi isn't at school.

"I don't know," Cameron says. "I'm not at school. I'm here, on death row."

Robbie laughs. "Use the index," he suggests. "It'll go faster."

"What do you think I'm doing?"

"Staring at a blank page."

Cameron looks down at his notebook. He didn't answer the first question. Something about the Big Club theory. Robbie throws his bandana on the table and leans into Cameron's space.

"How many questions?"

"Four." Cameron flips back to the index and looks up Monroe Doctrine. "Three for passing credit."

"If you get them right," Robbie agrees. "I'll help you."

"I don't need help."

"Mom won't leave you here and I'm starving."

"There's got to be some bread and water around here."

Robbie laughs. Cameron reads a little about the Monroe Doctrine, then writes a sentence into his notebook.

"You see any kids in front of the school?"

Robbie shakes his head. "The principal was there. Some

parents, too, I think. Cops. It looked like it was all over and they were trying to figure out what happened."

Their mother walks back into the room, the empty basket dangling from her fingers.

"Well?" she asks. "What have you learned about the Monroe Doctrine?"

"It was an exciting development in foreign policy." He made it up, but it sounds good and how is she going to know the difference?

"That's it?"

"It's a start," he says. "A pretty good start." He scans the page and then reads aloud, "Under the Monroe Doctrine European powers could no longer colonize America. That's my evidence."

His mother smiles. "Sounds good." She turns her attention to Robbie. "Maybe you should start your homework," she suggests. "You can do it right here, too."

Robbie pushes his chair back and protests, "My grades are good."

"I want them to stay that way," she says. "And that last math test was a D."

"I stayed after school and got help," Robbie reminds her.

"That's true." She pauses, thinks about it. "We'll see."

She ducks back into the laundry room and soon Cameron hears the sound of the washer filling.

"This sucks," Robbie says.

"Guilt by association," Cameron agrees and smiles.

"I stayed after school with Mrs. Harlodson. For an hour."

"You having a hard time in math?"

"Yeah. I hate it. You could help me, you know."

"I could, but then you'd have to look up to me."

Robbie chuckles. "That's not going to happen. How about a trade? I'll do that history assignment and you do my math?"

Cameron considers this. "I like the sound of that."

Robbie waves over the textbook. "What's the next question?"

"Number one."

"What?"

"I skipped it."

Robbie reads the question, flips through the book, and a minute later reads an answer off to Cameron.

"You write it," Cameron says and rolls the pencil toward him.

"You have to put it in your own writing," Robbie insists. "Otherwise Mom and your teacher will know you didn't do it yourself."

Cameron eyes him hard. "You know a lot about cheating," he says.

"Not really. Beginner's intuition."

"Sure." But Cameron picks up the pencil and starts writing. "Give it to me again."

Robbie reads from the book and Cameron edits out some of the words he doesn't think are absolutely necessary. He does it for answers three and four, too. They're just finishing up the last question when Randy walks through the door.

He doesn't knock. He stopped doing that a long time ago.

"What are you two up to?"

"Homework," Robbie says.

"Whose?"

"Mine," Cameron admits. "Robbie's helping me, then I'll help him with math."

Cameron decides it has to be the guy's uniform, the badge pinned to his chest, that pulls the confession from him. He and Robbie sit a long minute under Randy's considering gaze before their mother's boyfriend decides they're telling the truth.

"Where's your mom?"

"Upstairs. Getting ready for dinner," Robbie says.

"Good. I thought we'd go surf and turf tonight," Randy says. "Maybe Hanover's on the Lake." He walks across the room and says over his shoulder, "You boys will need to clean up a little."

He moves through the house, up the stairs. Cameron hears his keys and change jangling in his pockets.

"He's coming to dinner," Cameron says.

"He's been trying harder. I heard him tell Mom he wants to take us to an Eagles game. That's five months away."

Cameron thinks about this. When they first got together, his mom stayed with Randy three months straight. It never lasts longer than that.

"Maybe he'll stick around longer this time," Robbie suggests.

Cameron hears the way his brother's voice lifts, gets a little thin with hope. He remembers how he used to go to bed at night thinking that if Randy came around the next day maybe they could pass the football or play some one-on-one. It never happened. Just about the time Cameron started believing the guy had endurance, he always disappeared.

"He won't," Cameron says. It's better not to even start thinking it.

TUESDAY

6:15PM

They can't have Chinese or Italian. Cameron sits in the back of Randy's Dodge King Cab and pulls at the collar of his shirt. His mom made him button it until it was cinched around his neck. Bad enough if the shirt fit him, but he wore it last when he was thirteen, more than a year ago. *Yeah, Mom, even I do grow a little,* he thinks. "The shirt is too small," he told her. She suggested he roll back the cuffs; he did. Randy told him the collar would look better if he wore a tie, but he wasn't asking him to. Randy only wore the tie that came with his uniform; he didn't own any others and was real happy about that.

Randy never joined them on family night out. And they always voted on where they ate.

***

"Randy has veto power," Robbie had said, as they stood in their bedroom looking at each other in their navy blue pants and ironed shirts. His mom never ironed; she threw everything in the dryer. "This is getting serious."

The hope was back in his voice.

"We look like the Hardy Boys," Robbie said.

"Yeah." The biggest geeks ever. "He's not staying, you know."

"I've been counting," Robbie confessed. "They've been back together one hundred and eighteen days. They've never lasted that long."

"As your older brother I feel it's my responsibility to warn you — don't believe it. Don't buy into it. Mom won't keep him."

"Why?"

"After Dad?"

"Dad wasn't all bad."

Cameron spun away from the mirror. "You have amnesia," he said.

"He took us to ball games," Robbie pointed out.

"And got drunk on beer, slapped us if we complained about it, and forgot to feed us."

"He didn't forget," Robbie said and shrugged. "He said it was women's work to feed us."

"Whatever."

"I guess you're right," Robbie said. "I wouldn't want another guy around long-term after Dad."

"I think she wants Randy around," Cameron said, "but she's afraid that she'll get a repeat performance."

"Guys are assholes," Robbie decided.

"Most of 'em," Cameron agreed.

"I don't think Randy is. You ever see him mad?"

"No," Cameron admitted. "He probably puts all the mad into his job. By the time we see him he's low energy."

Cameron hasn't seen Randy do much more than eat and watch sports or the news on TV.

*

"Middle of the menu," Randy says now, pulling Cameron from his thoughts. "Okay, boys? I'm buying, so that means better than burgers but it's either steak *or* lobster."

Cameron can see him smiling in the rearview mirror. He's got good, strong teeth but a bunch of lines around his mouth and one long crease that reaches up to the corner of his eye.

He wonders how old Randy is. Older than his mother. His father, too. But not so old he's thinking about retirement.

Robbie says he's ordering the trout.

"Good choice. What about you, Cam?" Randy asks, with too much gusto in his voice.

"Maybe steak," he says. He needs to see the menu.

"I'm thinking a caesar salad with butterfly shrimp," his mom adds, too cheerful, and when Cameron looks at her profile he sees her smile is wider than usual.

They're trying too hard, Cameron thinks. They all turned on like a sudden blast of air conditioning and Cameron can feel it pressing against him, drying out his eyes and making the tips of his fingers numb. He's not the only one who notices.

So they're eating out. At a nice place on a night that's usually just Cameron and Robbie and their mom. They all know it. It makes Cameron's joints stick, his mom's voice flutter, Robbie's eyes bright, and Randy puff up like a hot air balloon.

It's not a big deal. They've had three years of Randy and Cameron knows it's always one step forward, two steps back.

Cameron releases the seat belt and pushes open his door. He starts toward the restaurant, but Randy's voice cuts him short.

"Hey, Cam, wait up, huh?"

Cameron stands on the curb in front of the Hanover's sign, pushes his hands into his front pockets, and tips forward on his feet. He watches them. Robbie shuts his door and their mother's, too. Randy waits at the front of the truck, then takes his mother's hand. They walk toward him, shoulder to shoulder, and Cameron gets a feeling in his gut he should be used to by now. He's looking at something he's not a part of, could never be a part of, but wants it so bad his teeth bleed for it.

He has a father already. No returns, no exchanges.

"Stay with us," Randy says when they reach him.

"Yeah, okay," Cameron says, but he thinks to himself: *How? What part of me fits here?*

A tall woman greets them at the door. She holds it open for all of them to pass and then discusses seating options with Cameron's mom. They decide on sitting outside, under a heating lamp for when the sun falls behind the mountains. They troop through the restaurant, which is dimly lit by ceiling fans and candles on the tables. Cameron notices there's not a lot of business on a Tuesday night; for every table that's full another's empty. He kind of likes that feeling, of people but not too many of them. Of the silence, but not total. That feeling in his skin, of being pinched, eases.

There's even more quiet on the deck. Cameron looks around and counts only two other occupied tables.

March on Lake Erie. Sometimes there's snow, but tonight the wind is almost nothing.

Randy pulls out his mom's chair. Robbie sits down next to her. This is when Cameron realizes he's back into voyeur mode — watching everything like he's not a part of it.

It happens so easily, he never knows until he's in it that he's a goner. That he's not really living, but stuck somewhere between that and dead.

He was going to try harder not to let that happen.

Especially after today, when he was the one better than the rest. The best. When all anybody could do was watch him, some of them probably wishing they could run like him. Have his speed. His endurance. He rode that high all day and even the thought of Patterson and his posse coming after him didn't ruin it.

Tomorrow he'll go to school and tell SciFi about Patterson's plan. He'll tell him to make sure he doesn't stand too long in one place. That's the number one rule for survival when you're one of the hunted. That's what friends do for each other. Warn them. Maybe they can hang out more, too. Not just in tech class. There's safety in numbers.

Maybe Cameron's days of being invisible are over. Maybe proof of life is right around the corner. And maybe Patterson will forget about SciFi.

"You decide, honey?"

His mom interrupts his thoughts and Cameron is in such a good mood he smiles at her.

"Steak, for sure," he says.

He has the menu open but hasn't looked at it.

"With a baked potato and a salad with blue cheese."

Cameron watches his mother's face warm, her hands flatten against the table.

"Which cut?" Randy asks.

"Which one won't kill your budget?"

Randy taps him with his menu and laughs. "Porterhouse, young man," he says. "You deserve the best. Your mom tells me you're headed for the Olympics."

He's not teasing. His face is creased into a toothy smile and his eyes are full of something that looks like pride.

"Two-ten." Randy shakes his head. "What's the fastest half mile in the world?" he asks.

Cameron doesn't know. He hasn't been keeping current. "Last year a guy from Sudan ran it in one-fifty-five."

"So you have to work on shaving fifteen seconds."

"Not so easy," Cameron says.

"I bet you can do it," Robbie says. "I've seen you run. You turn into someone else. Like a man with a mission."

Cameron feels his face warm. His heart slows and then falls over itself trying to catch up.

"Yeah. I feel like someone else when I run."

"You should work on it," Randy says. "You're young. Get the right training and see what you can do."

"He's going to be on the track team next year," his mom says. "The coach talked to him about it today."

"My PE teacher, really. He coaches the basketball team, but he was pretty amazed." Cameron can't help smiling.

"I never could run, not even fast enough to save my life," Randy admits.

"Cops don't run?"

"Most of my job is sitting in the car and writing about how one guy did this so the other guy did that. . . . We had a little excitement at the high school today, though."

Cameron stops breathing, feels the tightness begin in his chest. "What happened?"

"Mob fight, as best as I can make out. No one really knows. We got a 911 call about a fight, but by the time we got there the parking lot was empty, except the one casualty, and he isn't talking," Randy says.

"Someone died?" The menu slips from his mother's hands.

"No. The kid is going to be all right. Paramedics took him in, though. Big kid. I was surprised he got it so bad, as big as he is."

"SciFi? Was it SciFi?" Cameron's vision begin to darken around the edges.

"Who?"

"The big kid, what was his name?"

Cameron can hear the fear in his voice.

"I can't tell you that, Cam."

"Was it Elliott?"

Randy looks at him a long time. "What do you know about it?"

"I know the football team was planning on creaming us both. But Elliott was off campus today. He plays the clarinet."

Like that's going to save his life.

"The football team? Why?"

Cameron shrugs. "Patterson hates me. He plays front line. I lapped him today in PE and the coach called him out."

"But why would he go after the big kid?"

"Elliott's my lab partner."

Randy doesn't get it. His whole face twists into one big question mark and Cameron doesn't blame him. It sounds lame even to him. Since when does being someone's lab partner put a person in mortal danger? But it does when you're Cameron's lab partner. It does when the guy looking to kill you is Rich Patterson.

"Really, Cam?"

There's no way he can tell Randy about being Cameron Diaz, about half the school thinking he's a fag. He can't tell him about that afternoon and Patterson saying SciFi was Cameron's boyfriend. He can't do it, so he just looks at Randy and says nothing.

"Cameron, are you still having trouble at school?"

Cameron looks at his mom. *The trouble never stopped.*

He looks at Robbie. His brother dropped his menu on his plate and is watching them like it's a tennis match, but he keeps his mouth shut.

"Normal stuff," Cameron says.

"What happened today isn't normal," Randy says. "A kid was hurt. Bad enough they took him to the hospital."

"Is he going to be okay?" *Please let him be okay.*

Randy nods. "He was sitting up and talking when I saw him. Just not about what happened. He kept saying how his parents aren't even finished paying for the teeth he lost last year. He was real worried about that."

Cameron's whole body implodes with anger. His eyes are open, but the world is black and the loss of sight knocks him off his center of gravity. He clings to the table while around him the wind picks up and he hears the kind of sharp cry that comes from the eye of a hurricane, like a voice calling for help. He doesn't know it's him calling out until Randy's hand comes down on his shoulder.

"You all right, Cam?"

He peels his fingers off the table. Feels himself fall backward into that world where pain and fear are only ideas. Anything is better than here.

"Cameron?" His mom's voice, pitched with alarm, wraps around him like an iron claw. He bounces back to his reality like he's attached to a bungee cord and he realizes that he'll never really break away. Not when the weight of her voice can find him like a bolt of lightning.

"I'm all right, Mom."

TUESDAY

11:30PM

Cameron stands on the pedals of his bike and coasts down Bald Peak. From here he can see Commerce Street, lit up like an air strip and crammed with all-night grocery stores and diners. The hospital is on Commerce, too. It's seven stories with the emergency room up front and a parking structure that looks like an empty skull at night. His mom works on the fifth floor; SciFi was admitted and is on the third floor, in the pediatric wing. Room 315. Cameron knows the hospital well. He knows he can enter through the ER, get mixed up in the chaos of crying, bleeding people, and slip past the elevators to the staircase. Getting in to see SciFi after visiting hours won't be a problem.

Cameron can't get SciFi out of his head.

Patterson wouldn't have noticed him if Cameron wasn't talking to him.

The thought makes Cameron break out in a sweat. His blood thins, moves faster, hotter in his veins.

Everything he touches turns to shit.

He glides through the trough at the bottom of Bald Peak, where the road is broken up by an intersection. There's no one at the stop signs waiting, so Cameron sails through the four-way and starts pumping the pedals. He takes the s-curve in the road so tightly his tires sing. He eats up the half mile to town and then makes a series of turns so that he's traveling parallel to Commerce, not on it. The street is too busy. After eleven o'clock a kid Cameron's age is supposed to be tucked into bed. There's probably some kind of city ordinance about it. So Cameron tries to stay in the shadows.

Randy isn't working tonight, so there's no danger of bumping into him. In fact, when Cameron left the house in his bare feet, carrying his shoes and a flashlight, he saw Randy's truck still parked in their driveway. The house was dark. Randy's probably doing his mother, which doesn't bother Cameron. Thinking about it does. Wondering about when Randy's going to bail next gets to him, too. So Cameron pushes those things out of his mind and focuses instead on SciFi.

No one can hold up under an attack by the entire football team. Even if SciFi knew how to fight, even if he had the fire in him, which he doesn't, he's no match for thirty-plus guys. And SciFi has principles. He's a pacifist. The guy probably went down fast.

Cameron turns into the driveway reserved for deliveries and skirts the back of the hospital. Flowering bushes grow against the building and Cameron stashes his bike there, out of view. The flashlight, too. He follows his plan, getting lost in the packed ER waiting room, pushing through the sweaty crowd, and finding the door marked STAIRS. Once he reaches the third floor, he has to huddle in the doorway and wait for a nurse to swish past him. He passes a playroom full of furniture for little kids and a family lounge with a couch, a coffee maker, and vending machines.

SciFi is in the bed nearest the door. His face looks like the pulp of an orange. One eye is swollen shut and the eyebrow above it is shaved and stitched. The light is on over the bed and Cameron can see that SciFi's arms and legs are bruised but not broken. So maybe the damage isn't too bad.

"Hey."

SciFi's eye is open, the good one, which is bloodshot but at least working.

"News travels fast."

Cameron shrugs. "My mom dates a cop." Cameron moves into the room until he arrives at the foot of SciFi's bed. "But I'm sure the whole school knows about it by now."

"Gee, thanks. I'm starting to feel better."

"Patterson is the kind of guy who likes to share his accomplishments."

"Yeah. He has so little else to talk about."

"You lost a tooth."

"A few. My parents are pissed. Well, my dad is. My mom cried the whole time she was here." He shrugs. "I think I did a pretty good job holding onto the teeth I have left."

"It was the whole football team?"

"No. Half, maybe. And half of those lost interest. There's no fun in beating a punching bag."

"You didn't swing? Not even once?"

"I swung. My life was at stake. I didn't connect, though. No kidding, I have the coordination of a baby giraffe."

"Patterson has it in for me."

"I noticed."

"He never bothered you before."

"I think he was waiting for an invitation."

"Me."

"I've seen him work before. He's a class ass."

"You don't sound mad."

"I was. Now I'm thinking about ways to get even. You know, maybe put some instant glue on his chair. The only way to get up is to leave his pants behind." SciFi chuckles and Cameron joins in. "There's a compound called trioxide that will clear all the hair off a person in under ten seconds. And that's just from standing too close to the stuff."

SciFi smiles, baring a hole where a front tooth should be. His swollen eye bunches up and his grin twists in a way that makes him look almost maniacal.

"You're scaring me," Cameron says and laughs.

"I want to get a whole lot scarier," SciFi says. "I don't want Patterson or one of his buddies to think I'm the go-to guy for self-esteem building 101."

"You have a lot of work ahead of you," Cameron says.

"No way. I'm almost there." He turns his head into the light. "You think I could pass for Frankenstein's monster?"

"No. You're not that cool."

They laugh and in the silence after it Cameron wonders if maybe all is not lost. Maybe, when SciFi gets back to school, he won't act like Cameron has the plague. Maybe that's enough for now. Just the hope that he has a friend.

WEDNESDAY

9:10AM

"Mr. Grady? You didn't do your homework?"

Cameron jerks back to the present. Mr. Hart is standing in front of him, a pile of papers in his hand. Homework. Cameron can't concentrate. He keeps seeing SciFi's broken face in his memory. If Patterson can do that to a guy the size of SciFi, what will he do to Cameron?

He's dead. No doubt about it.

He's next. He knows it, but he doesn't care. In fact, he's looking forward to it. He'll fight this time. He'll throw more punches than Patterson can take. Even a guy as insulated as him, with more muscle than bone, will feel it. Cameron will make the first move, not wait for the Red Coats to get the jump on him. If he can get a few blows in he might have a chance.

"Well?" Mr. Hart prompts. "Homework, Grady?" An eyebrow lifts. He holds up the papers.

Cameron opens his notebook, turns the pages looking for where he might have written it.

"Tabs usually help," Mr. Hart says. "They cost about ten cents. Well worth the money."

Cameron's jaw snaps shut so his teeth meet with a sharp crack. Mr. Hart hears it and takes a step back. When Cameron looks into the man's face he sees it's as tight as it usually is when Hart's dealing with Eddie. Poor Hart; he has another lunatic on his hands. Cameron doesn't doubt that's what the guy's thinking. Even Cameron knows he's closer to that edge than ever before. He feels like he's standing on a tightrope, but it doesn't scare him. Not anymore. A person can be scared for only so long and then he stops caring.

Cameron finds his homework and pulls it out of his notebook. When Hart takes it from him the man is back to being in charge.

"Skimpy," he says and places it on top of his pile. "I'm sure I'll enjoy reading every word."

There's one big difference between Cameron and Eddie Fain.

Cameron feels no pull to carve up school property or himself with a straightened paper clip, but he would like to take one to Hart's smug face.

Cameron looks down from where he's balanced on that tightrope. It's a long way, and no net. He's so far up he can't see the people in the audience, or the clowns waiting to come out and divert attention from his mangled body.

He's so far up, the air is thin. He thinks about his victory yesterday; same high. Same life or death. Then he lifts one of his feet and stands like a flamingo, tempting gravity.

He looks into Hart's face and says, "You're an ass."

WEDNESDAY

9:20AM

Cameron holds the lighter under the balled-up paper towel. The fire doesn't spread fast, like Cameron wants it to, needs it to. The paper is wet. It smokes but doesn't flame. A dud. Like he is, only there's a lot more potential with fire than there is with a guy who's too afraid to bend over to tie his shoe, afraid he'll be like a duck with his head underwater, afraid a Red Coat will pluck him out of the pond and pick apart his insides.

Cameron tosses the piece of char into the trash and pulls a paper towel from the dispenser. Dry, like sandpaper. He ignites it and holds it between his fingertips. The first blush of heat is like a sweet song playing in his blood. The pulse in his wrists throbs heavily. It hurts. The flames eat away at the paper until there is almost nothing left. Cameron wishes he could go like that, in a blaze of glory. Yeah. Fast and with everyone watching. With everyone watching because they can't do anything else. Cameron stands over the bin and drops the fiery ball into it. It catches quickly. It's like he blinked and suddenly the trash can is an inferno, with flames jumping and smoke curling toward the ceiling. Cameron steps back. A tiny step. He wants to feel the burn on his skin.

It's hard to pull away. If Cameron went like that, everyone would have to watch. Fire has that much power.

The wall behind the trash can is turning black with soot and ash before Cameron does anything about it. Then he dumps the can over and stomps on the paper towels, what's left of them. When he's done, with the fire out and his hands trembling from the rush, he notices the rubber soles of his shoes have melted. He notices smudges of black on his face and hands. He notices the red pull fire alarm just inside the door and the ceiling spigots that didn't open up. And he laughs. A fire here at Madison High would burn without anyone noticing for a long time.

WEDNESDAY

9:30AM

The office, from the inside looking out, isn't as defeating as Cameron thought. He likes that. Suddenly the walls in this school aren't that high, the halls not so long. He feels a lot bigger. Like maybe he grew a foot and finally looks like he belongs.

He decides, before Mr. Elwood, the boys' counselor, calls him into his office, that he's not sorry and won't say that he is. Maybe he'll say nothing. Cameron knows how much adults hate that.

"Mr. Grady."

Elwood is tall and about as white as a cigarette. He smells like them, too. How does a guy who smokes try to get kids not to?

He doesn't.

Cameron stands up.

"Come on in."

He walks past Elwood and into his tiny ice cube of an office. Two plastic chairs sit empty in front of a metal desk. Cameron takes the chair closest to the door and looks around the room. A diploma in a plastic frame, a bowling ball, or at least its case, and photos of Elwood's golden retriever. He took the dog for a professional sitting. The retriever is sitting on a piece of carpeting, a football between his paws, with a blue background that looks like clouds smeared over a clear sky.

Nothing has changed since Cameron was here last.

"Mr. Hart says you called him an ass." Elwood is reading from the referral form. When he moves around his desk he lets the paper fall onto a stack of other referrals, then takes his seat. "He says it's possible you flipped him off as you left the room."

"I didn't do that," Cameron says. "I didn't flip him off."

"But you called him an ass?"

Cameron doesn't deny it.

"Does he list any witnesses?"

Elwood sits forward and reads from the referral, ". . . in front of the whole class."

Cameron laughs. Hart, the crybaby.

"Ass is a funny word, isn't it?" Elwood asks.

"I guess."

"Do you know what it means?"

Of course, but Elwood doesn't give him the chance to prove it. He reaches behind him for five pounds of Webster's definitions, flips to the beginning, and starts reading.

"'A long-eared mammal; a domesticated relative of the horse; uneducated; a foolish person.'"

Elwood looks at Cameron for confirmation.

"That sounds about right," Cameron says. "Well, except maybe the uneducated part. I mean, he went to school, right?"

Elwood nods. "He did. For a long time." He closes the dictionary and puts it back on the shelf. "You think Mr. Hart is a fool? Why?"

Cameron looks at him, thinking maybe this is a trick question. First of all, anyone who knows Hart has to know the guy's an ass. Second, why would Elwood want his opinion?

"What happened to crime and punishment?" Cameron asks. "You know I did it, so give me the consequence."

"We talk about things here, Cameron, so chances are it won't happen again." He pauses, hoping it'll sink in, Cameron's sure. "Look, I know you're new at this. The only other time you were in here was for a little squabble between you and an upperclassman. Remember? I called you both in here and we talked it out. That's how we work out conflicts at Madison: we talk. Sometimes

I bring all the parties together — do you feel like you need to talk to Mr. Hart?"

"No." Cameron feels he was pretty clear in the classroom. Anyway, he got a bloody nose the last time he tried to talk it out. It doesn't work. He wants to tell Elwood this. He wants the counselor to know what a failure he really is, but that would mean telling him about the punch he took, it would mean sitting in this office again with Patterson and later taking the punishment for opening his mouth.

"Okay. Sometimes I can get to the bottom of a conflict simply by listening to what a student has to say."

This is where Cameron is supposed to fill the silence with his innermost feelings. Not a chance of that happening.

"Or you could sit in Mr. Hart's class. See the way he talks to us."

"Did he say something that upset you?"

"Nothing I couldn't take care of myself." But Eddie's another story. And while Cameron thought it was funny before, he knows now that being lampooned by Hart is nothing to laugh about.

"What did he say?"

"Today?"

"Does this happen often?"

"No." He has another victim, one he prefers more.

"Okay, then. What did he say today?"

Cameron shrugs and realizes he's going to have to say something if he ever wants to get out of this office.

"It's the way he says it. Like I don't have a brain."

Elwood nods. "Have you seen *The Wizard of Oz?*"

"Yeah."

"You know the scarecrow didn't have a brain?"

Cameron is about ninety-nine percent sure that Elwood is missing some or all of his.

"I'm not a scarecrow," Cameron says.

"Exactly. Remember that whenever you think Hart is talking down to you."

"That's it?" Is this guy serious?

"No. Detention or Saturday school — which do you prefer?"

Right. Detention. Maybe that way his mom won't find out.

"I see those wheels turning," Elwood says. "I'm afraid I have to call her either way."

Great. "I'll take the detention."

"Three days, an hour after school today, tomorrow, and Friday."

Fine.

WEDNESDAY

9:55AM

By the time Cameron leaves Elwood's office, second period is over. The bell rings as he's walking through the hall. PE next. The thrill is gone. He thought last night about pushing his lap time even more. He knows he can shave a couple of seconds if he doesn't lose focus, but Patterson is all he can think about.

He stops at a water fountain, stalling. He never enters the locker room early. Before it was so he could avoid Patterson and his stooge. Now he's trying to psych himself up. He doesn't want to disappoint the coach. Doesn't want to look like a loser in front of the whole class after his victory yesterday.

He has to do pull-ups today, enough to pass the PT test, and push-ups, too. He's not worried about the running, the crunches, or the squats. The pull-ups and push-ups will be harder. His upper body strength sucks. Cameron has the thinnest chest in the whole ninth grade, except for Darcy Swimmer, the only flat-chested girl at Madison. That's one of the things Cameron notices a lot. His only reason for making it to physical science class, and passing it, is because his lab partner, Helen Gosset, wears shirts that are so small Cameron knows her belly button is pierced. And they're tight enough that Cameron can see the seams of her bra, the shape of tiny bows on the straps, through the cotton.

Cameron is still drinking when a hand comes down on his head and shoves his face into the stream of water. There's gum in the fountain and it connects with his chin. Cameron jerks backward, wipes at his face, and watches two Red Coats, Patterson's buddies, continue down the hall, their heads back, laughing.

"You make it too easy, Grady!" one calls back.

Cameron adds the colors red and gold, their school colors, to his hate list. He promises himself he'll never wear them again.

He pushes through the double doors, into the boys' locker room. Wet, dirty socks. The smell is the same every morning. Cameron stops at a urinal, pees and zips up, then finds his locker. He looks over his shoulder; the locker room is clearing out. He hears the coach's voice through the doors, lining kids up. He's later than usual and picks up his pace. He pulls his jock off the shelf, lets his underwear drop and is pushing his feet through the straps of his cup when the locker door next to his slams shut.

"I was wrong, Murphy. Grady here isn't a girl."

Cameron is pushed onto the bench; he shoves his hands in his lap to cover himself.

"You have nothing to hide, Grady," Patterson sneers. He bends over and plucks Cameron's jock from the floor. "What are ya doing with this?" He holds it up. "Look at that, Murphy. It's man-sized."

He laughs and taps Cameron on the head with it.

"Get off me." Cameron struggles against Murphy's hands, takes a swipe at the cup, but Patterson pulls it back.

"You're in the wrong locker room, Grady," Murphy says.

"He's not a girl, Murph." Patterson bends over, grabs Cameron's nipple, and twists. "No boobs."

"Darcy Swimmer doesn't have boobs, either," Murphy says.

"You're right, Murph. Looks like you have something to prove, Grady."

"I have nothing to prove to you," Cameron says. His tongue is dry and it makes the words stick to his teeth.

"You hear that, Murph? He has n-n-nothing to prove t-to us," Patterson snickers.

"How about to the school, Grady? Big mistake coming to sports night with your mommy. Wearing your hair like a girl's." He dips his head so he can snarl in Cameron's ear, "Big mistake yesterday. You know you run like a girl." Patterson pulls a cell phone from his pocket and flips it open. "I think you have a lot to prove. Once and for all. Is he or isn't he — a she?"

They laugh and it feels like scissors slicing through Cameron's ears.

Patterson nods at Murphy, who steps closer to Cameron, so close Cameron can feel his legs pressing into his back. The boy's hands tighten on Cameron's shoulders, the fingers grinding into his bones. There must be a pressure point there somewhere, because a hot, burning, tingling feeling runs down Cameron's arm right before it goes numb.

"I learned that in tae kwon do," Murphy says. "There are a hundred and seventeen points of destruction in the human body."

"Your girlfriend, the Incredible Hulk, went down like a tree," Patterson says.

Cameron feels a tearing in his chest, like his heart broke loose and is knocking against bone. He roars from the pain of it and tries to thrust to his feet. Patterson shoves him back down and digs his knee into Cameron's thigh, into the soft muscle, putting enough of his weight into it that Cameron feels the sting.

Murphy's hands tighten on his shoulders. Cameron tries to take a swing with his right arm, but it hangs useless at his side.

"Hold still, Grady," Murphy advises. "And say cheese."

"Get off me." Cameron twists, hoping to break lose, and Murphy's arms slither around his neck, holding him in a half nelson. Cameron swings at Patterson with his left arm, and glances off the cell phone in his hand.

"Pull his arm back, Murph."

"Doing it."

Cameron's arm is wrenched behind him, and he is completely exposed. Patterson snaps a picture. Cameron jerks up off the bench, frees his working arm, and tries again to knock the cell phone from his hand.

Patterson shoves Cameron back onto the bench, puts his foot on Cameron's leg to keep him there, and lowers his phone. Cameron hears a series of clicks. "A close-up. I don't think it'll do much for the girls, but it's worth a try."

Cameron screams in frustration and Patterson shoves a sock in his mouth. He gags on the cotton, which is too far down his throat, drying out his mouth. He breathes through his nose and switches to survival mode. Disconnect. He's got to get himself out of here, even if it's only as far as his mind will allow.

"Full frontal," Patterson says.

Cameron feels his legs pushed apart. Patterson is standing between them, holding the phone close to Cameron's body, snapping pictures.

"You want to impress the girls, Grady?" Patterson takes

Cameron's face in his hand, lifts it so that Cameron has to look him in the eye. "You have to pack wood for that."

"Are you going to do it, Grady?" Murphy asks, pulling on his arm. "Or are we going to do it for you?"

Patterson isn't waiting. Cameron sees the intent in his eyes, feels his own body shudder with an anger that's too big, that will split his skin, that will kill him for sure.

Patterson slides his phone into his shirt pocket and pulls out a glove.

"This won't hurt at all," he says.

"No! No! No!" Cameron's voice is muffled by the sock. He surges against Murphy's hold and then recoils from Patterson's touch.

If he doesn't die from this then he'll kill himself.

That's the last thing Cameron remembers thinking and then he checks out completely. His eyes hook on the white tiles leading to the showers. He thinks he can hear the steady drip of water from a shower head. A toilet flush. Water rushing from a sink faucet.

Tunnel vision. Patterson and Murphy become blurred; the white tiles sharp. And then a dark head. Small, bobbing over the half wall isolating the showers. It pops up and Cameron sees Pinon, just his head, his eyes wide, like the lids have been rolled back and pinned to his skull. Pinon. His glassy eyes and his teeth biting into his pink lips, like maybe he wears lipstick they're so pink. His hands come up, curl over the wall, and he swallows. Cameron can see his Adam's apple jerk, like the kid is choking on it.

He's real. Cameron isn't imagining anymore. Pinon is crouching in the showers, watching Cameron's humiliation. Not running for help. Not crawling into a small space. Hiding. Pinon is crouched in the showers, watching and not even blinking.

Cameron feels his body fall to the cement floor. A foot swings into his side. He cracks his head against the bench and squeezes his eyes shut. His hearing returns like the crashing of symbols.

"You're ours, Grady," Patterson warns. "This is just the beginning."

WEDNESDAY

12:35PM

Cameron makes it through the door of his computer class just as the bell rings. A group of kids are gathered around a computer work station. He starts toward them, when their teacher, Mrs. Marks, stops him.

"Cameron, when that bell rings you need to be at work, not just arriving."

He knows this, but it took him an entire hour to convince himself to finish the school day. After Patterson and Murphy were done with him, Cameron got back into his jeans and sweatshirt and bolted out of the locker room. He didn't stop running until he was off campus, until he found shelter under the canopy of some elm trees at the back of a strip mall, where he sat shaking and reliving the incident until he was so angry he was sure the rain sizzled when it hit his skin.

He despises Rich Patterson, his loser friends, all the pecker-heads in this school. He especially loathes Charlie Pinon. The next time Cameron sees him, he's going to let the perv know with his fists how much he doesn't like him. But even thinking about that isn't enough to cool him off, isn't enough to convince him that life is worth living.

His mom. When it comes right down to it, the image of her broken face, the moment she finds out he burned alive, is more than he can keep in his head. That's what Cameron thought about doing, lighting himself up. He sat under the tree, with the rain falling around him, and lit one match after the other. Letting the flame burn down to his thumb and finger, watching the skin bubble, feeling the pressure ease slowly from his body.

That helped, too.

"Mr. Grady?"

"Yeah. Sorry."

"Next time it's a tardy."

He is going to agree with her, but they're interrupted. Laughter. Deep, husky laughter and some nervous twittering. Then a girl's scream. That's how he'll remember it.

When Cameron turns toward the students crowded around a work station of three computers, he sees a screen flickering through a series of images. He doesn't need to step closer to know what they are.

He can't move. His heart is in his throat, thumping, crashing against his Adam's apple until he feels like he'll pass out from the pain. His blood is so hot, it's shrieking, his mouth too dry to spit. He watches the others as their faces, some of them horrified, some of them gleeful, turn somber or smirking. Until everything blurs, like he's looking through a window during violent rain.

"Mr. Grady?" Mrs. Marks. Is she whispering, or is he too far off to really hear her? "Mr. Grady?" Louder. Angry.

"Turn off those computers," she orders. "Now. All of you. Mr. Grady, step out into the hall."

That's the last thing he hears. Cameron is outside without knowing how he gets there. The sun glows behind a bank of heavy clouds, so that there's no more rain, but no blue skies, either. He's running. He feels the air burn in his chest. Feels it burst from his lips. He runs through long, wet grass, pushing through shrubs and between the thick trees that tower above and hide him, pushing, pushing.

WEDNESDAY

1:05PM

Cameron strikes a match against the carbon and watches it flare to life. He breathes deeply through his nose, that first acrid black-smoke taste on his tongue, then flicks the match through the front window of the Chrysler LeBaron. The car is an old wreck. It used to be gold, but most of that paint has peeled off or was eaten by rust. Must have been in the woods for years, Cameron figures. A great nesting place for squirrels, field mice, anything small enough to burrow into the backseat cushions and close its eyes or birth its babies. Today, Cameron doesn't see any animals. He can barely see anything in front of him. He wishes he could climb inside his head and rip out that last image of his humiliation. It's not enough to tell himself he won't think of it anymore, because it sneaks up and is right there, bigger than it was on the computer screen. It's like a damn accident, the way people just can't stop looking, no matter how gruesome it is. He'd rather shovel brain off pavement than see himself one more time, naked, stuffed with his own gym sock, with Rich Patterson's foot on his leg, holding him down.

"Peckerhead. Peckerhead."

His blood screams with the fury of it.

Rich Patterson is a peckerhead. A loser.

It doesn't do anything for him, thinking it or saying it aloud to the trees and the whitewashed boulders surrounding him. Once, he spray painted *Rich Patterson sucks dick* onto a road sign. But that was over Christmas, in Syracuse, when Cameron and his mom and brother visited his grandparents. For a few days he actually felt good about it. But no one in Syracuse knows Patterson. No one here knows about the sign.

Cameron lights another match, holds it under his nose. Too close. The smoke makes the small hairs burn and he feels it all the way down his throat, already hot and raw from the run here, from the screaming he did at the top of his lungs, his voice muffled by the thick leaves and columns of the trees: *RICH PATTERSON SUCKS DICK!* He wants to write it somewhere. Somewhere everyone in town will read it. Maybe on the overpass — there's only one in this part of town. All the way here, Cameron screamed it and the fire still seethes below his skin. He still tastes it, as thick as blood in his mouth.

Cameron flicks the match; it lands on what is left of the arm-rest inside the front door of the car. He wonders who drove this car. Who ditched it this far into the woods? Who wanted it that gone, that they drove it over the gnarled roots, the tall grass, the thick, scraggly arms of bushes grown into each other? What kind of life went on in the car? What kind of death?

Cameron lights another match and this time, leans inside the car. He tears a handful of foam from the backseat and places the flame to the material. It lights up immediately. Cameron lets it burn in his hand until it's a ball of fire. His fingers singe. He lays the coal on scraps of newspaper on the floor of the car, then tears another piece of cushion, lights another match, and ignites it. He keeps at it until flames jump in the front and backseats, touch the roof and spread. Until, like hands, they're curling around the outside of the car, trying to pry their way out. To fresher air. To lick the towering trees and eat up the leaves, grass. Anything for fuel.

Smoke billows from the car. Plastic melts, its sharp scent so close Cameron wants to gag. A whoosh of air, carrying fire, jumps from the car and Cameron falls back. A whole ceiling of fire is over his head. He lies in the grass and watches.

This is fire. He created it. It's his.

It seems to jump from the car to a tree branch thick with new leaves, curls their edges, and spreads in every direction. That's the beauty of fire, there's not a thing in the world it doesn't love. And it moves so fast it can trick the eyes.

It's almost too late when Cameron notices the fire is forming a circle around him. He jumps to his feet, dashes through an opening where the flames don't meet, stumbles over rocks and the clinging branches of scrub. He turns and looks back at the fire, more than twenty feet tall, reaching well into the branches of elm and maple, lighting them up like no freakin' Christmas tree he ever saw.

"Whooooweeeee!"

He hears his voice, its hoarse cheer. He stands at the rim of the fire, stuffs his hands into the pockets of his jeans, and grins full-faced at his creation.

WEDNESDAY

2:10PM

In the upstairs bathroom Cameron shrugs out of his coat and lets it drop to the floor. He'll have to trash it. The fire melted the Gore-Tex in places, making it shine like the skin of an apple. His mother would notice. He pulls his shirt over his head and drops it on top of his coat. Bad choice wearing a white T-shirt today, but then he didn't know he was going to become a one-man army against Smokey the Bear. He laughs at his own mental joke, kicks the pile of his clothes aside, and strips off his pants. These he can keep. There are no markings, but they smell like fire. He picks up the jeans, buries his face in them, and inhales deeply. It's in there, in the musty depths, all that power he unleashed in the woods. He can still smell it. He smiles, feels the jeans move against his face, take on the shape of his lips.

He's a firebug. He heard the term before and he likes it. A place to belong. Something he does well. He wonders if his mother would approve. Doubt it. *But Mom, you told me to find something I like to do.* He wonders briefly if Eddie Fain likes fire. If he carries matches, lights them just for the split second of acrid smoke, that calling it pitches into your blood. *Come to me. Light up. Burn.*

Cameron looks at his reflection in the mirror. The skin on his forehead is seared, red and puckered. *No pain, no gain,* he thinks. He wouldn't want the fire if it didn't leave its mark on him. He never felt as close to glory as he did shimmying through the flames. When he almost didn't make it. When the sky above him was a roof of unfurling red-orange waves. That beats a toasted fingernail.

I have to do something about my hair, he thinks. It stands straight up on his head, the ends fried by the fire. He runs his hands over it, feels the crackle, hears, in his memory, the crackling of the fire, the pop and hiss of branches as they caught, burned, dropped to the ground.

He carries a bigger punch than Rich Patterson. And has bigger balls, too.

Hell, he faced down fire.

He created a monster.

And got away.

He feels a zing shoot through his blood. Nerves. He's starting to feel them now. Now that he's home and safe. He holds his hands out in front of him. Steady. But his knee joints feel like mush, his throat like there's a butterfly in there. He doesn't know what time it is. How close his mom and Robbie are to walking through the front door.

Move. Gotta move faster.

In the woods, with the fire blazing, his brain was on speed. Felt like it, anyway. He didn't have to think a thing, he just did it.

Thinking is overrated.

For months all he thought about was the next time Patterson would land on him. Those days are over. He is the man now. Patterson doesn't know real power. But he will.

Cameron feels the smile on his face spread painfully. The crusty skin on his forehead pulls too tight.

He notices the shake in his knees. The hum in his calf muscles. His legs are vibrating, like a plucked wishbone.

He drops his jeans, tries to pick up the plastic garbage sacks he snagged on his way through the garage, but they're slippery, or his fingers don't work. He turns his hands over, looks. One blister, a tiny red balloon on the pad of his index finger that he got earlier, when he was just playing with matches. That's all. But he's losing feeling in his hands. Like a body part slept on too long.

Get a grip, he tells himself.

He doesn't know how he could be high as a kite then suddenly scraping dirt. Unless it is like taking speed, and this is the downside. He's coming off his high and these are the side effects. He stands for a minute more, gazing at himself in the mirror. It's not so bad, he decides. The shakes are worth it. Definitely. But as he watches, tears stream through the black soot on his face, drip off his chin, make thin murky rivers in the sink.

Maybe holding that kind of power in his hands was a little scary. But when he gets used to it, when it's like a cop or a soldier wearing his gun, this won't happen again.

He turns on the water, keeps it running until his eyes are clear, his knees solid. Then he splashes his face, rubs the soot free, and then pushes his head under the faucet. He needs a full shower, and he'll take one, but first he has to fix his hair, and it has to be wet in order to cut it. That's what the guy at Super Clips does.

WEDNESDAY

4:00PM

Cameron is toweling off his hair when he hears a knock at the bathroom door.

"Cameron, it's Mom. Open up."

He drops the towel and looks at his reflection in the mirror. His hair is about an inch long all over his head. All the sun-blond color is gone and at the root it's dark enough it's almost brown. No more Cameron Diaz. He wishes he had thought of it sooner.

"Come on, Cameron. I want to talk to you."

"I can hear you," Cameron says.

He bends over and scoops up some hair, dumps it into the trash. He can feel his mother on the other side of the door. Thinking. *What will get Cameron to come out?*

Not much. He's his own man now. He'll come out when he wants to.

He watches the doorknob move, just sink a little as her hand rests on it. She doesn't try to turn it.

"I got a call from your school today," she says. "I want to talk to you about it."

Her voice is thin, a notch below her normal. Her before-the-tears-come voice. In his mind Cameron hears his father yelling, "'Get it together, Maureen,'" and feels like laughing. Used to be his father's voice scared him. Made him want to hide. Not anymore.

He wonders if it was Elwood who called. If she knows Cameron called Hart an ass. Or maybe the principal called about the photos. Maybe both.

"Cameron," his mom stretches out his name.

Either way, what is she going to do? Nothing. His mom hasn't punished them, not really, since they left his father. And what can she do about Patterson? Another big zero there. It's up to him now. But he's ready. He's finally ready.

He holds his hands out in front of him; they're steady.

The new Cameron Grady. Fast. Fierce. And ferocious.

Talk won't change what happened today, but action will.

"I don't want to talk."

"We have to."

Cameron doesn't answer that. He bends for another handful of hair, brushes some off the vanity, and looks at himself again in the mirror. The haircut hasn't changed him so much that he's a new person. He'll go to school tomorrow and everyone will know who he is. But they won't call him Cameron Diaz.

"Cameron, I went to the school today. I had to. The principal called, Mr. Vega . . ."

Her voice is stronger. She waits for his response, but he's not biting.

"He told me what happened today," she says. "That's what I want to talk about."

Cameron doesn't need to talk. He already has a plan. He's going to kill Patterson and Murphy, and Pinon, too.

He hates Pinon. Probably as much as he hates Patterson.

More. Pinon watched him like he was an X-rated movie.

Cameron's going to get rid of them all. Then everything will be better. He can go back to thinking about normal stuff. He'll even get his homework done.

It'll be like today never happened.

Like in the movies, where they go in and cut out a scene that didn't work. What happened today definitely isn't working for Cameron. Cut and paste. It's that simple.

"Cameron, if you don't open the door . . ."

What, Mom? You're going to break it down?

He can't do anything about the pictures, but the way Cameron sees it, people will forget. If no one's around to remind them, people always forget.

No one remembers the atomic bomb until someone comes along and says, "Remember Hiroshima."

It's what the pictures don't show that Cameron has to wipe out of existence.

"You can't stay in there forever," his mom says. "I'll be downstairs when you want to talk." She pauses and Cameron feels the death in her next words before she even says them. "I saw the pictures, Cameron. Mr. Vega showed me the pictures and I want you to know the boys have been arrested. They're in jail."

She saw the pictures. Vega showed her the pictures.

An air pocket builds in Cameron's throat, threatening to suffocate him.

His mother saw the pictures.

He unlocks the door, swings it open.

His mother is standing at the top of the stairs, her hand on the banister. She turns toward him.

"No! No, you shouldn't have done that."

He's crying. Again. *Crybaby.*

That fast, he's back to being a girl.

Cameron Diaz.

He feels all that anger and the can't-do-anything-about-it hopelessness build inside him until he's sure he's going to burst.

"Why did you do that?"

Her hand lifts and flutters in front of her throat. "Look at the pictures? I had to, Cameron."

"No, you didn't. You didn't have to look at the pictures. He could have just told you what happened. He could have just shut up and not said anything and not showed you the pictures." He's standing in front of her, his fists balled up and shaking. "You definitely didn't have to *look* at the pictures."

"I'm sorry," she says, like that's going to fix it.

"But you can't forget them, can you? You can't get them out of your mind. You can't pretend it didn't happen."

"No."

"That's what I want. That's the only thing that's going to fix this."

He's screaming now. He hears it come back to him, high and sharp and nothing like in the woods when the fire was blazing and he was everything.

"Hey!"

Randy. Fuckin' Randy in his uniform and his know-everything attitude.

"What's going on?"

"Nothing!" Cameron screams. "Right, Mom?"

"Cameron." She reaches a hand out to him and he backs away.

"Nothing!"

He's tired of being a nothing.

Tomorrow he's going to fix that. Tomorrow, for just a minute, the world will go black and when he opens his eyes everything will be white. Like a clean piece of paper. He can start over. It'll be just like that.

"Cameron."

"Don't talk anymore, Mom. Don't say one more word."

He pushes past them, takes the stairs two at a time.

He shoves the kitchen door open, steps out onto the deck in his jeans and bare feet, and looks around him. Everything's the same. The too-quiet houses, bikes, Big Wheels and play sets in the yards, the trees tall and full and growing like a thatched roof over the world, the dogwoods blooming with pink and white flowers. Life. Nothing's changed.

WEDNESDAY

10:00PM

Cameron lies on his bed, above the covers, and flips through the stations on the TV. He refused to go down to dinner. Wouldn't talk to his mother, or look at her, when she came up with a plate of food. She stood in the center of his room, telling him how sorry she was that the kids at school picked on him. Telling him he was probably right, she shouldn't have looked at the pictures, but the principal handed them to her and she didn't know exactly what she was going to see, and then it was too late.

She put the plate on Cameron's nightstand and sat down on

Robbie's bed, her hands squeezing her knees, and tried to wait him out.

"I like your haircut," she said.

The lightness in her voice was forced. He felt her eyes in his hair, sifting through the short strands, looking for what was missing.

It's gone, Mom.

"I hardly recognize you," she admitted.

I'm gone.

He let her sink in the silence, counting the minutes on his alarm clock. She lifted her arms and let them drop, twisted her hands beneath her legs, tapped her toes, then surfaced in a fit of coughing. Three minutes, fifty-three seconds.

She gave Cameron's father a lot longer before she left him. But now she knows. She knows when she's going to lose, when to cut her losses and run. And that's what she did.

"I hope you'll eat something," she said.

She stood up. He felt her eyes on him, but not the usual burn when she's checking his mental health.

Then she turned and left.

He doesn't eat. She made chicken, a baked potato and broccoli. She forgot to bring him a drink and after a while he gets up and goes into the bathroom, dips his head under the faucet, and drinks. He returns to bed, scoops up the remote, and watches the flickering light from the TV as it spins through programs.

He presses the surf button on the remote and continues his

mindless search for nothing in particular. Then he hits on the local news, and for a moment the screen is alive with ribbons of red and orange flame.

The fire.

His fire.

His heart jumps and kicks into drive. Well, at least he has a pulse. He pushes the return button on the remote and stares at the screen, looking for himself in there. He recognizes the landscape of trees against the darkening sky, the shape of the boulders at the lip of the forest. He ran into the woods there, seeking cover. Like a rabbit chased by a wolf.

He'll never know that kind of fear again.

The camera pans out and suddenly the trees stop and smoke rises from the ground. The remaining stubs of once-towering elms and poplars still glow with flame deep inside them. It looks like a graveyard. He recognizes the heaviness in his chest as sadness and he's not surprised. He loved those woods but knew, even before today, that their loss was coming. Like knowing the cancer that's got your dog will soon take him. You can medicate, but it just prolongs life, puts off the inevitable.

The image on the screen shifts.

"The fire is contained now." A lady reporter stands with the woods at her back; the air is hazy with smoke. "But the loss is substantial. More than seventeen acres burned this afternoon, wiping out the dense forestry as well as the jogging path and children's park."

The newswoman is replaced with the scene of a melted climbing wall, the dripping plastic carcass of a slide. The only things left standing are the metal poles and chains of a swing set, now blackened by the fire.

"Those clumps of melted plastic were once children's toys," the reporter's voice continues. "All in all, officials say about two hundred thousand dollars in damage was sustained. The forest will need replanting, the park and jogging path rebuilding. And that's just the beginning."

The image shifts again, this time to a split screen focusing on a man sitting at a news desk and the woman reporter, who waves away the smoke in front of her face.

"But no one was harmed?" the man asks.

"No. No casualties."

"Any word on what started the fire?" the man asks.

"Arson, Mike. Fire department officials are very sure of that," she answers. "Apparently started in an abandoned car."

The guy goes on to say what a shame it is and then the news program moves into a commercial.

Cameron presses the continuous surf button on the remote and lies back against his pillow. He slips his hand under the mattress and comes out with a book of matches. He brings them to his nose, inhales the sulphur smell. The effect is calming.

He used to think about burning the school down, moving from bathroom to bathroom, lighting fires in the trash cans, in the trash cans in the halls, too, until the school was an oven and everyone on the inside was cooking. This was one of his favorite daydreams until he realized he was always pulling out one or two kids who didn't deserve to die; until his dream was ruined by the escape of Patterson and the other Red Coats.

Burning the school would not be one hundred percent effective. There's no guarantee his problems would end there.

He rolls off his bed and reaches under it for his collection of possible weapons. A pocket knife, a razor blade, a scalpel he took from his mother's work supply, an ice pick. He throws in the book of matches and then folds the white hand towel around them and stashes it in his backpack.

Patterson may not be at school tomorrow, but he will be back. And it'll be the same scene, take two. Only Cameron's not going to let Patterson or any of his chump friends make a bitch out of him.

"You're ours, Grady. . . . This is just the beginning."

No, I don't think so, Cameron thinks. *They're no match for me now. I'm new and improved.*

THURSDAY

10:10AM

The drive to Pittsburgh takes two hours. Cameron listens to his iPod. Coldplay. Kid Rock. Eminem. He used to like this music but realizes now that they're a bunch of whiners. He wants to take off his headphones and put himself out of his misery, but then either his mom or Robbie will talk to him, and he wants that even less. The only reason Cameron got in the car was because his father threatened to come all the way to Erie if he had to. And Randy stood over him, hands in his pockets, his tin star pinned to his chest. His gun clipped to his belt.

Cameron wonders briefly if there is any way he could get Randy's gun from him. There are school shootings all the time. They're in the news for a few days and then it's like they didn't happen.

He heard Randy tell his mom, after the last shooting hit the news, ~~that there'll be more of them. Cameron believed it even then.~~

But Randy always wears the gun when he's around; he never takes it off, never puts it down. Even when he's not in uniform the gun's holstered at his waist.

Cameron wants to be in school today. He wants it over with. When his mom came into his bedroom this morning and handed him the telephone, saying, "It's your father," he knew not to touch it. Not to put it to his ear. The fear caught him around the throat and as soon as Cameron realized what it was, he knew the only way to master it was to face it.

*

"What do you want?" Cameron had asked.

Pause. His father's face probably went all loose, surprised to hear his number-one son talk back to him.

"You're going to talk to your dad that way?" he finally asked, and his voice was like an elevator going up.

"I don't want to talk to you at all." Cameron felt the fear in his body change to something more, like riding a roller coaster that pulled at the rails, thundering toward liftoff.

"Well, you're going to talk to me," his father said. "You're going to sit your ass in your mother's car and drive two hours just to talk to me up close and personal." Cameron could hear the breath dragging through his father's nose, little bursts of it against the receiver. "If you didn't go get yourself beat up . . ."

Sissy boy. I'm not raising sissy boys.

". . . if you just stood up for yourself, landed one good punch, no one would mess with you."

Been there, done that, Dad. It had about the same effect as grease on a fire.

"Cameron? Did you hear me?" Cameron let the silence stretch, felt his father's anger pressing through the phone. "You get your ass in your mother's car . . ."

Cameron handed the phone back to his mother with his father still yelling.

✳

He wants to be in school. He wants to start all over again, almost. He knows enough not to expect everyone will forget the way Patterson put a big bull's-eye on his back. Not right away. It may take a week or two.

"Almost there," his mom says, turning briefly to look at him in the backseat. "Your father's anxious to see you."

She smiles like that's a good thing. How can she think that?

She's desperate. She doesn't know what to do with him and so it becomes a father-son thing. "Sometimes a boy needs his father," she told him this morning.

"He'll help you work this out," she says now.

No, he won't. But Cameron doesn't say so. He turns up the volume on his iPod and stares back at her, his eyes flat, and watches her smile fade. She turns back to the road, her fingers white now on the steering wheel. Inside, he reminds himself: *No fear.*

He is no longer afraid of his father. When you're ready to kill or be killed, fear curls up like a dog and lies at your feet. You can feel it breathing, know it'll wake up and howl at you if you don't take control.

His mom turns off the highway. The diner is built to look like it existed in the 1950s. You can park next to a speaker and order your meals brought to the car, or eat inside with a mini jukebox on your table. They do this, Cameron walking behind his mom and Robbie, stuffing his iPod into his coat pocket.

His father is sitting at a booth drinking coffee.

"What took you so long?" he asks.

Cameron refused to get into the car, until Randy showed up. But his mom doesn't say this. She doesn't leave them with their father and take a booth on the other side of the restaurant, either, which is what she usually does when their father wants to see them. She nudges Robbie so that he moves forward, prepared to sit next to their father.

"Traffic," his mom says.

His father stands up and Cameron notices that Robbie is just two or three inches shorter.

"Traffic? In the middle of a Thursday morning?" His voice is full of doubt and he stands with his hands on his hips waiting for an answer.

His mom ignores the comment and takes Cameron's arm. She wants him to slide into the booth ahead of her. She wants a fast escape if she needs it. Cameron gives it to her. He no longer lives afraid.

Still standing, his father looks down on him. "You lose that mouth between Erie and here?" he wants to know.

Cameron feels the shake in his knees. He presses his palms flat against his legs, tries to keep his feet from jumping, from pushing him up and out of the booth. He doesn't run anymore, he reminds himself.

No fear.

"Well, Cameron? You want to give it to me now?" his father challenges.

"Max," his mother protests.

Cameron doesn't doubt that his father will hit him right here, in the middle of the restaurant, with an audience. He keeps his voice low, but steady.

"I have nothing to say to you."

His father nods. "That's an improvement." He sits down. "I don't like the attitude. I gave up a day's work and drove three hours to take a look at you." He does this now, his small eyes shifting over Cameron. "You look pretty good to me. You get in any jabs?"

"A few," Cameron lies. Out of the corner of his eye he watches his mother's hands tighten around her purse.

His father pins her down with his eyes. "He looks fine. What's so damn important I had to take the day off of work?"

"Cameron was very upset last night," she explains.

"You still upset?"

"No," Cameron says.

"Boys get upset, Maureen. You never did have tolerance for that but that's the way it is. Men get pissed. We blow off a little steam and it looks like hell is taking over. Then we're fine." He turns to Cameron. "Are you fine now?"

Cameron nods.

"You know how you're going to deal with these boys tomorrow?"

Cameron nods again.

"Okay. End of story." His father turns to Robbie. "No one messes with you, do they?" he says. "You take after your dad. More muscle than anyone's willing to take on."

"That's about right," Robbie says.

"Too bad you have your mom's look," his dad says to Cameron. "I saw it the day you were born. Knew it would come to this. What you want to do," he suggests, "is take up some martial arts. Those guys are always small but they kick some mean ass."

"He needs more than that," his mom says. "Talk to him."

"You want me to hold his hand, Maureen? He doesn't want that. What Cameron wants is four inches and fifty pounds. That's the way a boy thinks. It's not going to happen, so I gave him the next best thing."

"Take a martial arts class," his mother repeats, her voice rising.

"Absolutely. They'll teach him ways of protecting himself you haven't even dreamed of. Ways that'll make the other boys turn tail."

Cameron likes the image his father created. He would like to see that, Rich Patterson running away with his tail between his legs.

"He has feelings about this, Max," his mother presses. "What about that?"

"He let them out last night, from what you told me. Over and done with."

His mother is beginning to realize what a wasted trip this is. A ring of white appears around her lips. Stress. This isn't turning out the way she planned. Her great white hope, dashed.

"You're not going to talk to him?" she says.

"I just did," his father says.

"And that's it?"

His mother stands up, pushes her purse under her arm, and tells Cameron and Robbie to get into the car.

"What the hell?" his father says.

"We're not going to eat?" Robbie asks.

"Not here."

"Damn it." His father stands up but blocks Robbie's exit. "I gave up a day's work and drove all the way down here to have lunch with my boys," he says. "We're having lunch."

Cameron's mom stands her ground. She turns her head slightly, keeping the boys' father in her sights, and says, "Get in the car, boys."

Robbie climbs over the table, shrugging off their father's hand, and gives Cameron a push. "Come on, let's go."

To their father, she says, "We didn't come for lunch, Max. We came for help."

"And I gave it."

Cameron's mom turns and herds him and Robbie toward the exit. Cameron hears his father swearing. Hears him shout, "It's never good enough, is it, Maureen?"

THURSDAY

5:30PM

Cameron is sitting on the deck, balancing the blade of his pocket-knife against his jean-covered thigh. He's not planning to hurt himself. He just likes holding the knife. He wants his palm to learn the feel of it, the same way blind people learn the feel of things.

He got the knife when he made Eagle Scout. He did that at fourteen, a month before his whole life went to hell. Most guys don't make Eagle until they're sixteen or seventeen. It was a big deal. His father didn't make it to the ceremony. His mom broke up with Randy the week before, but Cameron remembers taking the sash and the knife and looking out at all the parents and seeing Randy at the back of the room. Out of uniform, his arms crossed over his chest, the smile on his face looked about as comfortable as a sunburn. But he was there, and stayed until the ceremony ended, then left without saying anything to Cameron or his mother.

He's had the knife eight months. His mom had his name engraved on the steel blade and ever since it's been in his dresser drawer, inside a piece of bubble wrap.

He had forgotten he had it.

The blade is sharp enough to cut through the thick denim like it's air. It will slice easily though Patterson's skin, into his throat. Cameron won't have to hear the guy's smug laughter, his taunting voice anymore. That's why he's going for the throat. Patterson will die quietly. And Cameron can forget what he did to him in the locker room. Forget it all.

But even as a fantasy, Cameron is never able to watch Patterson's death through 'til the end. That's gotta change. He makes himself stand over Patterson until the guy's eyes roll back in his head, until his hands fall away from his throat and lay at his sides, his fingers curled into a wannabe fist.

"You're dead, Patterson. You're dead."

"You can't get him off your mind, huh?"

Cameron's body jerks until he nearly topples the chair. His pocketknife falls to the deck and scuttles a few feet.

"Sorry," Randy says. "I didn't mean to spook you."

Randy picks up the knife, pushes against the handle so that the blade snaps into its sheathing, then hands it to Cameron.

"I didn't hear you," Cameron says. His voice is thick with defense. "I wasn't spooked."

"Startled," Randy corrects. "Are you planning some revenge?"

Randy sits down in the chair next to Cameron's, stretches out his legs, and crosses them at the ankles.

"You want me to confess?" Cameron's fist closes over the knife; the sweat from his palm makes it slick.

"Before you even get a chance to knock the kid around a bit? No."

Cameron feels his heart slow. He strokes the smooth plastic handle of the knife with his thumb.

"He's bigger than me. Older. A junior."

"Yeah. That's usually the way it goes. The kid probably has about as much courage as a field mouse."

"I think I can get a piece of him. I just haven't tried yet."

"What are you waiting for?"

Cameron looks for sarcasm in Randy's face, but he's serious.

"You don't sound like a cop," Cameron says.

"I'm not trying to be a cop right now."

"You sound like my father."

"I'm not trying to be him, either. Your mom said he wasn't much help today."

"That surprised her?"

"Not really. She was hoping, though, that your dad would come through for you."

"He never has before."

Randy nods. "Not from what I've heard."

"Mom talks bad about him?"

"No. She doesn't talk about him at all. Good or bad. She does things, though, you know? And I can guess how she feels from watching her."

Cameron does know. As soon as they got home today his mother went through the house, opening windows, taking down curtains and tossing them in the washing machine. He hears the vacuum cleaner in the living room. Next she'll wipe down the bookcases and tables and the house will smell like a bushel of overripe lemons. Seeing his father has that effect on her — a need to clean.

"Yeah," Cameron says. "She won't be done 'til midnight."

Cameron turns, lets his gaze fall on Randy's profile. "Did she send you out here?"

"No. I came up with this idea all on my own. I figure you need someone to talk to even if you don't think so. You're at that age now where all hell breaks loose inside your body." He shakes his head. "I'd cut off a toe or two before I had to relive that."

"I'd give up an arm." If it would change things. If it would drastically improve his situation.

"Yeah, but later, when high school is just a memory, you'd want your arm back."

Cameron turns away, looks across the yard to the woods and follows the swooping ascent of a swallow with his eyes.

I don't think so. If losing my arm means Patterson never happened to me, no one calls me Cameron Diaz or fag or girly-boy, if I have friends again, losing an arm doesn't seem like much of a sacrifice.

"So if you're not talking to me as a cop or as my dad, what are you doing?"

"This is one man to another," Randy says. "A conversation on equal footing."

"Now you're trying to build me up."

"Because I called you a man?"

"I can't even drive yet."

"Experiences age a person, mature them faster sometimes than years," Randy says. "I think you already know that."

"Because my life sucks?"

"Does it all suck?"

"Pretty much."

"And you don't see how it's going to get any better. Not now."

"The whole school saw the photos," Cameron says.

"Probably," Randy agrees. "Next week they'll find something else to talk about."

"I doubt it."

Cameron flattens his hand against his thigh, the knife filling his palm perfectly. The curved handle against the meaty part of his hand feels right.

"It's hard at fourteen to pull yourself out of the moment, to see a few years, or even a few days down the road."

Cameron just wants to get through tomorrow.

"Life will get better," Randy says. "Sooner rather than later." He shifts, turns in his chair so that he's facing Cameron. "I've worked a lot of violent crimes. You're probably real familiar with the anger that follows an assault, but there's more than that. I think you should be ready for it."

"For what?"

"Delayed reaction. Victims of violent crime move through the aftermath in stages. You're going to be dealing with this for a while," he says. "It's part of moving on, getting past it."

"I'm only angry."

"Right now," Randy agrees.

"What else is there?"

"Fear."

Been there, done that.

"Anger and fear are a dangerous mix of emotions," Randy says. "Together they make a whole new person. Make a person do things they wouldn't normally do."

"Yeah? Like what?"

"Hurt someone. Hurt themselves."

Cameron feels like Randy is walking circles around him, that he knows something Cameron doesn't but needs to, and it's keeping him rooted. He thinks he should get up, walk into the house, into his bedroom and close the door. It's what he wants to do. Instead he says, "You think I would hurt someone?"

"I think you might," Randy agrees. "You might get yourself a whole lot of hurt, too. I don't want that to happen."

"Why?"

"The system is filled with lost boys."

"You're just doing your job."

"It's more than that. I have a special interest here." He places his elbows on his knees and leans forward. "You've already acted in fear and anger."

Cameron's hands loosen, fall completely without feeling against his thighs.

"How did you get that scab on your head?"

Cameron doesn't answer.

"It looks like a burn."

"It's not."

"You hear about the fire?"

"It was on the news," Cameron admits. "I saw some of it last night."

"Did you go anywhere near there yesterday? After you left school?"

"I went through the woods," Cameron says. "I go there a lot."

Randy nods. "Good answer. Someone reported a kid matching your description cut into the woods shortly before it went up."

148

"And you think I did it?"

"There weren't a whole lot of kids out of school yesterday. Sometimes anger can get the better of a person, can cause a whole lot of things to happen a person never intended."

"I think I'll remain silent," Cameron says.

"You'll need to do better than that," Randy advises. "The fire department found your school ID card not far from that burnt-out car. I'm just wondering, if you did do it, was it a reaction to what happened to you in the locker room? Is it going to happen again? I've been thinking a lot about it. Some firebugs, they get into it because it gives them a rush. It becomes an addiction. Others, especially kids acting out of anger, feeling helpless, find it by accident. It scares the hell out of them. They'll never touch it again."

Randy waits for him to work it out in his mind, to decide where he stands. An addict or an accident?

"You think if I did do it, I'm done with it now? I scared the hell out of myself and will never touch it again?"

It wasn't scary, not like Randy means. It was so much bigger than him and impossible to control. But he beat it. Something that big and wild and he beat it. That's power; it just about makes him a superhero. He knows it, wants it, won't give it up.

It's in his blood and he supposes that does make him an addict.

"That's where my money is. My job, too."

Randy's voice is so full of confidence that Cameron feels his guts twist. He doesn't want Randy's trust. He doesn't need the extra weight, another face in his head popping up and trying to turn him into Dudley Do-Right.

"Maybe you should arrest me," Cameron suggests.

Randy taps the arm of Cameron's chair to get his attention and then looks into his eyes almost like he's trying to drill for understanding.

"You don't want to be in prison, Cameron. What's been happening to you at school pales in comparison."

Cameron nods. He doesn't think prison could be worse, but it's probably more of the same. And Randy is right, Cameron doesn't want that.

"I'm trying to help you," Randy says. "You're still a kid. You'll get past what happened this week. One traumatic event doesn't have to make a kid a criminal."

Randy sits back in his chair, turns and stares into Cameron's face.

"I've read studies, real case reports that describe fire as a reaction to trauma and in every single one the flames seem to flow from the hand without conscious thought. Most of the respondents couldn't remember holding a lighter or a match. They couldn't remember how the fire started, only that it was." He turns to Cameron. "I'm going with that. For now."

Cameron likes the image Randy created, of fire shooting from his fingertips. That's exactly what it felt like, fire instead of blood in his veins.

"Don't talk to anybody about the fire," Randy says.

Cameron nods.

"Not your friends. Not your mom. Not the police."

"Okay."

"The police are going to come. I told them you're not talking unless I'm in the room."

He stands up, his gun belt creaking, and looks down at Cameron.

"You tell them what you told me. You were in the woods yesterday. You go there a lot. And that your ID card has been missing for days.

"They'll ask you why you go to the woods. Do you have an answer for that?"

"It's quiet there. I can think. Sometimes I hike the trails all the way to the lake."

"You go there to hike," Randy says. "And, Cameron, if you have a problem with them searching your room, your clothes, you go take care of that now."

Cameron doesn't jump to his feet, doesn't want to give himself away. He rolls the pocket knife under his palm, drying the sweat against his jeans, and holds Randy's gaze a few seconds longer.

"Listen to me, Cameron, sometimes we do things we never intended to do. Your whole life doesn't have to be defined by one mistake."

THURSDAY

8:00PM

The police didn't come.

Randy sat in a chair in the living room, first reading the newspaper and then a magazine on fly fishing, until after ten o'clock. Cameron sat at the kitchen table with his Spanish book and his mother and guessed the best he could at what might have been assigned. They completed a lesson on traveling from Barcelona to Madrid, using phrases that connected them with food, a bathroom, and a place to stay that wasn't too expensive. Robbie watched TV in their bedroom, canned laughter seeping through the floor.

Randy appears in the doorway. "They're not coming. Not tonight."

Cameron feels his mom grow tight, like every muscle went on instant standby. She places the English/Spanish dictionary on the table with too much care and then sits back in her chair.

"Maybe," she says, her voice at about thirty degrees below zero, "they found the person who really set that fire. They're busy arresting the *criminal*."

She accused Randy of being cynical. Of taking his work home.

✳

"Cameron did NOT set that fire. Have you ever seen him with matches? Does he seem like the type of kid who'd go out and deliberately destroy property?"

"No. But he went through a traumatic event yesterday —"

"He didn't set that fire, Randy. My son did NOT set that fire."

"The detectives are coming," Randy warned.

"Why?" his mom demanded. "Why do they think it's Cameron?"

Randy told her about the witness, about Cameron's ID card. He told her, when looked at from a police perspective, setting the fire was a natural reaction to what happened to Cameron in the locker room. "Victims of violent crime, of sexual assault, a lot of times they explode or implode."

"Sexual assault? No way! That didn't happen," Cameron

protested. He jumped up from his chair. His pulse slammed in his wrists, in his temples. "They didn't do that."

Randy turned to him. "We're treating it as a sexual assault, Cameron. They held you against your will, exposed you, and took pictures they later put on the Internet."

As if that settled it. As if that was all that mattered. Everyone knows sexual assault means rape. Everyone will know, will think that's what Patterson did to him.

"But they didn't *touch* me." Cameron heard his voice rising, turning sharp. "It was nothing like that."

"When are the police going to talk to Cameron about that?" his mom wanted to know. "*That* was a crime."

"We know that, and Cameron will give his statement, but the situation is contained. The boys were arrested."

"Are they still in jail?" Doubt dripped from his mother's voice. "They aren't, are they?"

"They were released to their parents this morning," Randy admitted. "Neither one has a history of trouble with police, or at school —"

"Neither does Cameron. But the police are still coming. Not because my son was hurt, but because they think *he* committed a crime."

"It wasn't sexual assault," Cameron tried to interrupt them. He wanted to scream but his heart wasn't cooperating. It kicked into slow and he couldn't get his breath to do more than whisper.

"The fire is an open case and the evidence leads to Cameron." Randy pushed his hands through his hair and looked down at both of them. "You need to know that. You both need to know that. This isn't about guilt. Right now, right here, our concern is damage control. The fire torched a lot of land, damaged public access, and came within three hundred yards of a domestic residence. The case will stay open until someone is arrested."

"Stop. Stop. Stop." Cameron raised his hands to his face, felt the tears, hot and sticky and *girly*, and curled his fingers, dug them into the skin around his eyes. "It wasn't sexual assault. They didn't do that. They didn't."

He felt his mother's small hands on his arms, pulling. Heard her call Randy's name and then Randy came at him from behind, pried loose Cameron's hands, and held them to his chest. He couldn't move. It was as good as wearing a straitjacket.

"They didn't rape me," Cameron sobs.

"We know that, Cameron," Randy said. "Assault isn't always rape."

"That's a lie. Everyone at school knows it's rape." He opened his eyes. His mom was standing in front of him, crying, her nose running. She knew. He could see it in her eyes. She knew exactly what it would mean to him if the police called it a sex crime. "Mom. Mom, don't let him do this. This can't be me. I want to die."

"Randy?"

He felt Randy's shoulders lift. "It's real clear. The attack meets the criteria for sexual assault."

"No! Make it go away, Mom. Please."

"Can we do that?" she asked Randy. "How can we do that?"

"You can drop the charges," Randy said. "But I don't think that's the way to go."

They argued about it, Randy insisting that Cameron needed to know that Patterson and his stooge were prosecuted. That what happened to Cameron was wrong and society said so, too.

"I can't be the boy who was raped."

His mom agreed with him. She promised she'd talk to the D.A.

"He can decide to prosecute without your cooperation," Randy said.

"But that's not likely," his mom pressed. "Is it?"

"You might get him to lessen the charges. Make it aggravated assault," Randy agreed.

✳

"He didn't do it, Randy," his mom continues, pulling Cameron from his memories. "I want you to believe that. I want to hear you say it."

Randy looks at her a long time, then lets his eyes connect with Cameron's.

"If the detectives come by in the morning, call me," he says. "Don't talk to them without me."

He didn't say so, but Cameron can tell Randy isn't relying on his mother for help. It's up to Cameron to save himself.

"I remember."

"I'm going home."

He leaves through the kitchen door. Cameron listens to his boots on the wood deck, in the gravel driveway, the slam of his car door and then the metallic scratch as the engine turns over. He turns to his mother. He feels a slow burn where his heart should be.

"He never said I did it," he tells her. "He never came right out and said I did it."

"But he thinks it," she insists.

"He's a cop and all the evidence points to me," Cameron says. He wants his mother to admit it, that her son is possibly a criminal. He wants to see what she'll do with it.

"He shouldn't think it," she says. "He knows you. He knows *me*."

"He doesn't know me that well."

"Apparently not."

Silence gathers.

"You won't ask me if I did it," he says. "If I started the fire. Why won't you ask me?"

"I don't need to. You're my son. *I* know you."

Cameron lets his face flood with the certainty of his crime. He wants to be as transparent as a ghost. He wants her to doubt him.

157

He wants her to know. His mother is great at escaping the truth and for once he wants her to face it.

She turns away.

"Ask me, Mom."

"No."

"I want you to."

She looks up from the counter she's wiping down. She's tired. Her skin always gets a shade lighter, her eyes darker, when she's worn out.

"Don't do this, Cameron," she says.

"What? Make you face the truth about me? Is that what you don't want?" he demands. "Could you still love me, Mom?"

"I love you," she says.

"Ask me."

"Okay. Did you? Did you start that fire?"

Her hand, still wrapped in the dish towel, trembles.

She already believes it. Part of her, anyway. Most of her refuses to let it be the truth. She's lived her life that way for as long as he can remember. She knew their father was a bully, a creep, but refused to let that be their reality until it was almost too late. Same thing with Patterson. She had to know that talking to the counselor at school wouldn't be enough. She had to know that the blood on his shirt the next day was from his nose. She knew that it wasn't over. And now it's too late.

"I'm taking the Fifth," Cameron says.

He leaves her standing at the counter. On his way out of the kitchen he flips the light switch. His last look at her shows half of her aglow from the range light, the other half in darkness, and he thinks that's about right. That's his mom.

FRIDAY

8:35AM

Cameron's mom insists on parking the minivan in the school lot and walking him into the principal's office.

"No way!" Cameron protests. "I'm not walking into school with my mommy."

"Then walk ahead of me," she offers. "I'm talking to Mr. Vega first thing. And I'm not letting you out of my sight until I hear what I need to hear."

"What's that?" Cameron asks, keeping a space of three feet between them, looking around him at the groups of kids. No one seems to notice him. Yet.

"That those boys aren't in school today. I won't be happy until I hear that they're never returning."

"They have to go to school, Mom. It's the law."

"But they don't have to go to *this* school," she says.

The halls are musty and damp. Too many bodies, too little air. Cameron increases his pace, wants to shake his mom loose, wants to go looking for Patterson, find him before the asshole finds Cameron. His blood throbs through his veins. He flexes his fingers. He's primed. He's ready. He'll take Patterson so fast the guy won't have a chance. He presses his hand against the outside of his pocket, traces the shape of the pocketknife, and feels his breath change. It becomes as fast and shallow as when he's running.

"Wait up."

His mother's heels click against the linoleum as she rushes to catch up. They're not even close to the office when he sees Vega's dark head turn toward them. Recognition plays with his face, makes it look happy to see them and sorry for it at the same time.

Vega extends his hand to Cameron's mother, but she ignores it.

"I'm dropping Cameron off for school," she tells the principal. "Those boys aren't here?"

"No. We've given them a formal suspension of five days. Like

I told you, there'll be a hearing. That'll help us determine the next step."

His mother nods.

Five days. That means Patterson and Murphy won't be back until Wednesday. Cameron will have to wait. He doesn't like that. His veins are swollen with anger.

"I'm holding you personally responsible for my son's safety," his mom tells the principal.

"You have my guarantee," Vega promises and places a cool hand on Cameron's shoulder. "I'm real sorry about what happened here Wednesday," he says to Cameron. "We're taking care of that. All you need to do is think about academics. And maybe you'd like to talk to Mr. Elwood?"

"No," Cameron says. "I'm okay."

"Well, I'll go now," his mom says.

She doesn't move, though, and stares at Cameron a long time. He starts to worry she's going to do something he'll regret. Like cry. Or try to kiss him goodbye. He takes a step back and she raises her hand in a small wave.

"Goodbye," she says.

"He'll be fine, Mrs. Grady," the principal says. "I'll make sure of it."

Cameron turns his back and moves into the crowd of kids, feeling like an ant in an ant farm. The halls aren't big enough and there are too many kids. He feels hot. Feels nerves pull tight inside him so that he's walking on his toes, though he tries not to. He lets himself be pulled upstream until he reaches his history class.

Even Hart is nice to him. Cameron doesn't like it. He doesn't like the way the other kids look at him, either. He stares at the whiteboard where Hart is writing dates and events, but feels the burn of eyes resting on his skin, wants so badly to turn and flip everyone off. Thinks Eddie would do it, no problem.

Cameron shifts in his seat, just enough so he can see Eddie Fain at his desk. The kid is drawing on his arm. That's one of Eddie's great talents. If he could get his mind straightened out, art school would be a slam dunk.

Hart walks away from the whiteboard with the suggestion that they use every available minute if they don't want the assignment to become homework.

Cameron opens his textbook. He scans the board for a page number, finds it, and paws through early American government until he arrives at a two-page spread of the justice system. Who does what, checks and balances . . . and then he loses focus. Feels the stares again, like his skin is about to blister, but when he finally gives in to the need and turns, he finds that most of the heads are down, looking at their books, or looking at the board.

He feels the seat next to him fill up. It's Eddie. He has a smile on his face that looks like pure vengeance. He rolls his arm over so Cameron can see the drawing. Patterson's face, two-dimensional and so lifelike it's frightening. Inserted in his mouth is a phallus, unmistakable, and when Eddie flexes his arm, Patterson's mouth moves so that it looks like he's sucking dick.

Cameron laughs aloud. It's so funny. So perfect.

"I'm making flyers, too," he says. "Going to paper the school with them."

"Mr. Fain, this isn't a group assignment," Mr. Hart says.

Eddie returns to his seat. He doesn't open his book and spends the rest of class either playing with his live art or staring out the window.

When the bell rings Cameron's paper is blank and Hart is standing over him.

"Why don't you hold onto that," Hart suggests and hands him a piece of lined paper with something written on it. "I saw you were having trouble concentrating," he says, "so I copied the terms from the board for you. Maybe you can work on that at home and turn it in on Monday?"

Cameron accepts the paper, slips it into his notebook.

"I've forgiven the quiz from yesterday," Hart continues. "No need for you to make that up."

Hart's voice has the irritating effect of making Cameron feel like his skin is splitting open. Cameron tunes him out, rises from his desk, and walks through the door, sure Hart is still talking.

English is a total bust. Cowan heard about the photos and moved Cameron's seat. First row, first desk. He's right next to the door and spends the entire hour watching the hall. He doesn't even pretend to read and she doesn't push him. They're twenty minutes into class when she asks him to step out of the room with her. He doesn't budge.

"Do you want to see the nurse?" she offers.

"I'm not sick," he points out.

"No, you're not." She lifts her hands, tucks them behind her. "Well, if you need anything . . ."

When the bell rings, Cameron is the first person out of the room. The halls are congested. He pushes through the kids; some move aside.

The locker room is full of guys, pulling shirts over their heads, tying shoelaces. Cameron doesn't remember ever entering early enough to walk into a flurry of elbows.

"Grady!" The coach's voice booms out across the rows of lockers.

Cameron feels his spine straighten so much it nearly cracks. He stops for a moment, like he grew roots, then pushes himself forward. Finds his locker. Spins the dial on his combination lock.

"Hey, Grady." The coach is standing beside him. "My office."

"No, thanks," Cameron says. Spins to the next number. The lock feels heavy in his hand. Cool. A dead weight that could do some damage. Why didn't he think to grab it when Patterson was all over him?

"It's not an invitation," the coach says.

Cameron spins to the final number and pulls on the lock. Nothing.

"Listen, Cameron," the coach starts and Cameron feels his skin pucker. He hates the way the teachers are his friends now. Hates that it makes him feel like a sorrier piece of shit than he was on Tuesday. "I moved your locker."

Cameron finally turns, looks the coach in the eye.

"Why?" he demands.

"You want to talk about it in my office?"

"No. I want to talk about it right here."

The coach nods. He looks over Cameron's head. "You boys clear out."

Cameron doesn't turn around. He hears locker doors slam shut, scrambling feet. Feels the warmth of too-close bodies give way to a cool absence.

The coach looks right at Cameron and says, "Scene of the crime. I thought you wouldn't want to come back here."

"Well, I do."

"My mistake." The coach lifts his arms until his hands are on his hips, looks at Cameron a bit longer.

"Forget it," Cameron says. "You can't win this one. I've had a lot of practice." His father was king of the one-minute meltdown. Cameron had learned from the best.

He puts his hands on his hips and pushes his chin forward and up.

"I'm not trying to win anything, Cameron." The coach steps back. "People been staring at you all morning?"

"Mostly teachers."

"Yeah, well, we're sorry about what happened. I'm real sorry. It happened right here under my nose. I feel a lot of responsibility for that."

Cameron shifts his shoulders, tries to loosen the tension. "Where are my clothes?"

"I put them in locker seventy. Two rows over." He checks his watch. "Join us when you're ready."

Cameron finds the locker, pops the combo, and holds the lock in his hand. Titanium. They put that in the knees of professional football players. It's that strong. That indestructible.

He sits down on the bench, curls his fingers over the lock, wishes he had knocked Patterson's head in with it. Feels the anger of missed opportunity slam in his veins so that his blood actually hurts with the knowledge that he had his chance and blew it.

He reaches for his gym uniform, sees again the dark spot growing across Patterson's back. He's dreaming it was a bullet that put it there when he looks over toward the showers. A movement. Darkness. A dark head. He's back in the moment again, Pervert Pinon peering over the half wall, watching him. He thinks he could crush the kid's head between his hands. Thinks he could flatten his head, until everything Pinon is comes oozing out. Cameron's guts twist painfully. Not because the image of a dead Pinon scares him, but because he feels it like a first breath. New life. His life.

He doesn't know his fists are curled until the lock is cutting into his skin. Doesn't know he's moving, flying toward the showers until he's there. Pinon's crouched behind the wall, looking up at him. Cameron doesn't even know it's real, not a dream, until his hand is around the kid's throat. Until his hand with the lock comes down on Pinon's skull. The harsh *swack* vibrates up his arm, almost knocks the lock from his hand.

He lifts his arm again, brings it down with the same crushing force.

Blood. Everywhere. He looks at his hands, dripping onto the white tile floor, the lock clenched so tightly he has to pry his fingers loose. He looks down at Pinon, blood pouring through the cuts in his head. He's dead. Cameron stands over him, looking for his chest to lift. It doesn't. He's not breathing. He's dead.

Dead.

Cameron's body jerks; he drops the lock. He moves toward the lockers, stops when he sees he's leaving footprints, bloody footprints. He needs a shower. He stands fully clothed under a spray of water and watches the pink runoff whirl down the drain. He looks over at Pinon's crumpled body.

He was a pervert. Cameron's heart dips, then jumps into his throat, threatening to strangle him. *He was a pervert.* He was. He stands under the shower, crying and telling himself it's the same thing as with the fire. Nerves.

He doesn't look at Pinon again. He strips off his clothes and bundles them in his arms. At his locker, he pushes his clothes into his gym bag, dries his body and hair with a towel, then changes into his PE clothes. From upstairs comes the muffled sound of basketballs hitting the wood floor.

He's late. Really late.

He ties his sneakers. Shuts his locker and slides the combo through it. He climbs the stairs to the gym and stands on the sideline, hands dangling at his sides, watching a game in progress.

"Grady!"

Cameron turns toward the coach's voice.

"You're over here."

Cameron's legs are heavy and it's an effort to shuffle along the sideline to where the coach is pointing. He pulls a blue jersey over his head, and takes position. He sucks at basketball. He probably won't get much play. The kids never throw him the ball.

FRIDAY

10:35AM

Cameron is the first one in the locker room. PE was a blur. He can't remember any of it. He opens his locker but doesn't change his clothes. He grabs his gym bag and heads back up to the courts, where the coach is collecting balls, pushing them into a mesh bag.

"I'm going home," Cameron says and walks past him.

"Hey, hold on, Grady." The coach jogs to catch up. "You want to talk?"

"No."

"You at least want to change your clothes?"

"No. I'm going to run the lake path. It's good for me."

"It is," the coach agrees. "But I can't just let you leave school in the middle of the day."

"You're not letting me," Cameron says.

The locker room door bursts open and several guys spill out, tripping over each other. Both Cameron and the coach watch them, their white faces, their mouths opening, stretching. Cameron can't hear them, with the blood rushing through his head again, sounding like the pounding surf, but the coach does and takes off.

Cameron pushes through the double doors and into the hall. It's empty. The closest door to the outside is fifty feet to the left. Cameron slips through it.

He keeps to the sidewalk, looking straight ahead, not turning even when he hears a horn blast, a guy yell out his store window, "You should be in school."

When he gets to the lake path he pushes his arms through the gym bag, wearing it like a backpack, and starts to run. It's seven miles to home. It's not raining, but the air is damp and sticks to him. He pushes his body through the motions until it remembers on its own exactly what it should be doing.

I killed someone today. The thought curls around his brain, picks at it like a piece of flint. His head hurts. Hurts worse than it ever did.

I killed someone. But it was only Pinon. The kid was a pervert.

He shouldn't have watched.

Cameron feels his life spin away from him, looks up at the sky and sees himself cartwheeling toward the clouds.

I took control. Today is the beginning.

The thought bounces off his brain, slips through his fingers. He doesn't feel in control. Control means calm. It means he's ahead of the pack, he determines the course of his life.

He thinks of Pinon, folded up like an accordion on the shower floor, washed in his own blood, and feels like heaving.

He shouldn't have watched, like I was a freak show. A porno freak show.

Cameron holds on to that. It makes the world stop spinning. When he remembers the Pinon who peered over the shower wall, watching him, he remembers there was no other way. He did the only thing he could do.

PART II

1:00PM

Cameron stands in Mrs. Murdock's backyard, shovel in hand. He wants to finish the job he started here, at least get her garden ready for seed, but he loses focus. He's been working on the same patch of dirt since he arrived, twenty minutes ago. It's like he falls asleep standing and startles awake to find himself here, covered with mud instead of blood, living a nightmare.

I killed a boy. Pinon.

He's not breathing normally anymore. He can't breathe at all.

It feels like a giant fist tore through his chest and pulled out his lungs.

Why did Pinon have to be so annoying? Why did he have to be there? There to witness my shame. There all the time, snapping at my heels. There when the anger boiled out of me.

He wants to forget Pinon; he knows he never will. He'll always see the guy, rolled up like a pill bug, his blood mixing with water and washing pink down the drain.

Cameron pulls air through his nose, hears the wet mucus, knows he's crying. Like a damn baby.

He can't take back what he did.

He can't even say he's sorry about it. There's no one to listen.

Cameron feels his body shake. Not just his hands or his legs, but his whole body shakes so hard he drops the shovel and when he bends over to get it, he sinks to his knees.

I killed a boy. A kid like myself. How could something be that wrong with me?

"Cameron?"

Cameron hears her wobbly voice. It's louder, stronger than usual. Mrs. Murdock must have been calling him for a while. When he looks up, she's standing in the grass, leaning on her cane, her head bouncing like a bobble toy.

"Are you alright?"

Cameron wipes his face with his arm.

"No," he says. "There's nothing right with me."

Her eyes flare and he can tell he startled her. He usually doesn't talk about himself. He watches her gnarled hand twist in the pocket of her apron.

"Don't be so hard on yourself," she says. "Sometimes the world gets ahold of us, doesn't it?"

"I think I'm going crazy," he admits.

"I don't think so. You're a good boy. I see that in you."

"I don't feel good." He hasn't felt good in a long, long time. "I did something. I want to take it back, but I can't."

"Sounds like a situation where you have to learn from your mistake," she suggested. "Life is full of moments like that."

Cameron feels like he exploded in the locker room, and it wasn't just anger that erupted from him, but the good parts, too. The parts of him he liked and he can't even remember what they were. He only knows that he'll never be that boy again.

"It was a big mistake."

"Then there's a lot to learn."

He doesn't like thinking about what he's lost. It makes him sad, and then angry. Like the two emotions can't exist separate from each other.

He doesn't want to think about what comes next.

"I won't be able to finish." He nods at the solid ground, where she wants to plant zucchini and tomatoes. "I want to."

She nods.

Cameron picks up the shovel and heads to the hose. It doesn't feel the same anymore, all the things he used to do. Rinsing the shovel, hanging it in the garage, climbing on his bike, pedaling into the wind, none of it. He isn't Cameron Grady anymore. He hasn't been for a long time.

FRIDAY

5:30PM

Cameron sits at the table, folding paper towels into napkins.

"Make a few extra," his mom says.

She came home from work with an already-cooked chicken, poured wild rice into a pot she filled with water and set on the stove, then started a slaw salad. Cameron was at the kitchen table then, with Robbie, working out a math problem the long way so his brother could see every step. It was slow, but he didn't feel the plucking at his skin to move, go faster, run, outrun the fear. He didn't have that anymore. The boil in his blood, the bubbles rising to the surface and popping against his skin, were gone. The weight on his chest, that made every breath an effort, evaporated.

He looked up. His mom stood in the door and smiled at them. She had a grocery bag in each arm.

✳

"What?" Cameron wanted to know.

"Nothing," she said. "I just like what I see."

"Great," Cameron said, but it felt right. Robbie never did well with numbers and before this year, before Cameron's life became a heap of twisted metal, he had helped Robbie after school. They sat at the kitchen table just like this and Cameron set up problems and Robbie solved them.

Cut and paste. The thought stuck in his mind. It was possible to go back, to edit out what didn't work and then stitch together the two sides. He was proof of that. This moment was proof. He was back to being Cameron Grady. He fit.

"He's a genius, Mom," Robbie said. "I'm really starting to get it."

She walked around with that smile on her face another fifteen minutes.

Robbie got up, closed his book, and went to organize his stuff for Monday. Cameron used to do that, too, get ready for school ahead of time.

"How was school today?" His mother's voice breaks through his thoughts.

"I have history homework," Cameron says. Mrs. Cowan gave an assignment in English, but Cameron can't remember what it is. That was before, when his world was still cloudy, when he was hearing from a distance and even that was scrambled. "I need to read some of my English book, too."

She nods. "Good. We'll start right after dinner. How about Spanish?"

He knew it would come to this and he decided he would tell the truth. Or some of it, anyway.

"I ditched," he confesses. "I left after PE and went running."

He needed to clear his head. Needed to ditch the gym bag and his clothes that were covered with Pinon's blood. That part wasn't easy. He dove into the woods, crashing through the branches of trees grown too close together, and then dug a hole in the packed earth with his hands. He marked the tree, because he knew he'd have to go back.

He watches his mother's back grow stiff and she takes her time placing the big stirring spoon on the counter. When she turns to him he can see she's ready to back him. Her face is soft and open. Willing to believe in him.

"Has school been bad all year?" she asks.

"Pretty much," Cameron admits.

Her lips fall into a flat line somewhere between anger and sadness. "I'm sorry, Cameron. I should have done something."

Too little, too late. But he gives her points for finally arriving.

"What, Mom?" he asks. "Guys like Patterson run the school."

"It's not supposed to be that way," she says.

"It's reality," Cameron says, then he shrugs. "Maybe it'll get better. At least until Wednesday."

"Those boys aren't going back to Madison."

They'll be back, Mom, he thinks. That's the way the world works. He went back. SciFi will be back. Patch them up and put them back on the lines. Patterson and Murphy will spend a few days planning the next attack, and how not to get caught this time. But they'll be back and they'll be ready to fight.

He looks up from the paper triangle in his hands, lets his eyes touch hers briefly, then skitter away.

The silence snaps in his ears like fire.

Funny, that he doesn't feel that pull anymore. It was with him all the time, the sulphur smell in his nose, the burn on his fingertips. But he hasn't thought about fire since this morning.

"It'll get easier," she says. "The first day back was probably the hardest."

"It started off bad," Cameron agrees. "I feel okay now."

"Monday you'll stay the whole day?" she asks.

"I think so." No promises. He doesn't know what will happen.

He might need to leave to clear his head.

To find a foxhole.

He figures the only way to stay alive now is to take the offensive. In this case, he knows there are plenty of Red Coats left and one might decide to take over where Patterson left off. He'll be prepared for that.

"Call me if you feel like leaving, okay? I'll come pick you up."

He shrugs. If he leaves he'll go running. By the time he got home earlier he had everything settled inside. His stomach had stopped heaving, his eyes had stopped tearing, and he had known life was all about the survival of the fittest.

He wanted to kill Pinon. He wanted to live. Black and white. Gray is for the people who stand outside Wal-Mart holding up pictures of deformed lab animals and asking for signatures. Black and white. Life or death. Choose.

"You want to get your brother? I'll put dinner on the table."

FRIDAY

10:45PM

Cameron is in his bedroom, splayed across his bed, when he begins to feel the silence in the house. It touches his skin like snow flurries. At first, his body heat zaps them, until there are too many, until a storm hits and he's sure he's living inside a snow globe that someone's shaking. The layers build against his skin, pinning him to the bed. He feels the cold so deeply that his body slows down. Less oxygen in his blood, less blood pumped through the heart. Hypothermia. Embalming fluid. *So this is dead.* Cameron feels nothing. Like lying in a coffin.

Robbie walks in, closes the door, and stares at him.

"You all right?" he asks.

He's asked that a lot since Wednesday. His big little brother really cares about him.

Cameron finds this so funny his mouth opens: thunder. Not really laughter, but a dense sound, with blunt edges that knock into each other, erupts like a twister rising from his throat.

It scares him; his heart kicks against his ribs looking for a way out.

It scares Robbie. His brother's voice rises above the sound he's making. "Cameron?" He turns back to the door, opens it so that it bounces against the wall, and yells for their mother.

There's nothing she can do, Cameron thinks. *Don't you know, Robbie? Nothing. Nothing. Nothing.*

She runs into the room, her black hair airborne, and stops inside the door.

Cameron's still laughing. His body moves like something is coming out of his mouth, but he doesn't hear it, unless that's him. That sharp, shearing noise that could be scissors or hedge clippers, but not human.

"What is it?"

She sits on the edge of his bed, places a hand on his shoulder. "Cameron?"

She shakes him, like that'll get him to talk.

I've had worse, Mom, and still kept my mouth shut.

"Cameron? What's wrong, honey?"

He feels her hands on his face, rolling his head to the side so that he has to look at her. Dead man's stare.

"Stop this right now," she says. "Stop it."

He can hear the panic in her voice, feel it tremble in her hands.

"This is about those boys," she says. "Sometimes our reactions are delayed. Sometimes it takes a while to catch up with us."

He believes that. He's a killer. It's just catching up with him now.

"Remember what Randy said yesterday?" she prompts. "Delayed reaction."

She runs her hands down his arms. "You're shivering. Robbie, get that blanket."

Cameron feels the wool descend on him, scratch his skin.

"You're better than those boys. . . . They're cowards. . . . They pick on people because they don't feel good about themselves. . . . You're better than that, Cameron. . . . You're going to be okay. . . ."

No, he's not. He's not better than them. But he wants to be. He wants to believe her and he falls asleep listening to her talk, her voice drifting in and out of his brain like the melody of a song.

SATURDAY

8:30AM

Cameron and Robbie are clearing the breakfast dishes from the table and stacking them next to the sink when the radio switches from an Alan Jackson song to the news. Charlie Pinon is the headline, though they don't say his name.

MORE SCHOOL VIOLENCE IN THE NEWS TODAY AND, LADIES AND GENTLE-MEN, THIS ONE HITS HOME. THE BODY OF A YOUNG MAN WAS FOUND BEATEN TO DEATH IN THE BOYS' LOCKER ROOM AT MADISON HIGH YES-TERDAY AFTERNOON . . .

Cameron stops in the middle of the kitchen, orange juice glasses clutched in each hand. If he looks down he's sure he'll see his heart beating through his T-shirt. It's knocking as loudly as someone at the door and he wonders if Robbie or his mom can hear it. He looks at them, caught by the announcement coming from the portable radio.

"Geez," Robbie breathes.

"Quiet." His mother's voice is tight, her hand twisted at her throat. "Quiet," she breathes.

POLICE SPOKESMAN MARTIN HOWER SAYS THE DEATH IS CERTAINLY CRIMINAL IN NATURE. QUOTE, "IT'S CLEAR THE BOY WAS MURDERED." ANOTHER SCHOOL MURDER, THIS TIME HERE IN ERIE. HOPED WE'D NEVER SEE THIS DAY . . .

The DJ can't stop talking about Pinon. His voice is low, and a couple of times he has to stop and clear his throat, like he knew the kid personally and the loss is too much for him.

THE POLICE ARE STILL ON SCENE, PROCESSING EVERY PIECE OF EVIDENCE THEY CAN GET THEIR HANDS ON. . . . THEY'RE ASKING THAT PARENTS HAVE THEIR KIDS VOLUNTARILY GIVE THEIR FINGERPRINTS. . . .

Cameron tunes out the broadcast, moves himself to a point where he's watching rather than living the moment. He's finally gotten a handle on that, too. Used to be his mind did that all on its own; now Cameron can lift himself outside his body, floating around, touching the walls, nothing touching him. *Nothing.* Not Patterson. Not Pinon and his bulging eyes, watching. Not Randy and his *knowing* so much about him.

"What was his name?"

His mom snags his attention. Somehow she snuck up on him, is standing nose to nose with him, pulling him back to life.

"What?"

"What was the boy's name?"

Cameron shakes his head.

"They didn't say."

Robbie's voice is thin and when Cameron looks at him he notices his chest rising and falling, fast. Too fast. His brother is scared.

"Cameron?"

His mother's voice presses against him, the sharp edge peeling through the layers of memory.

"Did you know about any of this?"

"Know about it?"

"You left school yesterday," his mom says, rubbing a hand against her chest like she's trying to ease a tightness there. "That was good. That school's not safe."

"The locker room isn't, anyway," Robbie says. "Did you see anything happen?"

"No."

"Why did you leave?" Robbie asks.

"I went running." Cameron hears his voice rise a notch and turn hard. "What are you, junior cop?"

"You left school to go running?"

"That's right. What's your problem with that?"

"Nothing."

"If I'm going to the Olympics, I have to train." *Remember.* "I'm a man with a mission," he quotes Robbie from dinner.

Cameron leaves the room. He pushes through the kitchen door and takes the steps down from the deck two at a time. He hits the gravel driveway with both feet. He needs to run. His heart is already stampeding in his chest. He sprints across the yard, into the trees, pushing through leafy branches and scrub oak. He doesn't stop until the air turns heavy, smelling of the closeness of the lake and of something else. Ash.

He draws in a breath and the air tunnels through his nose, dries his throat. There's still ash in the air, kicked up by the wind. Cameron slows to a walk. Though he is still surrounded by trees, they feel thinner, the air around him paler and growing white.

Cameron's eyes fall on landmarks, clusters of wild cabbage that release a stink like that of a spraying skunk, a Japanese maple tree with a knot the size of a fist at eye level, an abandoned possum den. Then the woods stop abruptly. Cameron looks down at his feet, rubs the toe of his sneaker through soot two inches deep. The dirt beneath it is black. He digs through it with his shoe, piercing the top layer, looking for clay-colored earth. His ears begin to ring; his center of gravity tilts. He throws his arms out to regain his balance. His whole body feels like the chord of a guitar, plucked and vibrating but making no sound.

The silence. No birds. No rustling in the bushes. No life.

He looks around him, walking slowly, turning 360 degrees. The trees still standing in a ring around what could have been a gigantic campfire are all black. Patches of missing bark make them look like they caught a skin disease. Some trees still standing are naked. No leaves. Their scraggly arms stretch above Cameron's head. The wind makes the limbs creak and close by a branch breaks loose with a crack like lightning and plummets to the forest floor.

Cameron's lungs expel a final breath and stop.

He's standing still, but the world around him is moving. The empty treetops, the sky where there should be oak and maple, spinning over his head. His stomach heaves. He closes his eyes, pushes the heels of his hands into them, hoping to stop the dizzy collapse of the world around him.

It doesn't work. He's falling. The ground shifts under his feet and he throws his hands out again, grasping air.

It's the end of the world.

Cameron's body slams against something solid. His ribs ache. His lungs burn. The tips of his fingers press against the scabs on his forehead and he digs in with his nails. Not pain, but feeling. He's alive. He opens his eyes enough that he can see a blank sky.

A steady sky. He lets his hands fall to his sides and his eyes roll around in his head, touching again on the bony claws of leftover trees. Not moving. As still as time.

The ringing in his ears fades to static. He hears the whistle of air in his throat; the fire in his chest cools. He pushes himself up to his knees and looks again at the empty sky, the charred stumps of trees poking out of the earth like talons. Then he wipes at the ash on his clothes, but all that does is smear it into the fabric. He gets to his feet, shoves his hands into his pockets, and doesn't look up.

Don't look at what isn't there.

He walks until he reaches the epicenter. The old LeBaron burnt down to a black skeleton of few bones — even some of the metal is missing. No tires, the car sunk into the ground, the doors gone.

"Hey, kid!"

Cameron's head jerks back. A man in a blue uniform, with a clipboard of papers that flutter in the wind, is walking toward him. Patches are sewn onto his sleeves, a badge is pinned above the pocket on his shirt. Fire Department.

Cameron can't move.

"What are you doing here?"

"Walking." He pushes the word past his lips without stuttering.

"Walking?" The guy looks him over. "You take a fall?"

"Yeah. I was running, lost my balance."

192

"Running?" His eyes look at Cameron's jeans, sneakers, back up to his blue T-shirt. "I thought you said you were walking."

"I sprint and walk when I need to," Cameron says.

"You're not dressed for a run."

For a fire cop the guy is pretty much a nothing.

"I needed to get out of the house." *Fast.*

"Feeling the heat at home?"

"It's all about what's happening at school." Cameron looks the fire cop in the face and shrugs his shoulders. "My mom doesn't think it's a safe place."

"A lot of parents are thinking that right now." He tucks his clipboard under his arm and rolls back on his feet. "You come here a lot?"

Cameron nods. "I run the trails."

"You like running?"

"I'm good at it."

"What's your name?"

Cameron tells him.

"You have some ID on you?"

"No."

"Where do you live?"

Cameron gives the guy his address, but he doesn't write it down, just looks at Cameron real steady and says, "I was going to come by and talk to you today. Your mom's boyfriend tell you that?"

"He said you might come by."

"You were here on Tuesday."

"That's right. I was here on Saturday and Sunday, too."

"What were you doing?"

"Walking."

"And sprinting," the fire cop says, doubt all over his voice.

"I run the half mile in two-ten," Cameron says. "That's a fact."

"You want me to write that down?" Anger whittles the cop's words into shrapnel.

"I guess you don't like sports," Cameron says.

"I don't like punk kids who set fires," he says. "That's what I don't like. It's good having a cop in the family, isn't it?"

"He's not in the family."

Cameron gives the guy his back, walks a few feet.

"We'll be talking again," the fire cop says. "Real soon."

SATURDAY

2:00PM

Keegan's Liquor doesn't get busy until dinnertime. Then the glass doors never really close, with people going in and out so much. Cameron leans against the side of the building, his hands pushed into his back pockets. He called out to a woman about his mother's age, who held a bottle of booze in her arm like it was a baby and struggled with her car keys. She asked him if his parents knew what he was up to. *Probably.*

No one's come in since. The sun is hot enough that sweat pools around his hairline, slides behind his ear, down his neck.

He lifts the hem of his T-shirt and wipes his face. There's ash in his clothes, from his fall in the woods, from his run through the underbrush still coated in soot. He left that fire cop standing at ground zero, searching for evidence he can use against Cameron. He wanted to tell the guy, *Don't waste your time. I'm going down. And for something much bigger than torching a few trees.*

Wind blows dust across the parking lot. The day has grown heavy with heat and the clouds overhead are a gray so dark they're almost black. It's not unusual to have dry storms in Erie. For lightning, in shades of green and pink and purple, to drop out of the sky and lie flat over the lake. It's a whole lot of energy that has nowhere to go but down, and Cameron feels it pushing on his shoulders. His knees go soft. He smells the earth, too close and sweet.

A green car with a Penn State pennant attached to the antenna pulls into the parking lot and hits the curb before it stops. A blonde girl jumps out of the passenger side, laughing. She's wearing jeans and a short-short top. A butterfly is tattooed above her belly button.

She looks like sunlight, Cameron thinks, bright and clean. He wipes his palms against his jeans and watches her move toward the liquor store.

She seems to be floating.

The words he wants to say knot in his throat. *Buy me a beer?* She's at the door before he can draw the breath to speak.

"Hey!" He waves at her and she stops and looks at him. "You want to buy me a beer?"

"You want a beer?" she asks.

"That's right."

She curls her hand into a fist and props it on her hip. "How old are you?"

"It's one beer," he says, like it's no big deal.

She thinks about it. "I wasn't much older than you when I had my first drink."

"It's not my first drink."

"Really, big guy? So what's your beer?"

It's a quiz. One he can ace. Even if he never tried the stuff before, the TV is full of beer ads. He voted online for the coolest Super Bowl beer commercial in February.

"Coors," he says.

She lifts her chin. "Light?"

"Sure. I'm watching my figure."

She looks him over and laughs again. "You're cute," she says. "In a few years you'll be old enough to use that."

She walks into the store. The door closes, sweeping a draft of cool air into the afternoon. Cameron turns back to the parking lot, tries to see through the spotted windshield of the green car. There's a girl sitting in the driver's seat. Dark hair in a ponytail and white teeth. She could be smiling at him. Or she could be laughing. The windows are rolled up, the air conditioning on so that the engine hums.

"What's your name?"

The blonde girl is back and Cameron turns to her voice. She's carrying two six-packs of Coors Light.

"Never mind," she says. "I'll forget it the minute you tell me. It's been that kind of day."

"Cameron," he says. "You should remember it. I'm going to be famous one day."

"Yeah? Me, too. I'm going to write songs. What are you going to do?"

"I've already done it."

"And you're not telling?" Her pink lips press into a pout and Cameron feels it like a sucker punch. For a moment it hurts to breathe. He doesn't feel even half as good sitting next to Helen Gosset.

"What if I give you that beer?" she asks. "Will you tell me then?"

"Yeah, I'll tell you."

She puts a six-pack on the sidewalk and pulls a bottle from the pack she's still holding. It's already built up a sweat from the heat. She holds the brown bottle up in her hand, and Cameron notices her fingernails are bitten short, the pink nail polish peeling.

"What did you do?" she asks.

"What's my name?" he tests her.

She laughs, pressing the back of her hand to her mouth. "I told you I'd forget."

"It's Cameron." He says it slow, hoping it will stick. Names are important.

~~He plucks the bottle from her hand.~~

"You read the newspaper?" he asks, and takes a step back.

"I try not to."

"I made the front page."

"The front page is all about a dead boy," she says.

Cameron nods. "That's me."

He holds the bottle of Coors by its skinny neck and dashes across the street. He turns only once and the blonde girl is standing where he left her, her soft face puckered with doubt. He likes that. She doesn't even know him and she wants to believe he's a good boy.

He takes the beer into the city park and finds a picnic table with a shelter and sits under it. He uses his teeth to pry off the cap then lifts the bottle to his lips. Mist from the beer curls up his nose. It's thick, wet, and makes him cough before he even takes a swallow.

He drinks it like it's a dare, trying to swallow fast enough that he doesn't gag on the bitter kick, not stopping until all that's left is foam.

He should have eaten something. He sits perfectly still on the edge of the picnic table but feels the liquid swirl in his stomach. He won't throw up. He doesn't do that anymore.

A car circles the block, rap music on the radio. Cameron lets his mind focus on the bass pumping like blood through an artery, thick in his ears, scratchy as the beat leaves the speakers. The key is not to dwell on what's happening in his body.

The tingling in his fingers begins, not as strong as touching an electrical current, but close. His mind slows, and thoughts and feelings become like pennies you throw into a wishing fountain. Then blast off. There's more than one way to fly.

He lays back on the picnic table and stares at the gray clouds rolling across a pale blue sky; at the tail of a lightning bolt, pink and then purple, squirming in the thunderheads.

SATURDAY

7:00PM

At seven o'clock Randy arrives at the house. Cameron watches him from his bedroom window. The sun is beginning its descent behind the mountains to the west and the sky is purple.

Randy climbs out of his truck, shuts the door, and leans against it. He's still in uniform. His gun is holstered to his right hip; hand-cuffs hang from the back of his belt. He has a can of Mace, too, in a leather clip, and a Taser. He doesn't wear this but keeps it stored in the trunk of his cruiser along with a high-powered rifle and ammunition. Once, when Cameron asked him, he said he

has more than a hundred bullets back there and two speed load-
ers. *You have to be prepared.* Even here, in Erie, where the greatest
danger comes from domestic disputes.

Randy shoves his hands into his front pockets, tips forward
on his toes and back, then reaches through the window of his
truck. Cameron watches his hand move along the dashboard
like a white wing, fluttering. When he withdraws it, he has a
cigarette clenched between his finger and thumb. Randy quit
smoking last year.

He doesn't light up. He rolls the cigarette between his fingers,
stares at it, raises it to his nose, and draws a heavy breath.

Cameron doesn't hear the cell phone ring, but he sees it light
up on Randy's belt.

Randy is always on call. He's a sharpshooter. Twice since Cameron's known him Randy has set up on the rooftops of buildings during hostage negotiations, prepared to but never having to shoot.

He pockets the cigarette, flips open his phone, and listens.
Cameron can tell Randy's hearing something he doesn't like. His
shoulders get stiff and he bends into the phone to hear better.

It's about him. The call is about Cameron. He's sure of it.

Randy ends the call, slips the phone back on his waist, and
tosses the cigarette through the truck window. Then he looks at
the house, the kitchen where Cameron's mom is cooking dinner,
hands on his hips, his mouth heavy.

Cameron takes the stairs slowly and hits the bottom as Randy enters the kitchen. He listens to his mom greet him. Frosty. She's still mad at Randy. Mad at her world spinning out of control.

"Where's Cameron?"

"In his bedroom, studying," she says. "Or hatching a plot to end the world."

"Maureen."

Cameron hears fatigue and frustration in Randy's voice.

"I'm trying to help him," he says.

"Because he's innocent? Or because he's guilty?"

"Either way, he needs help. A lot of it."

"Why? What's happened?" Worry makes his mother's voice breathless.

"You need to stay out of this," Randy says. "Right now, it's me and Cameron. That's the way it has to be."

"I'm his mother."

"You're too close to him to do him any good."

He's giving you what you want, Mom. An out.

He's surprised she doesn't take it. That she doesn't run with it.

"I can help him, Maureen. You're going to have to trust me," Randy says.

"Why?" she asks. "Why do you want to help him? You've been so in and out. Remember? You're not father material."

"Maybe I'm not," Randy concedes. "I guess we'll find out."

His mom is quiet a long time. Cameron moves until he's standing just outside the kitchen and leans his head against the wall.

She's crying. She can't help him. She knows that. But how much help can Randy be? He's a cop. At some point the law is going to mean more to him than Cameron does.

"He'll die in prison," Randy says. "If he goes maximum security, we'll never see him again."

His mother breaks. Her tears catch in her throat and she makes a strangling noise and then finally manages to choke out, "Okay. You're right. Okay."

Cameron steps out of the darkness of the living room and into the kitchen. His mom is leaning into Randy, her hands curled into his shirt and her face wet with tears.

"I don't want his help," Cameron says.

"Cameron," Randy says his name with purpose, the kind that would push him into a chair and into answering questions. Good cop, bad cop, Cameron thinks. Yesterday, on the deck, Randy played it cool. Tried to make Cameron think he was a friend. Today, he's all about his job. Cameron can feel it before he says anything about Pinon.

"I'm not talking to you," Cameron says.

"You're going to talk," Randy promises. "You're going to tell me everything that happened at school yesterday. You're going to give me a chance to help you."

Randy leaves his mother and walks to where Cameron stands, invading his space. He's taller, wider than Cameron, and when he draws breath his chest, still wrapped in his Kevlar vest, almost touches Cameron's chin.

"I'm going to help you, Cameron."

"You're going to do your job," Cameron says.

"If you made a mistake," Randy says, "then we need to fix it."

He puts his hands on Cameron's shoulders and keeps them there even as Cameron tries to shrug him off.

"Let him help you, Cameron," his mom says. "You need help."

"So you think I did it, too?" Cameron says, his voice sharp and rising. "You think I killed that boy? I'm a killer, Mom? A pyro and a killer?"

His voice hits a pitch that hurts his ears. The tears on his face feel like shards of glass.

"I don't think that," she says.

"But I need help. You think I need help."

"Yes."

Randy keeps his hands on Cameron's shoulders, moving him toward the table, and says to his mom, "Leave us alone, Maureen. We'll talk later."

Cameron resists Randy's strength, tries to pull away from his heavy hands.

"You're going to sit at the table with me and we're going to go over your day at school. What happened. What you can remember."

He pushes Cameron into a chair.

"If you want, I can put the cuffs on you."

Cameron sits in the chair, not looking at Randy.

Looking at the wall with its pictures of his grandmother and grandfather in oak frames and pictures of him and Robbie when they were younger, babies through their Scout years. He sits for a long time, waiting for Randy to talk, to ask his questions, to pretend he knows Cameron better than Cameron knows himself. But he's silent and Cameron tries to focus on the pictures of him when he had something to smile about.

"I wasn't at school yesterday," Cameron finally says. He won't tell Randy everything. Some things he already knows. The things he doesn't, Cameron won't confess. "Not the whole day."

Randy sits back in his chair. Cameron listens to his steady breathing, to the creaking of his leather holster.

"Long enough that you went to PE."

"Yeah, I went, but I had an argument with the coach."

"You took PE," Randy insists.

"I suited up. I didn't get a lot of play and I decided to leave. I told the coach I was leaving."

Cameron looks at Randy. He has a notebook out but no pen. He runs his finger down the page, looking at the details that made up Cameron's day.

"I spoke to the coach. He said he moved your locker and you were upset about it."

"That's right."

"Tell me about that."

"Didn't the coach already tell you?"

"I want to hear it from you."

"Fine. He moved my locker and it pissed me off. It wasn't a big deal. Not like you're making it."

"Why were you pissed?"

"Why did he move my locker?"

"He didn't think you'd want to go back there, to the place Patterson and Murphy assaulted you."

"He thought it'd be easier for me to forget what happened if I wasn't standing in it every day."

"Maybe. That's what pissed you off?"

"That and him being so nice to me. All the teachers were too nice. It was bad enough with everyone looking at me, thinking about those pictures and looking at me. I just wanted everything to be the same. I wanted it to be like Patterson and Murphy died at birth and never had a chance to do that to me."

"But you got to school and your teachers treated you differently?"

"That's right."

He looked at his notebook. "Your English teacher changed your seat."

"Yeah."

"You know why she did that?"

"She wanted me closer to her desk?" Cameron guesses.

"She wanted to keep an eye on you." He looks again at his notes. "She said you seemed really angry."

"She wanted me to talk to her, in the hall," Cameron says. "She wanted to pull me out of class and talk to me while all the kids sat inside knowing what we were talking about."

"And you refused."

"That's right. But I didn't say anything to her. I didn't do anything."

"No," Randy agrees. "She said you were quiet, but ready to blow. That an accurate description of the way you were feeling?"

Cameron shrugs. "I kept myself in check."

"Yes. She said as much." He flips a page in his notebook. "Your history teacher is a talker."

"He's an ass."

"He told me about that. He said on Tuesday, before Patterson and Murphy attacked you, that you exhibited behavior he's never seen from you. He attributes it to the trouble you were having."

"No. Hart really is an asshole."

Randy nods. "But he was nice to you yesterday?"

"Yeah."

"That pissed you off?"

"Everything pissed me off, okay?"

"Let's go back to the locker room. You walk in and find out the coach moved your stuff. Pick up there."

"He wanted to talk to me in his office. He's never done that before. Probably wanted to hold my hand and tell me everything was going to be all right."

"You wouldn't go to his office?"

"No way."

"So he met you at your locker."

"My old locker. He told me he moved me. I told him I didn't like it. He told me to suit up. The tardy bell was going to ring."

"Were you late to class?"

"Yeah."

"The coach says you were maybe ten minutes late to class."

"Maybe."

"The timing is important, Cameron," Randy says. "Really think about how long it took you to find your new locker, open it, dress . . ."

"Finding my new locker wasn't hard," Cameron says. "I opened it and sat on the bench and just stared at my clothes."

"Why?"

"I was thinking."

"About what?"

"How I'd like to kill Patterson. All my troubles would be over, then, you know? Most of them anyway. Then I started thinking about what they did to me. I got caught up in it like it was happening all over again."

"Then what happened?"

"I don't know. I guess I just sat there thinking that. Then I got dressed and went upstairs. I remember hearing the balls bouncing against the gym floor and thinking I was really late. They were already through stretching."

"And nothing else happened?" Randy asked. "You didn't see or hear anyone else in the locker room?"

Cameron shook his head. "I didn't see anything. Just what was going on inside my head."

"Sometimes it's hard to separate that from what's really going on."

"I don't have that problem."

"You've never felt disconnected?" Randy asks. "It's not unusual for someone who's been the target of abuse to lose focus, drift from reality. It's called post-traumatic stress disorder. We see it a lot in people who suffer from domestic violence."

"You mean because Dad was violent? You think maybe I check out when things get tough?"

"I'm just saying it's common."

Cameron shakes his head. "When Dad hit us, after a while I just put myself somewhere else when it was happening. Is that what you're talking about?"

"You say you have no problem separating dream from reality?"

"I might have a little bit of that," Cameron says. "Sometimes I watch my life happening like I'm in the audience and not living it."

Randy nods. "Does that happen a lot?"

"I can't control it. I don't even know when it happens, just suddenly I'm seeing myself from the outside."

"And not feeling what's going on inside?"

"Sometimes I don't feel anything."

"Do you know a boy named Charlie Pinon?"

"Yeah. He's a perv."

"Why do you say that?"

"He hides out in the showers and watches us."

"You've seen him do this?"

Cameron nods.

"Was he doing it yesterday?"

"He did it every day."

"The coach said he wasn't good at sports. That he didn't always make it to class."

Cameron shrugs. "I don't know about that."

"You know he's the boy who was killed?"

"I think so."

"Why?"

"It was either him or me," Cameron says.

"What does that mean?"

"We were Patterson's favorites."

"You think Patterson did it?"

It never would have happened if Patterson didn't exist.

"Patterson wasn't in school," Randy points out. "He was suspended."

"Patterson runs the school."

"Did you see him on campus yesterday?"

"I didn't look for him."

"Did you see him?"

"No."

"Your PE lock is missing," Randy says. "It's not on your locker."

"It's not missing. I have it."

"You have your lock?"

"Yeah. I didn't put it back on. The coach said he'd move me back to my old locker."

"Where is the lock now?"

"In my backpack."

"Where's your backpack?"

Cameron was going to say here, in his bedroom, where he always keeps it when he's not in school. But then he sees the last minutes in the locker room play out in front of his eyes. He grabbed his bag, stuffed with his jeans and T-shirt, slammed the locker door shut, ran up the stairs to the gym.

"It's in my PE locker. The new one."

Randy nods. "We have it," he says. "We went through it. The lock isn't there."

"You went through my backpack? You're not allowed to do that!"

"It was left at the crime scene and taken as evidence." Randy pins him with his eyes. "You had a lot of sharp objects in the bag. A razor, a scalpel."

Cameron nods. "I thought Patterson was going to be in school."

"What we're you going to do with them?"

"Protect myself."

"You don't know what happened to your lock?"

"No. You do," Cameron guesses.

"I think it was used to kill Pinon," Randy says. "A combination lock was found close to his body. There's a number on it. The coach keeps a list of all lock numbers and combinations." He pushes aside his notebook. "The number matches your lock."

SUNDAY

4:00AM

He wakes up out of breath, a fist locked around his throat, and realizes he's still stuck in his dream. A dream where he died. He knew it was coming and didn't run. It passed through him, stealing the air from his lungs, silencing the scream that burned his lips.

Cameron lies still in his bed, eases his fingers from their twisted grip in the sheets, and waits.

He thinks about all the things he'll miss. His mother moving around in the kitchen. She hums when she cooks and taps the spoon against the counter keeping time. Robbie's face. There's something a little off with having a soft, believing face and a body as big as his. It makes Cameron think there is hope. The view from his bedroom window. Treetops all the way to the lake.

He draws a breath that stabs him in the chest.

Cameron realized last night, after talking to Randy, that his life is over. He was right from the beginning, there are no do-overs.

He slides out of bed, gathers his running clothes, and changes without turning on the light. Robbie is sleeping, the air whistling in his nose. It used to be his brother flopped around in bed, caught up in nightmares that featured their father, painted red, taller than he really is, and swinging hands that were iron mallets or ax blades. But time has been good to his brother. Cameron doubts he'll ever stop dreaming about his father. He was too old when his mom finally left him; his memory is solid.

He slips out the door, down the stairs, and through the kitchen. On the deck, with the sun burning the edge of the night sky, he's able to make out the lighter shadows of chairs and tables, and walks around them. His footsteps stir the gravel in the driveway, but the sound is no louder than a whisper.

He wonders if, when he dies, he'll be able to come back, live among his family, unseen but close. The ghost he didn't want to be.

The air is cool, cleans out his lungs. He walks until he finds the woods and then uses his hands, in the deeper shadows under the trees, to feel his way to the trail that winds through the park and down to the lake. Owls hoot at one another. He disturbs a flock of bats that squeal and wheel off against the black night. When he reaches the trailhead it's light enough that he can see the mist of his breath in the air.

He doesn't have to speak to his body. His knees lift and his legs follow through like the pistons of a train. He wants to feel the burn in his lungs and the moment of takeoff. He doesn't let his mind drift to images of him bursting through tape, to the feel of a gold medal around his neck.

Dreams are a thing of the past.

He wonders what Pinon dreamed of. Did he want to move the world forward in some way? When he wasn't jumping at Cameron's heels or being pushed around between Red Coats like a ball in the paws of a Doberman, or lurking in the showers, he was in class smoking everyone else. He was easily a better math student than Cameron. Was he going to use that to make a dent in the world?

Cameron doubts it. It takes courage to go the distance. Confidence. Pinon didn't have it. Not an ounce of it.

He killed Charlie Pinon. He makes himself hold the thought, just Pinon, pushing Patterson and his flunkies, and his own anger and fear down and out, and seeing only Pinon in his mind. A small kid, like him, with arms thinner than Popsicle sticks. And no friends. Cameron's breath bottles up in his throat; he runs through it. He wipes the mucus from under his nose, not slowing.

At the beginning of the year, Cameron felt sorry for Pinon. He even covered for him once, standing in the way of a tide of red while Pinon streaked into the restroom and cowered in a stall, standing up on the toilet and shaking so much the toilet seat clattered. By Christmas, Cameron thought to himself that someone should put the guy out of his misery. It was an idle thought. Not something he ever planned to be a part of. But in the end, Pinon bothered him. Even looking at the guy filled him with anger. Pinon on the outside was what Cameron felt like on the inside: small and weak. He hated looking at the kid and seeing himself. He hated that the Red Coats thought he and Pinon were the same breed of scared.

Cameron runs through a patch of sunlight. As the trail slopes downward he catches his first glimpse of the lake, the water the color of steel. There are others on the trail now. Bikers pass him, a mother pushing a jog stroller. His eyes focus on a pair of runners ahead; he picks up his pace, lengthening his stride, planning to overtake them, blow past them, run until his heart explodes in his chest.

SUNDAY

1:30PM

"Let's sit down," the cop, the one with the tie that's braided like a noose, says and points to the couch.

Cameron takes the chair and watches Randy walk around the coffee table, settle into the end of the couch closest to him. The two cops stand a minute longer, both looking at Cameron, silent and accusing.

Cameron returns their stare. He's not afraid of them. Name, rank, and serial number.

"You're a sophomore at Madison High?"

"Freshman," Cameron corrects them, knowing they already know this. It was a lame attempt to challenge his honesty.

"Freshman." The cop writes it down in his notebook then asks, "How do you like school?"

"I don't," Cameron admits.

"There's nothing wrong with that. A lot of kids don't like school," Good Cop says.

Cameron doesn't respond. He lets the silence build and though his shoulders begin to ache, he knows now is not the time to move them.

"You have a good man on your side," Bad Cop says, nodding toward Randy.

"That's what he tells me."

Cameron's mom enters the room with a glass of soda on ice and places it in front of Cameron.

"You might get thirsty," she says.

She looks at the cops, her face stiff. She folds her arms over her stomach and seems to grow a few inches.

"Nothing for us," Bad Cop says.

"That's good, because that's exactly what you're getting."

She turns to Randy and places a hand on Cameron's shoulder.

"Let me know when they get around to asking about the attack on Cameron. *The crime against my son*," she repeats and turns back to the cops. "It happened on Tuesday, in the boys' locker room."

"We're aware of it, ma'am. I believe arrests were made in that case."

"Arrested and released," Cameron's mom says.

"That's the law," Bad Cop says and tweaks his noose-for-a-tie. "Last I heard, the D.A. plans to take the case to court. You'll get your justice."

His mom knows this. Cameron heard her on the phone, talking to the D.A., twice last week. She doesn't like the law that allows violent criminals on the street and when the D.A. told her that's the reality, she hung up on him.

"The thing I keep asking myself is will Charlie's parents get justice?" Bad Cop asks.

His mom's face turns to stone.

"You can speak to my son for ten minutes." She checks her watch. "Not a minute more."

She walks out of the room and even Cameron can feel the temperature go up. This isn't the first time she's defended him. Before they left his father, she stood in front of him and Robbie, her skinny hands reaching behind her, pushing at them, trying to get them to run out the door to safety. They never left her.

"Your mom's a good one to have in your corner," Good Cop says.

"You're wasting time," Randy barks.

"You took a beating last week," Bad Cop says. "Did it make you mad?"

"Yeah. I was pretty much pissed off all week after that."

"What did you do about it?"

"Nothing."

"But you planned to do something," Good Cop says.

"Yeah. I was going to kill Patterson. I wanted to, anyway. But he wasn't at school."

"Want isn't the same thing as intent," Randy points out.

"And intent isn't commit. We know it," Good Cop says.

"We found weapons in your backpack."

"I know."

"Where did you get the scalpel?"

"I took it from my mother's work bag."

"She's a doctor?"

"No. She works in the lab at the hospital, though."

Bad Cop nods. "Straight blade razor. What were you going to do with that?"

"Ask another question," Randy says.

"I want to establish intent."

"You already did."

"Your teachers say you were angry and non-communicative on Friday," Good Cop says.

"Okay."

"You agree with that?"

"I was angry."

"How many times do you want him to say it?" Randy asks. "Move on."

"You fought with your PE coach?"

"It wasn't a fight," Randy corrects. "It was an argument."

"You had an argument with your PE coach on Friday?"

"Yes."

"What was it about?"

"He changed my locker and I didn't like it."

"What did you do about it?"

"I told him I wanted my old locker back."

"Did he agree?"

"He didn't disagree. He said he was sorry he had acted without asking."

"Did you suit up for PE?"

"Did the coach say I did?"

"Answer the question."

"You know the answer."

"Answer the question, Cameron," Randy says.

Cameron sighs. "I suited up for PE on Friday."

"You get there on time?"

"No."

"Why?"

"I was talking to the coach. By the time we were done I had two minutes to change."

"The coach says you got to the gym when play was already in motion."

"That's right."

"So you were about ten minutes late?"

"Maybe five minutes late."

"The coach says it was closer to ten."

Cameron shrugs.

"Move on," Randy says.

"Why did it take you so long to dress?"

"I was pretty steamed about the locker change. I guess I sat a while thinking about it."

"What were you thinking?"

"That I didn't like it."

"Why?"

"I wanted everything back to normal," Cameron says. "I wanted to forget about everything and no one would let me."

"You wanted to forget that Patterson and his friend attacked you?"

"That's right."

"Did they touch you? Your genitalia?"

"That's it," Randy says, standing up. "We're done."

"No," Cameron says, "we're not done." He stands up and moves in front of Randy. "They didn't touch me. I told him that, too." He jerks his finger at Randy. "And I don't want anyone thinking they did."

"Okay. Okay," Good Cop says. "They didn't touch you. Not like we were saying."

"No."

"It's just that when a victim puts a lot into denying something happened, it usually means it did."

"It didn't."

"We heard different," Bad Cop says.

"That's a lie." Cameron's hands curl into fists. "And you better stop saying it."

"Enough," Randy says. He puts a hand on Cameron's shoulder. "They're trying to upset you, Cameron. It's what they want."

"Did you know Charlie Pinon?" Bad Cop asks.

"We're done," Randy repeats.

"I'll answer that," Cameron says. "Yes. I knew him."

"Some of the boys in your PE class say Pinon hid in the showers," Good Cop says. "Did you ever see him do this?"

"He did it all the time. He watched us dress."

"You think Pinon was gay?"

"He was a perv."

"Was he hiding in the showers the day Patterson attacked you?"

"I think so."

"Was he there on Friday?"

"Probably."

"Did you see him?"

"I didn't look for him," Cameron says.

"That's not an answer."

"Maybe I saw him. I had my mind on other things."

"He was in there the day Patterson beat on you," Good Cop says. "You know how we know?"

Cameron shrugs. "You're going to tell me."

"He told the principal all about it. Us, too. On Wednesday, when you were AWOL."

Pinon told. He waited, watching, never ducking back behind the shower wall, not missing a moment of the show. Pinon watched him like it was some kind of porno horror movie, then he ran through the halls, bleating like a scared sheep. And he told.

Too little, too late.

"Your coach says Pinon hid in the showers because he was no good at sports. He got harassed a lot by the jocks in the class. But never by you."

"So I guess he wasn't really a perv," Good Cop says.

"He watched," Cameron says. "I saw him watching."

"When Patterson had you down?"

"That's right. He watched and did nothing about it."

"Maybe he was as scared as you."

"He lived his whole life scared."

"And that's no way to live, is it?"

"I've been living scared all year," Cameron says.

"And that's why you decided to kill Patterson? Is it why you killed Pinon? Because he was part of the whole thing, too?"

225

Randy moves so that he stands in front of Cameron, blocking the cops and their questions. "This is over. You're going to leave now. If you want to talk to him again it'll be with his attorney present."

The cops stand up.

"You can't make people forget, so you take them out of the game? Is that right, Cameron?"

"Out," Randy says, taking a step toward Bad Cop.

"It's my last question. Will you answer it, Cameron?"

Randy keeps moving, herding the cops to the front door.

Cameron feels like he's inside a toaster, his skin burning. He doesn't care that they figured him out; he's pissed that they think the whole thing was his fault. The tone of Bad Cop's voice, the way he made it heavy with sarcasm, makes it clear he thinks Cameron is the bad guy and that his way of making it all stop was a bad decision, a fool's decision. Like it never would have worked.

Cameron lets the truth settle on his face. Lets the cops see it. Yeah, he did it. It was the only thing left to do.

"Now that's a real shame," Good Cop says, reading Cameron's expression like his face is a map. He pulls out a small plastic box and holds it up. "We need his fingerprints, Randy."

"You have a warrant?"

"You're going to make us get a warrant?" Bad Cop asks, like maybe Randy is joking.

"We're doing this by the book," Randy says. "He answered your questions in good faith, but it's clear you have an agenda."

"You knew that coming in."

"I thought so," Randy agrees. "Get a warrant."

"You know that will happen."

"I know."

SUNDAY

5:40PM

Cameron's attorney is short and about as thick around as the trunk of a redwood. His hair is shaved on the sides with a clump of curls on top that tumble over his forehead and into his eyes. He pushes at it a lot and Cameron wonders why he doesn't get it cut. His arms are solid, even through his suit jacket, his triceps so puffed up they make his shoulders look too close to his ears. The guy lifts weights. He has to. There's no other natural explanation for the thick muscles that wrap around his body. Cameron is wondering if the guy uses steroids when his thoughts are interrupted.

"Look, you're going to have to talk to me," Mr. Jeffries says. "I'm your attorney and everything you say is in confidence." Then he throws his hands up like he's trying to stop traffic. "But I don't want to know if you did it. I don't want to know if you didn't. I'm not a priest. You can take that up with the clergy."

"You defend the innocent and the guilty?" Cameron says.

"That's right," Jeffries says. "I'm equal opportunity. That's how this lawyer business works. Answer my questions and feel free not to add anything."

"What was your question?"

"How well did you know Charlie Pinon?"

"Not well."

"You weren't friends?"

"No."

"You had PE class together and what else?"

"Spanish and math."

"You ever interact with him in any of those classes?"

"No."

"Why not?"

"I didn't like him."

"Why?"

"He was a sissy."

"A sissy?"

"Yeah. He cried a lot. Whenever the Red Coats picked on him he teared up like a girl and ran to the office."

"Who are the Red Coats?"

"The jocks. They wear their red letter jackets and hunt us in the halls."

"You included?" Jeffries asks. "Were you one of the hunted?"

Cameron shrugs. "I guess so."

"You don't like thinking of yourself that way."

"Would you?"

"No." He writes a few notes. "This Patterson boy, he had it out for you?"

"I guess so."

"Did he go after Pinon, too?"

"Yeah."

"Was it a case of, 'no one was safe'?"

Cameron shakes his head. "Mostly it was me and Pinon. A couple of times I saw him pushing around someone different." Cameron tells him about SciFi and Jeffries makes a few notes, then asks, "But he had his favorites?"

Cameron nods.

"I hate dirtbags like that."

Cameron hears the angst in Jeffries's voice and guesses that, being as short as he is, he was probably messed with in high school, too.

"Did you see Pinon on Friday?"

"I answered this already." Cameron shifts in his chair, stretches his legs out under the kitchen table.

"You spoke to the police. Now you're talking to the man who's going to save your ass."

Cameron doubts it. It's too late to save him. There's no going back. When soldiers return from battle their lives are forever changed.

"Yeah, I saw Pinon on Friday. He was hiding in the showers."

"You see anyone else? Hear a door open, maybe, while you were dressing? Hear people talking?"

"No. None of that."

Jeffries frowns. "It would help if you remembered one of those things."

"It didn't happen."

"Right." He looks down at his notepad. "Did you ever have an altercation with Pinon?"

"No."

"Even anything small?"

"No."

"Ever see anyone other than Patterson pick on Pinon?"

"A lot of people picked on him."

"All of those Red Coats?"

"I guess."

"The police have your combination lock. They believe it was used to kill Pinon. Why wasn't it on your locker, like everyone else's?"

"I guess I left it off."

"That's not good enough," Jeffries says. "Unless you have a death wish."

He doesn't get it. He's already talking to a dead man.

"I was changing lockers," Cameron explains. "Going back to my old locker. So I guess I left it off so the coach could make that happen."

"Do you remember exactly where you left it?"

"No. On the bench?"

"I don't know." He sets his pen down. "You remember for sure that you didn't see or hear anything else in the locker room, but you don't remember what you did with your lock?"

"That's about right."

Jeffries nods. "Do you ever feel like you're not a part of this world? Disconnected, maybe?"

Cameron stares at him.

"Your mom's boyfriend, the cop, thinks you're suffering from a dissociative disorder. Something like post-traumatic stress disorder."

"Soldiers get that," Cameron says.

"That's right. People who lived a long time with domestic violence, too."

"Yeah. Maybe I have a little of that. A little of living but not feeling it."

"You're going to see a psychologist," Jeffries decides. "There are some good ones, but your mom will have to take you to Philly for that." He tears a blank piece of paper off his pad and writes down a name. Then he consults his BlackBerry and jots down a phone number. "Don't talk to the police again without me. Not even your mom's boyfriend."

He hands Cameron the slip of paper.

"Go to school tomorrow," Jeffries says. "Like it's just another day."

MONDAY

8:42AM

The street in front of the school is swarming with teachers, Elwood and his better half, Mrs. Maroni — the girls' counselor, Vega and the vice principal, all of them bent toward car windows, mouths and hands moving.

Cameron sits in the passenger seat of his mother's minivan, listening to Mr. Ferguson, the shop teacher, explain that all students are expected to go to the auditorium first. They have counselors, specialists in trauma, waiting there.

"We want parents to stay, too," Ferguson says. "For as long as you can."

"I plan to," Cameron's mom says.

Ferguson walks away from the van and to the car behind them. Cameron turns in his seat and watches the shop teacher bend at the waist and lean into his announcement.

"I don't like this school," she says. "It's not safe."

No kidding.

"Do you think you could ever feel safe here?"

Cameron shrugs. Watches the drizzle spray the windshield, the slow lift of the wipers on intermittent. Three seconds. The wipers lift every three seconds.

The truth is, he won't feel safe until Patterson is dead. And nothing that's happened, nothing the police have said, that his mom or Randy have promised, has changed that.

"I'm going to find a place to park," his mom decides.

She pulls into the heavy line of traffic, tapping the brakes every yard or two. When they pull even with the parking lot Cameron notices cop cars, two with bars on the roof, though they're not flashing, and several unmarked cars with lights on the dashboard. Were they still in the locker room? Was Pinon still in there, his body slumped against the wall, his eyes open, watching? He feels an ache in his kidneys. His breath whistle in his throat. He has to go to the bathroom. Now.

"Mom —"

"I don't know how they plan to fit all of us into the auditorium. Students *and* parents?" She pulls on the steering wheel, making a sharp cut into a vacant space between a police cruiser and an SUV.

Too close. They were too close to the cars, to Pinon, too close to the school.

"Mom!"

It's too late. Cameron feels a flood of hot liquid squirt between his legs. He stares at his lap, the growing stain on his jeans. He can't stop himself. He tries to put a mental vice on his bladder, but it doesn't work.

"Cameron?" His mom's voice is sharp, startled.

"No." He looks at her, helpless.

"It's okay, honey," she says. "You're scared."

Her hands wring the steering wheel, the knuckles growing white.

"Delayed reaction," she says. "Remember?"

A car horn blasts and Cameron jumps in his seat.

"Let's get out of here," he says.

"Do you remember, honey? Being attacked the way you were is something that you'll deal with in stages. Randy said it could even be like those sneaker waves that catch you by surprise. It'll feel like you've been hit from behind." She leans toward him, her eyes questioning. Even she has trouble believing herself. "Right, honey? This is all about the attack. Those boys will go back to prison. They're not coming to this school again."

Cameron wants to tell her. He wants to confess, not just about Pinon, but all the stuff that's happened. The way Patterson walked through the halls, sniffing him out. Patterson has a nose for fear and Cameron was afraid of him. Afraid, but he refused to give into it. He wasn't like Pinon, running scared. Isn't that something to be proud of? He never ran. He opens his mouth, but the words pile up in his throat. He coughs like he's choking on a chunk of food. Tries to gasp for air around it and feels his mom's hand hit his back.

"Cameron?"

The alarm in her voice reels him in. He pulls in a breath, coughs again, then eases back into his seat.

"Take me home," he says.

She stares at him. "Mr. Jeffries says you have to go to school today."

"I can't go like this." His hands spread out over his lap.

"I'll take you home and you can change."

She puts the van in reverse.

"I'm not going back," Cameron says.

He takes another gulp of air and stares out the window. His throat is raw but the fear is ebbing. He feels it loosen its hold on him, draw back until it's just a speck of black in the center of his heart, just waiting to bloom again.

The Toyota in line behind them brakes and Cameron's mother pulls them back into traffic. They're letting people park in the staff lot and on the football field, but his mom turns the van around and heads back to the street, where a campus security guard is waving cars into the lot. He stops them and his mom rolls down the window.

"There's parking in the rear lot," he says.

"We'll be back," his mom says and closes the window.

She turns left into the street and accelerates. There's no traffic heading west.

"Are you cold?" She leans over the console and turns the heat up. "You're shivering," she says.

His pants are cold and stick to his skin and the smell of piss sears his nose. He pissed his pants.

Like a baby. A scared baby.

"I'm not coming back," Cameron says again.

"You have to."

MONDAY

12:35PM

SciFi catches up with Cameron in the hall.

"I've been looking for you all day," he says.

"I just got here," Cameron admits. He keeps walking, down tech alley toward their computer class. If it'd been up to him he wouldn't be here, but his mom called Randy and Randy drove by the house in his cruiser. He practically tossed Cameron in the backseat then wasted no time getting him to school.

＊

"Don't I at least get a phone call?" Cameron asked.

"You think this is funny?" Randy demanded. "You think this won't happen for real? Only you won't be going to school, you'll be going to jail."

"What's the difference?"

"In jail you'll become some scum's bar of soap."

Cameron was quiet after that.

So there was a difference. Not much, but one he could appreciate.

"When are you going to realize I'm trying to help you? When are you going to start helping yourself?" he wanted to know.

"I am helping myself," Cameron said.

"Jeffries thinks you have a death wish. He thinks you have your mind made up and there's no changing it. You know what he thinks?"

"He told me."

"*Jail.* He thinks you want to go to jail. Is that true?"

"I think that's where I'm going."

"You killed that kid," Randy said. "That doesn't mean you're a murderer."

"I know."

✳

"My mom wanted to keep me home," SciFi says, snagging Cameron's attention. "Statistically, this is the safest school in the nation right now."

Cameron tries to process that as they push past a handful of kids knotted in the hall. He notices that some have black bands tied around their arms.

"What are those for?" Cameron asks.

"They're in mourning," SciFi says. "A lot of kids are wearing them."

"No one liked Pinon."

"I know. It's screwed up."

Cameron wants to take a good look at SciFi's face. He wonders if he's still bruised, if his teeth are fixed.

They slip through the door to their computer class and take their seats. Then Cameron turns on his swivel stool and looks into SciFi's face. Not as dramatic as he was expecting. A faint splotch of lavender and robin's egg blue is spread across his cheekbone, under his left eye, and into his hairline. Definitely an improvement over the last time Cameron saw him.

"Not so bad," Cameron decides.

"I was a one-eyed Cyclops on Wednesday," SciFi says. "And watch this." He opens his mouth and pulls on a front tooth. It comes off in his hand. "This is temporary. I lost four veneers. My parents went through the roof. Made me spill names, called a lawyer, and now Patterson's parents are footing the bill for a new set." He pushes the temporary cap back in place. "Where have you been?"

Cameron shrugs. "Home."

"You didn't want to come back, huh? I don't blame you. Patterson

241

is a prick. What he did to you, and putting those pictures on the 'net, now *everyone* knows he's a prick. Even if he does come back to Madison he has nothing and no one to come back to."

Cameron feels a knife twist in his chest when SciFi brings up the photos. He tries to focus instead on the idea that Patterson is ruined.

"Why do you say that?"

"He's out of control," SciFi says. "The reason I look so good —" he stops and rubs a hand over his face, "is that his friends realized it, too. They came at me, pushing and pulling, swinging, and Patterson yelling. Some guy rolled under my legs and I went down like a brick house and Patterson was kicking me and foaming at the mouth. He was so red in the face he looked like he came right out of hell. His friends started backing off. I looked at their faces and saw it there. Patterson scared them. Some of them pulled him away, even before the cops got there."

"Maybe things will get better," Cameron says. "Maybe not."

"They'll get better. Patterson's gone and we have a killer among us. It's got to get better."

"Yeah. I guess so."

"We're walking in a combat zone," SciFi says.

"It's always been that."

Their teacher, Mrs. Marks, walks through the door with a stack of papers in her arms. She passes them out as the bell rings and then explains that, due to the tragedy they're all experiencing, they won't begin work on their next project — which she handed out on Friday.

"We're going to read about software programs today," she says. She passes out articles photocopied from a computer magazine. "I want you to write a brief statement identifying the value of each product."

Her thoughts seem fragmented, at least to Cameron. He feels his mind drift. He thinks about Patterson at home, kicking back, laughing at the memories he has of Cameron, stuffed like a pig. He thinks about the locker room, the cops in there scraping DNA off the shower floor. He doesn't know Marks is standing in front of him until she taps his desk with her knuckles.

"You weren't here on Friday," she says to Cameron. "I hope you're feeling better. What happened, well, it's inexcusable and I'm sorry for it." Her face is soft. She looks like she's about to cry. "The whole world is going crazy, isn't it?"

She walks away but turns and says, "I paired you up with Elliott for the next project. I hope that's all right. The two of you work well together."

Then she drifts off, toward her desk, and Cameron feels like maybe she's a little lost. A boat without a captain. And that's how it is the rest of the day. Cameron's Spanish teacher writes a page number on the board and asks them to work quietly at their desks. She doesn't explain the assignment and no one asks questions. Cameron takes out his notebook and writes down the page number at the top. He scratches in the Roman numeral I, counts out ten spaces and then fills in the Roman Numeral II, planning to do both exercises, but then he's back again, in the locker room, watching the cops collect ceramic tiles and poke through the shower drains.

MONDAY

4:00PM

Robbie is already home when Cameron walks through the door. He's sitting at the kitchen table, a textbook open, but he's not reading it and the paper in front of him is blank except for a large X carved by the sharp point of a pencil. His face is doughy, his cheeks rubbed pink. Cameron can't let himself look at his brother too long. Doesn't let himself think about what's going on inside Robbie's head. His brother is a worrier. Always has been. And for days he's been walking around the house, sometimes at Cameron's heels, saying nothing, but staying close.

"Mom called," Robbie says, breaking into Cameron's thoughts. "Twice. Where have you been?"

"At school."

It's four o'clock. He took the bus home, got off, and walked into the woods. March is almost over and that means that just about every tree has a bird's nest in it, filled with eggs or babies who don't know how to fly yet. He sat beneath a sugar maple with a handful of its green pods and separated their sticky joints, stuck his fingertips into their pockets, and wore them like feathers. He wants to fly away. That would be his superpower, if someone was handing them out. He's almost there already. Sometimes, when he's running, when the air is cool and snaps against his skin and he no longer feels his feet hit the ground, he's almost there.

"Your lawyer is coming. Mom wants you to know that. The cops are coming, too. They're going to take your fingerprints."

The beginning of the end.

"Randy says all that'll prove is you touched your own lock," Robbie says. "The police think you killed that boy."

"I know."

"Did you?"

Cameron lets his gaze hit Robbie square in the face. He sucks up his brother's uncertainty. Robbie wants to believe in him.

"You think I did?"

"No. But everybody else does. Even the newspaper is making predictions."

"Yeah? What does it say?"

"It says the police have one suspect, another boy who attends Madison High."

"And the police are coming here. So I must be it."

"They have a warrant."

"Yeah. Randy made them do that."

"The paper says whoever did it will be tried as an adult. They're going to try to do that."

"Lethal injection," Cameron says. He feels the slow burn up from his wrist, his veins on fire. Fire won't be so bad. "What's in that stuff?"

"Sodium chloride."

"You're a smart kid, Robbie."

"It was in the paper. I don't know what it does. I mean, if it hurts."

"I think maybe it'll burn a little," Cameron says. "And then there's nothing. You ever wonder what happens to birds who fly too high? You know, they break through the atmosphere and are suddenly in outer space?"

"They die." Robbie is crying. "They suffocate and die."

And maybe that's how it is. The chemicals hit your heart, freeze it when you're still alive and know it's over, and you have that one moment to hold onto forever.

Cameron focuses on his brother, wiping his eyes with his shirtsleeve and looking about six years old. Looking like he did when their father was raging and they were locked behind their bedroom door with their mother, praying the wood wouldn't splinter.

"Don't cry, Robbie. Everything's going to be okay."

MONDAY

6:10PM

Mr. Jeffries knocks on the kitchen door, then opens it and sticks just his head through.

"Hi. Your mom told you I was coming?"

He slips inside, carrying a leather briefcase too packed to close all the way. Cameron doesn't get up from the table. He nudges his half glass of milk back and forth between his fingertips and watches his lawyer walk toward him in a kind of slow motion that's really a trick of the mind. Cameron can't alter the rotation of the world. The end is coming, and not on his terms.

"The police are pulling into the driveway," Jeffries says. "They're going to take your fingerprints. They want to ask you a few questions. I told them we'd listen. I didn't promise answers."

He sets the briefcase on a chair and sifts through it until he comes to a stack of yellow papers stapled together.

"I have a couple of questions, too," he says. "The cops found a second blood type in the locker room. More specifically, on a single shower tile, on the combination lock, and in the hair of the victim," he reads from his notes. "Could that blood belong to you?"

"Anything's possible," Cameron says.

Jeffries steps closer. "Turn your hands over."

Cameron releases the glass and turns his palms up. There are marks on his right hand, a small circular bruise where maybe the spin notch of the lock pressed against his skin. Worse, between his middle and ring fingers there's a purple gash now covered with a thin layer of new skin. Cameron watches the sun set in Jeffries's face.

"How did you get that?" he asks.

"Don't ask, don't tell, remember?"

Jeffries sinks into a chair at the table. From outside come the sharp clicks of car doors slamming.

"Okay. We're going to have to regroup," Jeffries says. "For now, do exactly as I tell you." He pauses, rubs a hand over his forehead, and pushes back his hair. "Unless stated on the warrant, you don't have to show them your hands. So don't. Keep your palms down while they roll your prints."

Cameron sees the cops through the window before they knock. Good Cop and Bad Cop again. And Randy. He's standing behind the other cops, in full uniform, his face about as flat as a plate. Cameron wonders why Randy doesn't open the door. He never knocks anymore.

Jeffries stands up and moves toward them. "Don't answer any questions without my approval," he warns. "They ask, you wait for me to tell you it's okay. Got it?"

Cameron nods. He pushes himself up until he's sitting tall in his chair. His fingers curl into his palms and he taps his fists against his thighs under the table.

Jeffries opens the door and holds it wide and then the room is too full and the air is suddenly thin.

"Hi, Cameron," Good Cop says. "How you doing today?"

Cameron looks at Jeffries.

"You can answer that."

"Fine," Cameron says.

"You have him on a tight leash," Bad Cop says. "Why's that?" He looks at Cameron. "You hiding something?"

"Shut up, Finney," Randy says and walks around the two cops and takes a seat next to Cameron at the table. "Take the prints."

Good Cop pulls the plastic box from his coat pocket and asks Cameron if he wouldn't mind standing and walking over to the counter. Cameron waits for Jeffries' nod and then rises from his chair. His legs are full of the tired that comes after running seven or eight miles at full speed. He shuffles to the counter where Good Cop is setting up.

"Let's see the warrant," Jeffries says. "And then you can take the prints."

"We showed it to Randy."

"Great. Now show it to me," Jeffries says, and takes his place next to Cameron.

Bad Cop tosses the warrant to Jeffries. "You're not going to like it," he warns.

Cameron feels his gut clench but breathes through it. He watches Jeffries eyes shift as he reads, lifting several pages, taking his time.

"Fingerprints, blood, and house," Jeffries says. "We're fine with that."

Good Cop takes Cameron's left hand, rolls each finger through an ink pad and then onto a piece of paper that's separated into a grid. Cameron holds his hand stiff, breathes through his nose, feels his pulse slam against the veins in his wrist.

"Loosen up." Good Cop shakes Cameron's hand, rolls his thumb over the paper, then reaches for his right hand.

"Not used to holding hands with a guy?" Bad Cop asks.

"Shut up," Randy says again, his voice so tight Cameron thinks it might snap in two.

"You need to loosen up, too," Bad Cop tells Randy. "You know what's coming."

"You're not going to find anything," Randy says.

"You've already been through the house?" Bad Cop asks. "We figured as much. Figured we'd find it super clean. That's okay. The prints and the blood will probably be enough."

Good Cop runs Cameron's fingers through the ink and across the paper. He feels the cop's fingers move on his palm, over the peeled skin of his healing cut.

"You're right-handed, Cameron?"

"Yes."

"Feels like you cut up your hand."

Good Cop tries to turn over Cameron's hand, but he holds it steady and then Jeffries places his hand on top of Cameron's.

"You a nurse now?" Jeffries wants to know. "Just take the prints. The warrant doesn't entitle you to a search of his body."

"Well, maybe we'll just go back and get that," Bad Cop says.

"You do that," Jeffries invites. "I like it when we go by the book. Everything's so neat and tidy."

Good Cop tucks the card with Cameron's prints on it into a plastic bag and slips it into his pocket. He packs up his plastic box and turns to Jeffries.

"We like it that way, too. Keeps the cases in the courthouse."

"Adult court this time," Bad Cop says. "The D.A.'s already talking about moving this one out of the juvenile system."

253

"That's premature," Jeffries says.

"But likely," Good Cop says. "All these cases are getting tried in adult court."

"Some of them," Jeffries says. "Not all."

Good Cop shrugs.

"My money's on adult court," Bad Cop says. "What do you think about that, Cameron?"

"You can ask him about the clothes," Jeffries says. "That's it. Then I'm taking Cameron down to the lab for the blood sample."

"You left your backpack in your gym locker," Good Cop says. "You know we found that. But we haven't found your PE clothes, or the street clothes you were wearing on Friday."

"I had my PE clothes on when I left," Cameron says. "I went to the lake. I went running."

"Yes, your PE teacher says you left in your PE clothes, but where are they?"

"In the wash, I guess."

"What about your street clothes?"

"In the wash?"

"Then you left wearing your PE clothes and brought your street clothes home with you?"

"Yes."

"You sound positive about that."

"I brought my gym bag home instead of my backpack," Cameron says.

"Why?"

"It was a mistake."

"You wanted to take your backpack?"

Cameron nods. "I had homework for history I wanted to do."

"Your teachers say you don't do homework," Bad Cop says.

"I do some of it."

Good Cop checks through his notes. "Hit and miss, that's what your history teacher, Mr. Hart, says about your homework."

"Move on, then," Jeffries says.

"Did your mom do the laundry this weekend?" Bad Cop asks.

"Maybe."

"How is he supposed to know?" Randy asks.

"It doesn't matter," Bad Cop says. "You know you can't wash blood out of clothes, Cameron? It's set for life, even if you can't see it with the human eye."

"Where are we going to find your clothes," Good Cop asks. "Your room? The laundry room?"

"My room, maybe."

"What about the gym bag? Where's that?"

Cameron shrugs. "My room?"

"You don't sound sure about that."

"I'm pretty sure."

"Maybe you could go get it for us," Good Cop suggests.

"Get it yourself," Jeffries says. "You've got a warrant, use it."

He puts his hand on Cameron's shoulder and says to him, "Go

get your jacket. We'll pick up your mom on the way to the police lab."

Cameron walks into the living room and picks up his coat from the couch. He can hear them talking, Randy mostly. His voice is raised and strained.

"The city's really pushing this into adult court? They don't even know yet who they're trying."

"They're making noise." Jeffries sounds confident.

"They can and will move it," Bad Cop says.

"We don't know that this case is going there or that it will even involve us," Jeffries cautions. "It's insane, really, to be talking about adult court when a viable suspect isn't even in the picture."

"Well, that's a matter of opinion, isn't it?" Good Cop says.

"Opinion is all we have," Jeffries says.

TUESDAY

2:30AM

The cops (Cameron counted thirteen of them) weren't done searching the house until two in the morning. Cameron stuffed the cushions back into the couch and curled up there while they picked through his bedroom. Robbie spent the night at a friend's house and his mom dozed in the armchair close by. Randy stood outside, in the glow of halogen lamps, and watched cops dig through the garage, which included the laundry area and the trash cans lined up against the outside wall. When they were done, Randy shoveled the trash back into the cans, picked up the clean clothes that were in the dryer but were tossed around by the detectives, and loaded them back into the washer, then he straightened the furniture on the deck and came inside.

"They're just about done," Randy says, looking Cameron in the eye, even through the dimness of the room.

"Good."

"They didn't find what they're looking for," he says.

"My clothes."

"That and your gym bag."

"I know." *Because they're buried in the woods. For now.*

Randy nods. "Your lawyer told you not to talk to me about the case. That's a good idea."

"Yeah, I think so, too."

"Are you scared?"

"Sometimes," Cameron admits. "Mostly, I don't feel anything at all."

"Your mom made an appointment with a doctor in Philadelphia. You know that's a confidential relationship? Not even the court can break it."

"Okay."

"I just want you to be straight with the guy."

"I'll try."

"Sorry to break up the pillow talk," Bad Cop says, walking into the room. "But we're done."

"You're an ass, Finney," Randy says.

Cameron sits up on the couch.

"This is the first I've heard of it," Bad Cop says. "You're taking this personally."

"Real personally," Randy agrees.

Good Cop walks into the room, smiles, and says. "We're leaving. Empty-handed."

"Bull. You're too happy. You found something," Randy says.

"We're confident the blood is all we need. We'll let you know the preliminary results on that later today."

"You mean you'll either clear Cameron or you'll be back to arrest him?"

"That's right," Good Cop says.

"We'll see you tomorrow, Cameron."

Randy lets them walk themselves out. Cameron hears them packing up. The halogen lamps outside are shut off, plunging the room into darkness. Car doors slam shut. Engines turn over and tires crunch on the gravel, skidding on the last patch of driveway before making the state road and clinging to the blacktop. His eyes adjust and he finds Randy, sitting now in a chair near the window.

"I'm going to jail," Cameron says.

"Maybe."

"Am I going to die?"

"It wasn't murder," Randy says. "It wasn't planned."

Cameron didn't know he was going to kill Pinon. It wasn't a decision but an action. And maybe this will save his life.

TUESDAY

9:45AM

His mother is in the kitchen, sitting at the table drinking a cup of coffee, when Cameron enters from outside. She's still wearing the makeup she didn't wash off the night before, but her hair is combed into a ponytail and she changed clothes. She's not going to work. He thought maybe she'd go in late, but she's wearing a velour sweatsuit and is in no hurry to get out the door.

She told him not to go to school today. Last night, after he gave his blood at the police lab, they sat in Jeffries's car in the parking lot and talked about the immediate future. They no longer talked in days but hours. Cameron shouldn't go to school. Before the end of the day the police would return and if the blood was a positive match, Cameron would be arrested.

"And if his blood isn't a match?" his mom asked. "What then?"

"The police will move on, look for another suspect," Jeffries said. He paused and tapped the steering wheel with his stubby fingers, then looked into Cameron's mom's face and warned, "We have to think about what we'll do if the blood does match. We need a plan for that."

His mom's face got tight, smaller somehow. Air rattled in her throat as she drew a breath. "You're supposed to believe he's innocent."

"He has bruising, a pretty deep cut on his right hand. They're consistent with having handled a combination lock." *Violently.* Jeffries didn't say it. He didn't have to.

His mom's lips peeled back from her teeth. Cameron thought she was going to defend him, but the words never came. Instead, he heard a thin hiss like air escaping out of a balloon and even as he watched her she grew distant, out of reach.

When Jeffries dropped them off at home she got out of the car and walked toward the house, surrounded with halogen lamps on tall metal poles and strangers picking through and setting aside their stuff. She stopped on the deck, a dark, haloed figure, her fingertips pressed to the railing, and swayed on her feet.

"She's in shock," Jeffries said. "She won't give up on you."

She stood in his bedroom door that morning, her fingers barely touching the doorjamb, as if testing its reality, and told him to stay home. He already knew that so he guessed she was finally accepting that she had a killer for a son. She looked at him a long time, so long he felt like she was trying to memorize him. He felt her eyes on his hair, cut so short now and the color of bark. Her gaze settled on each feature of his face individually. She didn't just look into his eyes, she dove in. Stayed. Searched. Then she approached him, cupped his face with her hands, and kissed his forehead, beneath the burn scabs. She loved him no matter what he did.

✳

"What are you doing?"

His mother's words break through his thoughts. Her voice is high and thin and charged with accusation. He takes another step toward her, clutching the blue gym bag to his chest.

"You shouldn't bring that in here," she says. "They're coming back, the police."

"I don't want to die," Cameron says. His voice breaks and so he says it again.

She pushes up from her chair. Coffee spills and pools around her cup.

"Give me the bag."

She opens her hands but Cameron clings to the bag and instead he moves into her arms. He puts his face on her shoulder, his nose turned into her neck, and smells her flowery powder, watches his tears wet her jacket.

"I wish this had never happened," Cameron says.

She lays her hands on his head, strokes her fingers through his short hair, rubs his temples, and promises him she'll try to fix it. All of it. And Cameron doesn't mind that she seems to include him in that statement or that her record for repairing what's broken is unimpressive.

TUESDAY

7:00PM

Cameron watches from his bedroom window as his mom removes the steel rack from the grill, stuffs his jeans into the trough, and pours lighter fluid on them. His gym bag is on a deck chair, the zipper open, T-shirts, shorts, and socks falling out the top. His mom steps back from the barbecue and strikes a match. The fire catches fast, flames a foot long leaping into the air. She waits with her arms folded over her stomach, bent a little at the waist, like she's leaning into a muscle pull. He can't see her face, but he knows she's crying. He knows her eyes are dark, unfocused, confused. She looked like that a lot of times when they were still with his father.

She burns his clothes and the gym bag, then scrapes melted plastic off the barbecue while it's still hot, gathers the metal zippers and buttons, dumps the hot ashes into a brown grocery sack, and leaves the deck.

He hears the garage door open. She had told him she was going to burn it all, that he should stay in his room and not think about it. She didn't tell him what she planned to do with what's left over.

He had told his mom that he did it. He had killed Pinon. But she'd already known. It was like she had just been waiting for him to say it. Her hands had shaken a little. The breath caught in her throat and tears spilled off her cheeks, but she hadn't said anything. Not then, and not much since. He could tell, though, that he had broken her heart. She had that bruised, scared look she wore living all those years with his father.

And maybe that hurt him more than all the beatings he's taken this year. It might even hurt more than knowing that he killed a boy.

Confessing was, at first, like losing all the marrow from his bones. It was excruciating, but he felt suddenly weightless. Able to soar above it all. Now his heart is kicking against his ribs, and he thinks about how some birds die scared, their hearts bursting in their tufted chests even as they're flying.

He doesn't want to be a killer.

He doesn't want Pinon dead.

But there's no way to change who he is and what he's done.

He hears his mother's feet in the gravel driveway and then she's in the yard, carrying the brown bag and a shovel. She walks through the grass then slips between the trees and into the woods.

TUESDAY

7:50PM

They're finishing dinner when two police cruisers pull into the driveway. His mom gets up from the table and walks to the window.

"Randy is here," she says. "And those two cops." She turns and looks at Cameron. "Jeffries is going to meet us at the police station. Remember not to say anything."

Cameron nods.

"The therapist, from Philadelphia, he'll drive out the day after tomorrow."

His mom believes that what happened in the boys' locker room is the culmination of a year's abuse. It makes sense to Cameron. His freshman year of high school made him a soldier.

"I'll talk to him," Cameron promises.

Robbie stands up, bounces on his feet, pushes his hands into his pockets then pulls them out again. His mom walks to him, places her hand on his arm and says, "Remember, we're thinking positive."

Cameron looks at his brother's face, the fear in it making Cameron's stomach lurch. He remembers how he wanted Robbie to be afraid of him, just a little. Now it feels as wrong as everything else. Anyway, Robbie is afraid *for* him, not *of* him, and that's even worse.

"You worry too much," Cameron tells Robbie.

"That's the way I am," he says.

"I know."

Randy knocks on the door. Everything by the book. Cameron's mom has to open the door, give her permission for them to ask Cameron questions. She lets them in but tells them, just as Jeffries instructed, that Cameron isn't speaking about the crime with which he is charged.

"That's murder," Bad Cop says. "Just so you know, the arrest warrant says 'for the murder of one Charles Pinon, a minor.'"

"That's your opinion," Cameron's mom says.

Good Cop puts the handcuffs on Cameron. The metal is cold

and tight. Then he turns Cameron around and Bad Cop reads him his rights, stopping after each one to ask if Cameron understands it.

Randy says, "Don't talk, Cameron."

"I know."

"Not in the cruiser. Not in processing. Not at any time your lawyer isn't with you."

Cameron nods.

Good Cop goes through Cameron's pockets, runs his hands under Cameron's armpits, between his legs and all the way down to his feet, his long fingers squirming into the tops of Cameron's sneakers.

"We have a room waiting for you at the Ritz," Good Cop says.

"It's going to feel like the Ritz after they move you to adult court."

"If they do," Randy says.

"Give it up," Bad Cop says. "You know which way the wind is blowing on this."

"Mr. Jeffries will see you tonight," Randy says, putting a hand on Cameron's shoulder. "He's going to make sure they're treating you right."

"With gloves on," Bad Cop says.

Cameron's mom slips her arms through his. She pulls him into her embrace, sniffling through her tears, and says, "I'll be there to see you as soon as they let me. Maybe tomorrow."

"Okay." Cameron hears his voice break but remembers that killing Pinon was the only action he could take. The only one available to him. "I'll see you."

He looks at Robbie. "You going to come visit me?"

"No kids allowed in the jail," Good Cop says.

EPILOGUE

SENTENCING

"No one really knew my son," Mrs. Pinon says. "Not at that school. No one gave Charlie a chance."

She stands with her husband at a podium in the middle of the courtroom. They don't look at Cameron. They don't take their eyes off the judge who sits with his hands folded, his maroon tie looking like a drop of blood above a black so dark it has to be death.

"He was a great kid. I want you to know that. I want them to know that. All the kids at Madison High who decided because he didn't look like them, didn't play football, didn't belong to a team, he wasn't of value. He was smart and funny. For my birthday he made me a swan. An origami swan." Her voice gets thick and wet and she stops and clears her throat. "He was scared to go to school. No child should ever be scared to go to school."

Beside him, Mrs. Roth, Jeffries's legal assistant, rubs Cameron's arm. She did that a lot during the trial, whenever anyone on the stand had something bad to say about him. When his father was up there, talking about how hard he tried to make sure he raised sons who would be real men, she put her arm around his shoulders and whispered to him, "That's as close as he's going to get to you."

She understands what it was like for him growing up with his father. Cameron doesn't know how. Mrs. Roth is at least as old as his grandmother.

Cameron knows he's going to stay in jail. He's already put in eight months and six days, waiting for his trial, waiting for his trial to end. But it won't be for murder. The psychologist his mom hired to evaluate him, Mr. Lau, diagnosed him with a stress disorder. He told the court he believed, one hundred percent, that Cameron killed because he felt he didn't have any other choice. Lau said, being back at the scene of his assault, Cameron's reality blurred.

So he hasn't been tried for murder. He won't spend twenty-five years in a tiny room with a tin can toilet.

Cameron knows that memory and reality blurred that day in the locker room. But only for a moment. Cameron believed his life was in danger; with Pinon alive to talk about what really happened in the locker room, the stuff the pictures didn't show, Cameron would have had no life. But that's not self-defense, is it?

Lau told the court that Cameron didn't even know it was Pinon he was harming. Not at first. He resorted to the survival instincts of a soldier in combat.

A medical doctor, a specialist on how the brain works, told the court that Cameron's brain was not fully formed. He showed MRIs of three brains: Cameron's, another kid Cameron's age who never committed a violent crime, and the brain of a twenty-four-year-old man.

✳

"The region where we decide between right and wrong, the human threshold of morality," the doctor said, "is not fully formed until we're in our mid-twenties."

"Who can argue with science?" Jeffries asked the court.

In the moment, Cameron didn't think about death and how it was forever, but he had thought about it before, and after, and forever was what he wanted.

Jeffries appealed to the jury, "Cameron's brain is no different than any other kid's his age. It is humanly impossible, at the age of fourteen, to know the complete ramifications of an act that was spontaneous and defensive in nature."

✳

"We didn't want this tried in adult court." Mr. Pinon is talking now. He's a small man in a dark suit. He pushes his hands into his front pockets and digs up the coins he finds there. "We don't want to see another child's life ruined."

Jeffries scribbles something on his yellow legal pad and Cameron waits for him to stop writing so he can read it: LET MR. PINON'S COMPASSION LEAD YOU AS YOU SET MY CLIENT'S PUNISHMENT.

Jeffries will get his turn to talk after Cameron's mother.

He has organized a list of all the things the judge knows about Cameron:

—BOY SCOUT

—STRAIGHT-A STUDENT BEFORE HE ENTERED HIGH SCHOOL

—ABUSIVE FATHER

—BULLIED/RICH PATTERSON GUILTY OF ASSAULT

Under the heading TESTIMONIES, Jeffries wrote:

—HART: CAMERON DOESN'T CARE ABOUT MUCH OF ANYTHING

—SPANISH TEACHER: WORRIED ABOUT SPIRALING GRADE

—PE COACH: DESCRIBED A LOCKER ROOM OF LITTLE/NO SUPERVISION

—Father: admitted to physical and verbal abuse

—Sgt. Lucas: details of Pinon's "unplanned" killing

—Psych: "A stress disorder where the victim actively disengages from reality"

—Elwood: counseled regarding attack/October

Under this, Jeffries has written: No adult intervention

"Charlie talked about Cameron," Mr. Pinon says. "He said the kids who picked on him picked on Cameron, too. I remember that." He rolls onto the balls of his feet and bounces nervously. "The truth is, I should have done more to help my son. I keep thinking, why are we in adult court when no adult ever stood up and did anything to help these boys?"

"Cameron Grady killed my son," Mrs. Pinon says. "I want you to remember that. But he didn't do it alone."

Cameron's mom speaks next. She's light on her feet and holds onto the edges of the podium. She apologizes for not being a better mom. She thought her son was having a difficult time adjusting to high school; she didn't know every day was a living hell for him. She didn't know he would kill an innocent boy. She apologizes for that twice. She turns and looks right at Pinon's mom and dad and says, "I'm sorry." Then her face breaks up into the mismatched pieces of a puzzle and she pushes her next words though tears, "Sorry just isn't enough."

She turns back to the judge and says, "But he's still a boy. He's my boy. And there's so much about him you don't know." And she tells him about all the hours Cameron put into the community, as a Boy Scout, more volunteer hours than he needed.

Cameron listens to her voice warble. Her hands lift off the podium and flutter in front of her throat. When she runs out of good things to say about him, she stands gasping for breath. The judge tells her to sit down.

Cameron watches her move through the gate, into the gallery. Randy is sitting toward the back. He takes her hand and whispers something to her. Words that give her a lift. She dries her eyes with a tissue and then looks at the judge.

Jeffries stands and pleads for a soft sentence. The judge listens, taps a pencil against a pile of papers, then tells Jeffries to sit.

"Will the convicted please rise."

Cameron's legs won't cooperate and Jeffries pulls him up and keeps a hand on his elbow until he's steady.

"Cameron Grady, a jury sat in this courtroom and listened to testimony about the death of a young boy whose only offense was to be in the wrong place at the wrong time. They heard about your troubles. They were given expert testimony on the biology of a brain that is moved to kill and testimony that described a trend in America that scares us all. And they found you guilty. It is my job now to decide the legal consequences of the crime for which you are convicted: manslaughter."

Beside him, Jeffries and Roth stand close enough that he can feel their body heat, but he can't feel the floor beneath his feet. He knows now what triggers his ability to move in and out of his body: mental and emotional stressors. He loses feeling in his hands and feet and then he's like a kite, banking in the wind, looking down on himself and feeling that whatever is happening, it can't be too bad.

"Four years in the New Castle Youth Development Center in Pittsburgh," the judge says. "This is a maximum security detention facility for juvenile offenders. It's a rigorous program, and rehabilitation will be your first responsibility. You'll use the four years to reflect on your actions. To find a way of living peacefully with what you've done and form a plan for how you'll make the best of this second chance you've been given."

A second chance. That's what he wanted, from the beginning. But he knows there's no way to really start over new. Tomorrow, he'll wake up and still be Cameron Grady, killer. And Pinon won't wake up at all.